Mazda Automotive Repair Manual

A K Legg

T Eng (CEI), AMIMI

Models covered

UK:

All versions of Mazda Montrose and 626 Saloon and Coupe:
1586 cc and 1970 cc

USA:

All versions of Mazda 626 Sedan and Coupe; 120 cu in (2.0 liter)

ISBN 0 85696 996 6

Printed in England

ABCDE
FG

HAYNES PUBLISHING GROUP
SPARKFORD YEOVIL SOMERSET BA22 7JJ ENGLAND
distributed in the USA by
HAYNES PUBLICATIONS INC
861 LAWRENCE DRIVE
NEWBURY PARK
CALIFORNIA 91320
USA

Acknowledgements

Thanks are due to Toyo Kogyo Company Limited for the supply of technical information and certain illustrations. The Champion Sparking Plug Company supplied the illustrations showing the various spark plug conditions. The bodywork repair photographs used in this manual were provided by Holt Lloyd Limited who supply 'Turtle Wax', 'Dupli-Color Holts' and other Holts range products. Castrol Limited very kindly supplied the lubrication data, and Sykes-Pickavant Ltd provided some of the workshop tools. Special thanks are due to all those people at Sparkford who helped in the production of this manual.

About this manual

Its aim

The aim of this manual is to help you get the best from your car. It can do so in several ways. It can help you decide what work must be done (even should you choose to get it done by a garage), provide information on routine maintenance and servicing, and give a logical course of action and diagnosis when random faults occur. However, it is hoped that you will use the manual by tackling the work yourself. On simpler jobs it may even be quicker than booking the car into a garage and going there twice to leave and collect it. Perhaps most important, a lot of money can be saved by avoiding the costs the garage must charge to cover its labour and overheads.

The manual has drawings and descriptions to show the function of the various components so that their layout can be understood. Then the tasks are described and photographed in a step-by-step sequence so that even a novice can do the work.

Its arrangement

The manual is divided into thirteen Chapters, each covering a logical sub-division of the vehicle. The Chapters are each divided into Sections, numbered with single figures, eg 5; and the Sections into paragraphs (or sub-sections), with decimal numbers following on from the Section they are in, eg 5.1, 5.2 etc.

It is freely illustrated, especially in those parts where there is a detailed sequence of operations to be carried out. There are two forms of illustration: figures and photographs. The figures are numbered in sequence with decimal numbers, according to their position in the Chapter – Fig. 6.4 is the fourth drawing/illustration in Chapter 6. Photographs carry the same number (either individually or in related groups) as the Section or sub-section to which they relate.

There is an alphabetical index at the back of the manual as well as a contents list at the front. Each Chapter is also preceded by its own individual contents list.

References to the 'left' or 'right' of the vehicle are in the sense of a person in the driver's seat facing forwards.

Unless otherwise stated, nuts and bolts are removed by turning anti-clockwise, and tightened by turning clockwise.

Vehicle manufacturers continually make changes to specifications and recommendations, and these, when notified, are incorporated into our manuals at the earliest opportunity.

Whilst every care is taken to ensure that the information in this manual is correct, no liability can be accepted by the authors or publishers for loss, damage or injury caused by any errors in, or omissions from, the information given.

Introduction to the Mazda Montrose/626

The Mazda Montrose/626 was first introduced in the UK in April 1979. It was initially known as the Montrose, but in early 1981 this was dropped in favour of the American market model name 626.

In the UK two engine sizes are available. The 1600 cc engine was fitted to saloon models with GL or GLS trim options up to 1981, and to the DX saloon from 1981 on. The 2000 cc engine was fitted to saloon and coupe models with GLS trim up to 1981, and to the SDX saloon and coupe from 1981 on. A four-speed manual gearbox is fitted to 1600 cc models and a five-speed manual gearbox to 2000 cc models. Automatic transmission was available on 2000 cc saloon models only up to 1981, but on 2000 cc saloon and coupe models from 1981 on.

In the USA the 626 is available in sedan or coupe form with the 120 cu in (2000 cc) engine. A five-speed manual gearbox is fitted as standard with automatic transmission optional.

Standard equipment on all models includes an electric boot lid release, reclining front seats, tinted glass, and servo assisted brakes.

Contents

4

Mazda Montrose Saloon

Mazda 626 Coupe

General dimensions, weights and capacities
Refer to Chapter 13 for revisions and information related to 1982 models

Dimensions
Overall length:
    UK models with small bumper .... 4360 mm (172 in)
    UK models with large bumper .... 4415 mm (174 in)
    US and Canadian models .... 4465 mm (176 in)
Overall width:
    UK models with wide protector .... 1690 mm (67 in)
    All other models .... 1660 mm (65 in)
Overall height:
    Saloon (Sedan) .... 1370 mm (54 in)
    Coupe (Hardtop) .... 1345 mm (53 in)
Wheelbase .... 2510 mm (99 in)
Track:
    Front .... 1370 mm (54 in)
    Rear .... 1380 mm (54.3 in)
Minimum turning radius .... 4.8 m (15 ft 7 in)

Kerb weight (nominal)
UK .... 2321 lb (1055 kg)
USA .... 2565 lb (1163 kg)

Capacities
Engine (including filter):
    1600 .... 3.2 Imp qt; 3.6 litre; 3.8 US qt
    2000 .... 3.4 Imp qt; 3.9 litre; 4.1 US qt
Cooling system (with heater) .... 6.6 Imp pt; 7.5 litre; 7.9 US qt
Manual gearbox:
    4-speed .... 1.2 Imp qt; 1.4 litre; 1.5 US qt
    5-speed .... 1.5 Imp qt; 1.7 litre; 1.8 US qt
Automatic transmission .... 5.5 Imp qt; 6.2 litre; 6.6 US qt
Rear axle .... 1.1 Imp qt; 1.2 litre; 1.3 US qt
Fuel tank .... 12.1 Imp gal; 55 litre; 14.5 US gal

Use of English

As this book has been written in England, it uses the appropriate English component names, phrases, and spelling. Some of these differ from those used in America. Normally, these cause no difficulty, but to make sure, a glossary is printed below. In ordering spare parts remember the parts list may use some of these words:

English	American	English	American
Accelerator	Gas pedal	Locks	Latches
Aerial	Antenna	Methylated spirit	Denatured alcohol
Anti-roll bar	Stabiliser or sway bar	Motorway	Freeway, turnpike etc
Big-end bearing	Rod bearing	Number plate	License plate
Bonnet (engine cover)	Hood	Paraffin	Kerosene
Boot (luggage compartment)	Trunk	Petrol	Gasoline (gas)
Bulkhead	Firewall	Petrol tank	Gas tank
Bush	Bushing	'Pinking'	'Pinging'
Cam follower or tappet	Valve lifter or tappet	Prise (force apart)	Pry
Carburettor	Carburetor	Propeller shaft	Driveshaft
Catch	Latch	Quarterlight	Quarter window
Choke/venturi	Barrel	Retread	Recap
Circlip	Snap-ring	Reverse	Back-up
Clearance	Lash	Rocker cover	Valve cover
Crownwheel	Ring gear (of differential)	Saloon	Sedan
Damper	Shock absorber, shock	Seized	Frozen
Disc (brake)	Rotor/disk	Sidelight	Parking light
Distance piece	Spacer	Silencer	Muffler
Drop arm	Pitman arm	Sill panel (beneath doors)	Rocker panel
Drop head coupe	Convertible	Small end, little end	Piston pin or wrist pin
Dynamo	Generator (DC)	Spanner	Wrench
Earth (electrical)	Ground	Split cotter (for valve spring cap)	Lock (for valve spring retainer)
Engineer's blue	Prussian blue	Split pin	Cotter pin
Estate car	Station wagon	Steering arm	Spindle arm
Exhaust manifold	Header	Sump	Oil pan
Fault finding/diagnosis	Troubleshooting	Swarf	Metal chips or debris
Float chamber	Float bowl	Tab washer	Tang or lock
Free-play	Lash	Tappet	Valve lifter
Freewheel	Coast	Thrust bearing	Throw-out bearing
Gearbox	Transmission	Top gear	High
Gearchange	Shift	Torch	Flashlight
Grub screw	Setscrew, Allen screw	Trackrod (of steering)	Tie-rod (or connecting rod)
Gudgeon pin	Piston pin or wrist pin	Trailing shoe (of brake)	Secondary shoe
Halfshaft	Axleshaft	Transmission	Whole drive line
Handbrake	Parking brake	Tyre	Tire
Hood	Soft top	Van	Panel wagon/van
Hot spot	Heat riser	Vice	Vise
Indicator	Turn signal	Wheel nut	Lug nut
Interior light	Dome lamp	Windscreen	Windshield
Layshaft (of gearbox)	Countershaft	Wing/mudguard	Fender
Leading shoe (of brake)	Primary shoe		

Buying spare parts and vehicle identification numbers

Refer to Chapter 13 for revisions and information related to 1982 models

Buying spare parts

Spare parts are available from many sources, for example: Mazda garages, other garages and accessory shops, and motor factors. Our advice regarding spare parts is as follows:

Officially appointed Mazda garages – This is the best source of parts which are peculiar to your car and are otherwise not generally available (eg complete cylinder heads, internal gearbox components, badges, interior trim etc). It is also the only place at which you should buy parts if your car is still under warranty; non-Mazda components may invalidate the warranty. To be sure of obtaining the correct parts it will always be necessary to give the storeman your car's engine and chassis number, and if possible, to take the old part along for positive identification. Remember that many parts are available on a factory exchange scheme – any parts returned should always be clean! It obviously makes good sense to go to the specialists on your car for this type of part for they are best equipped to supply you.

Other garages and accessory shops – These are often very good places to buy material and components needed for the maintenance of your car (eg oil filters, spark plugs, bulbs, fanbelts, oils and grease, touch-up paint, filler paste etc). They also sell general accessories, usually have convenient opening hours, charge lower prices and can often be found not far from home.

Motor factors – Good factors will stock all of the more important components which wear out relatively quickly (eg clutch components, pistons, valves, exhaust systems, brake cylinders/pipes/hoses/seals/shoes and pads etc). Motor factors will often provide new or reconditioned components on a part exchange basis – this can save a considerable amount of money.

Vehicle identification numbers

Modifications are a continuing and unpublicised process in vehicle manufacture quite apart from major model changes. Spare parts manuals and lists are compiled upon a numerical basis, the individual vehicle numbers being essential to correct identification of the component required.

Whichever source of parts is used it will be essential to provide correct information concerning the model and year of manufacture, plus other pertinent information given in the vehicle identification numbers.

The model plate is located in the engine compartment on the right-hand side of the bulkhead (photo).

The chassis number is stamped next to the model plate.

The engine number is located on the right-hand side of the cylinder block above the alternator.

The safety information and tyre pressure chart is located on the trailing edge of the driver's door.

The colour code plate is located on the inner side of the bonnet, on the front left-hand corner.

On USA models *the vehicle identification plate* is located on the left-hand side of the dashboard and can be viewed through the windscreen.

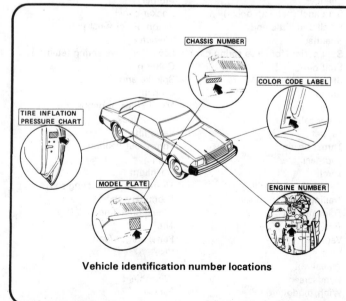

Vehicle identification number locations

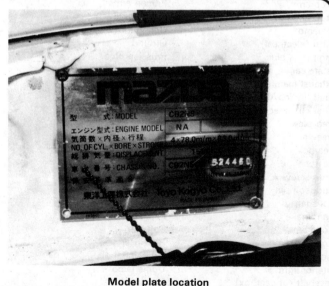

Model plate location

Tools and working facilities

Introduction

A selection of good tools is a fundamental requirement for anyone contemplating the maintenance and repair of a motor vehicle. For the owner who does not possess any, their purchase will prove a considerable expense, offsetting some of the savings made by doing-it-yourself. However, provided that the tools purchased meet the relevant national safety standards and are of good quality, they will last for many years and prove an extremely worthwhile investment.

To help the average owner to decide which tools are needed to carry out the various tasks detailed in this manual, we have compiled three lists of tools under the following headings: *Maintenance and minor repair, Repair and overhaul,* and *Special.* The newcomer to practical mechanics should start off with the *Maintenance and minor repair* tool kit and confine himself to the simpler jobs around the vehicle. Then, as his confidence and experience grow, he can undertake more difficult tasks, buying extra tools as, and when, they are needed. In this way, a *Maintenance and minor repair* tool kit can be built-up into a *Repair and overhaul* tool kit over a considerable period of time without any major cash outlays. The experienced do-it-yourselfer will have a tool kit good enough for most repair and overhaul procedures and will add tools from the *Special* category when he feels the expense is justified by the amount of use these tools will be put to.

It is obviously not possible to cover the subject of tools fully here. For those who wish to learn more about tools and their use there is a book entitled *How to Choose and Use Car Tools* available from the publishers of this manual.

Maintenance and minor repair tool kit

The tools given in this list should be considered as a minimum requirement if routine maintenance, servicing and minor repair operations are to be undertaken. We recommend the purchase of combination spanners (ring one end, open-ended the other); although more expensive than open-ended ones, they do give the advantages of both types of spanner.

> *Combination spanners - 8, 10, 11, 12, 13, 14 & 17 mm*
> *Adjustable spanner - 9 inch*
> *Rear axle drain plug key*
> *Spark plug spanner (with rubber insert)*
> *Spark plug gap adjustment tool*
> *Set of feeler gauges*
> *Brake bleed nipple spanner*
> *Screwdriver - 4 in long x $\frac{1}{4}$ in dia (flat blade)*
> *Screwdriver - 4 in long x $\frac{1}{4}$ in dia (cross blade)*
> *Combination pliers - 6 inch*
> *Hacksaw (junior)*
> *Tyre pump*
> *Tyre pressure gauge*
> *Grease gun*
> *Oil can*
> *Fine emery cloth (1 sheet)*
> *Wire brush (small)*
> *Funnel (medium size)*

Repair and overhaul tool kit

These tools are virtually essential for anyone undertaking any major repairs to a motor vehicle, and are additional to those given in the *Maintenance and minor repair* list. Included in this list is a comprehensive set of sockets. Although these are expensive they will be found invaluable as they are so versatile - particularly if various drives are included in the set. We recommend the $\frac{1}{2}$ in square-drive type, as this can be used with most proprietary torque spanners. If you cannot afford a socket set, even bought piecemeal, then inexpensive tubular box wrenches are a useful alternative.

The tools in this list will occasionally need to be supplemented by tools from the *Special* list.

> *Sockets (or box spanners) to cover range in previous list*
> *Reversible ratchet drive (for use with sockets)*
> *Extension piece, 10 inch (for use with sockets)*
> *Universal joint (for use with sockets)*
> *Torque wrench (for use with sockets)*
> *Mole wrench - 8 inch*
> *Ball pein hammer*
> *Soft-faced hammer, plastic or rubber*
> *Screwdriver - 6 in long x $\frac{5}{16}$ in dia (flat blade)*
> *Screwdriver - 2 in long x $\frac{5}{16}$ in dia (flat blade)*
> *Screwdriver - 1$\frac{1}{2}$ in long x $\frac{1}{4}$ in square (flat blade)*
> *Screwdriver - 3 in long x $\frac{1}{8}$ in dia (electricians)*
> *Pliers - electricians side cutters*
> *Pliers - needle nosed*
> *Pliers - circlip (internal and external)*
> *Cold chisel - $\frac{1}{2}$ inch*
> *Scriber*
> *Scraper*
> *Centre punch*
> *Pin punch*
> *Hacksaw*
> *Valve grinding tool*
> *Steel rule/straight-edge*
> *Allen keys*
> *Selection of files*
> *Wire brush (large)*
> *Axle-stands*
> *Jack (strong scissor or hydraulic type)*

Special tools

The tools in this list are those which are not used regularly, are expensive to buy, or which need to be used in accordance with their manufacturers' instructions. Unless relatively difficult mechanical jobs are undertaken frequently, it will not be economic to buy many of these tools. Where this is the case, you could consider clubbing together with friends (or joining a motorists' club) to make a joint purchase, or borrowing the tools against a deposit from a local garage or tool hire specialist.

The following list contains only those tools and instruments freely available to the public, and not those special tools produced by the vehicle manufacturer specifically for its dealer network. You will find occasional references to these manufacturers' special tools in the text of this manual. Generally, an alternative method of doing the job without the vehicle manufacturers' special tool is given. However, sometimes, there is no alternative to using them. Where this is the case and the relevant tool cannot be bought or borrowed you will have to entrust the work to a franchised garage.

> *Valve spring compressor*
> *Piston ring compressor*
> *Balljoint separator*
> *Universal hub/bearing puller*
> *Impact screwdriver*

Micrometer and/or vernier gauge
Dial gauge
Stroboscopic timing light
Dwell angle meter/tachometer
Universal electrical multi-meter
Cylinder compression gauge
Lifting tackle (photo)
Trolley jack
Light with extension lead

Buying tools

For practically all tools, a tool factor is the best source since he will have a very comprehensive range compared with the average garage or accessory shop. Having said that, accessory shops often offer excellent quality tools at discount prices, so it pays to shop around.

There are plenty of good tools around at reasonable prices, but always aim to purchase items which meet the relevant national safety standards. If in doubt, ask the proprietor or manager of the shop for advice before making a purchase.

Care and maintenance of tools

Having purchased a reasonable tool kit, it is necessary to keep the tools in a clean serviceable condition. After use, always wipe off any dirt, grease and metal particles using a clean, dry cloth, before putting the tools away. Never leave them lying around after they have been used. A simple tool rack on the garage or workshop wall, for items such as screwdrivers and pliers is a good idea. Store all normal spanners and sockets in a metal box. Any measuring instruments, gauges, meters, etc, must be carefully stored where they cannot be damaged or become rusty.

Take a little care when tools are used. Hammer heads inevitably become marked and screwdrivers lose the keen edge on their blades from time to time. A little timely attention with emery cloth or a file will soon restore items like this to a good serviceable finish.

Working facilities

Not to be forgotten when discussing tools, is the workshop itself. If anything more than routine maintenance is to be carried out, some form of suitable working area becomes essential.

It is appreciated that many an owner mechanic is forced by circumstances to remove an engine or similar item, without the benefit of a garage or workshop. Having done this, any repairs should always be done under the cover of a roof.

Wherever possible, any dismantling should be done on a clean flat workbench or table at a suitable working height.

Any workbench needs a vice: one with a jaw opening of 4 in (100 mm) is suitable for most jobs. As mentioned previously, some clean dry storage space is also required for tools, as well as the lubricants, cleaning fluids, touch-up paints and so on which become necessary.

Another item which may be required, and which has a much more general usage, is an electric drill with a chuck capacity of at least $\frac{5}{16}$ in (8 mm). This, together with a good range of twist drills, is virtually essential for fitting accessories such as wing mirrors and reversing lights.

Last, but not least, always keep a supply of old newspapers and clean, lint-free rags available, and try to keep any working area as clean as possible.

Spanner jaw gap comparison table

Jaw gap (in)	Spanner size
0.250	$\frac{1}{4}$ in AF
0.276	7 mm

Jaw gap (in)	Spanner size
0.313	$\frac{5}{16}$ in AF
0.315	8 mm
0.344	$\frac{11}{32}$ in AF; $\frac{1}{8}$ in Whitworth
0.354	9 mm
0.375	$\frac{3}{8}$ in AF
0.394	10 mm
0.433	11 mm
0.438	$\frac{7}{16}$ in AF
0.445	$\frac{3}{16}$ in Whitworth; $\frac{1}{4}$ in BSF
0.472	12 mm
0.500	$\frac{1}{2}$ in AF
0.512	13 mm
0.525	$\frac{1}{4}$ in Whitworth; $\frac{5}{16}$ in BSF
0.551	14 mm
0.563	$\frac{9}{16}$ in AF
0.591	15 mm
0.600	$\frac{5}{16}$ in Whitworth; $\frac{3}{8}$ in BSF
0.625	$\frac{5}{8}$ in AF
0.630	16 mm
0.669	17 mm
0.686	$\frac{11}{16}$ in AF
0.709	18 mm
0.710	$\frac{3}{8}$ in Whitworth, $\frac{7}{16}$ in BSF
0.748	19 mm
0.750	$\frac{3}{4}$ in AF
0.813	$\frac{13}{16}$ in AF
0.820	$\frac{7}{16}$ in Whitworth; $\frac{1}{2}$ in BSF
0.866	22 mm
0.875	$\frac{7}{8}$ in AF
0.920	$\frac{1}{2}$ in Whitworth; $\frac{9}{16}$ in BSF
0.938	$\frac{15}{16}$ in AF
0.945	24 mm
1.000	1 in AF
1.010	$\frac{9}{16}$ in Whitworth; $\frac{5}{8}$ in BSF
1.024	26 mm
1.063	$1\frac{1}{16}$ in AF; 27 mm
1.100	$\frac{5}{8}$ in Whitworth; $\frac{11}{16}$ in BSF
1.125	$1\frac{1}{8}$ in AF
1.181	30 mm
1.200	$\frac{11}{16}$ in Whitworth; $\frac{3}{4}$ in BSF
1.250	$1\frac{1}{4}$ in AF
1.260	32 mm
1.300	$\frac{3}{4}$ in Whitworth; $\frac{7}{8}$ in BSF
1.313	$1\frac{5}{16}$ in AF
1.390	$\frac{13}{16}$ in Whitworth; $\frac{15}{16}$ in BSF
1.417	36 mm
1.438	$1\frac{7}{16}$ in AF
1.480	$\frac{7}{8}$ in Whitworth; 1 in BSF
1.500	$1\frac{1}{2}$ in AF
1.575	40 mm; $\frac{15}{16}$ in Whitworth
1.614	41 mm
1.625	$1\frac{5}{8}$ in AF
1.670	1 in Whitworth; $1\frac{1}{8}$ in BSF
1.688	$1\frac{11}{16}$ in AF
1.811	46 mm
1.813	$1\frac{13}{16}$ in AF
1.860	$1\frac{1}{8}$ in Whitworth; $1\frac{1}{4}$ in BSF
1.875	$1\frac{7}{8}$ in AF
1.969	50 mm
2.000	2 in AF
2.050	$1\frac{1}{4}$ in Whitworth; $1\frac{3}{8}$ in BSF
2.165	55 mm
2.362	60 mm

Jacking and towing

To change a roadwheel, remove the spare wheel and tool kit from the rear luggage compartment. Block the wheel diagonally opposite the wheel to be changed and apply the handbrake firmly. Loosen but do not remove the wheel bolts, then use the jack to raise the car until the wheel is clear of the ground. Remove the bolts and lift off the wheel. Fit the spare wheel using a reversal of the removal procedure.

The jack supplied with the car should only be used for changing a wheel. When using a trolley jack, position it under the front suspension crossmember or rear axle. Position axle stands as shown in the illustrations.

The towing hooks provided at the front and rear of the car are for emergency use only for towing or pulling the car – do not use the rear hooks for towing another vehicle. Automatic transmission models may be towed at speeds up to 30 mph (45 kph) for distances up to 10 miles (15 km) provided the transmission is not faulty. When being towed, remember that more effort will be required for braking because the servo is inoperative with the engine stopped.

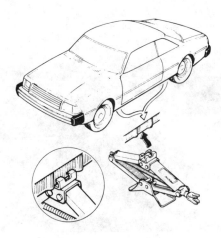

Jack and jacking points

Using a trolley jack under the front suspension crossmember

Using a trolley jack under the rear axle

Axle stand positions at the front of the car

Axle stand position at the rear of the car

Spare wheel location

Tool kit location

Jack location on sill

Front towing hook location

Rear towing hook location

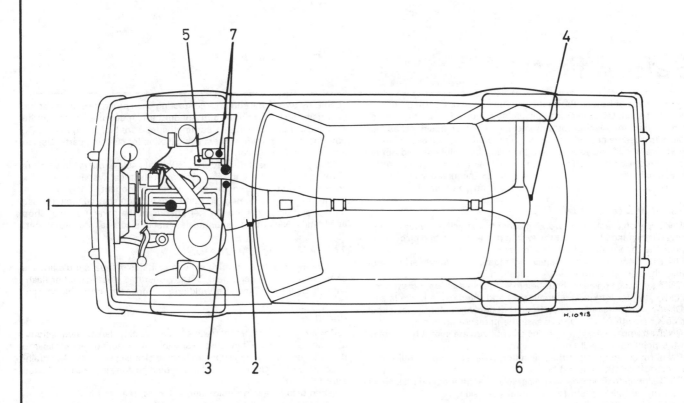

Recommended lubricants and fluids

Component or system	Lubricant type of specification	Castrol product
Engine (1)	SAE 20W/40 or 20W/50 multigrade engine oil	**Castrol GTX**
Manual gearbox (2)	SAE 90 EP hypoid gear oil	**Castrol Hypoy EP90**
Automatic transmission (3)	Automatic transmission fluid type F to M2C33F	**Castrol TQF**
Rear axle (4)	SAE 90 EP hypoid gear oil	**Castrol Hypoy EP90**
Steering gear box (5): Manual Power-assisted	SAE 90 EP hypoid gear oil Automatic transmission fluid type F to M2C33F	**Castrol Hypoy EP90** **Castrol TQF**
Wheel bearings (6)	Multipurpose lithium-based grease	**Castrol LM**
Brake and clutch fluid reservoirs (7)	Hydraulic fluid to SAE J1703, FMVSS 11, DOT 3 or DOT 4	**Castrol Girling Universal Brake and Clutch fluid**

Note: *The above are general recommendations only. Lubrication requirements vary from territory to territory and depend on vehicle usage. If in doubt, consult the operator's handbook supplied with the vehicle, or your nearest dealer.*

Safety first!

Regardless of how enthusiastic you may be about getting on with the job at hand, take the time to ensure that your safety is not jeopardized. A moment's lack of attention can result in an accident, as can failure to observe certain simple safety precautions. The possibility of an accident will always exist, and the following points should not be considered a comprehensive list of all dangers. Rather, they are intended to make you aware of the risks and to encourage a safety conscious approach to all work you carry out on your vehicle.

Essential DOs and DON'Ts

DON'T rely on a jack when working under the vehicle. Always use approved jackstands to support the weight of the vehicle and place them under the recommended lift or support points.

DON'T attempt to loosen extremely tight fasteners (i.e. wheel lug nuts) while the vehicle is on a jack — it may fall.

DON'T start the engine without first making sure that the transmission is in Neutral (or Park where applicable) and the parking brake is set.

DON'T remove the radiator cap from a hot cooling system — let it cool or cover it with a cloth and release the pressure gradually.

DON'T attempt to drain the engine oil until you are sure it has cooled to the point that it will not burn you.

DON'T touch any part of the engine or exhaust system until it has cooled sufficiently to avoid burns.

DON'T siphon toxic liquids such as gasoline, antifreeze and brake fluid by mouth, or allow them to remain on your skin.

DON'T inhale brake lining dust — it is potentially hazardous (see *Asbestos* below)

DON'T allow spilled oil or grease to remain on the floor — wipe it up before someone slips on it.

DON'T use loose fitting wrenches or other tools which may slip and cause injury.

DON'T push on wrenches when loosening or tightening nuts or bolts. Always try to pull the wrench toward you. If the situation calls for pushing the wrench away, push with an open hand to avoid scraped knuckles if the wrench should slip.

DON'T attempt to lift a heavy component alone — get someone to help you.

DON'T rush or take unsafe shortcuts to finish a job.

DON'T allow children or animals in or around the vehicle while you are working on it.

DO wear eye protection when using power tools such as a drill, sander, bench grinder, etc. and when working under a vehicle.

DO keep loose clothing and long hair well out of the way of moving parts.

DO make sure that any hoist used has a safe working load rating adequate for the job.

DO get someone to check on you periodically when working alone on a vehicle.

DO carry out work in a logical sequence and make sure that everything is correctly assembled and tightened.

DO keep chemicals and fluids tightly capped and out of the reach of children and pets.

DO remember that your vehicle's safety affects that of yourself and others. If in doubt on any point, get professional advice.

Asbestos

Certain friction, insulating, sealing, and other products — such as brake linings, brake bands, clutch linings, torque converters, gaskets, etc. — contain asbestos. *Extreme care must be taken to avoid inhalation of dust from such products since it is hazardous to health.* If in doubt, assume that they *do* contain asbestos.

Fire

Remember at all times that gasoline is highly flammable. Never smoke or have any kind of open flame around when working on a vehicle. But the risk does not end there. A spark caused by an electrical short circuit, by two metal surfaces contacting each other, or even by static electricity built up in your body under certain conditions, can ignite gasoline vapors, which in a confined space are highly explosive. Do not, under any circumstances, use gasoline for cleaning parts. Use an approved safety solvent.

Always disconnect the battery ground (−) cable *at the battery* before working on any part of the fuel system or electrical system. Never risk spilling fuel on a hot engine or exhaust component.

It is strongly recommended that a fire extinguisher suitable for use on fuel and electrical fires be kept handy in the garage or workshop at all times. Never try to extinguish a fuel or electrical fire with water.

Torch (flashlight in the US)

Any reference to a "torch" appearing in this manual should always be taken to mean a hand-held, battery-operated electric light or flashlight. It DOES NOT mean a welding or propane torch or blowtorch.

Fumes

Certain fumes are highly toxic and can quickly cause unconsciousness and even death if inhaled to any extent. Gasoline vapor falls into this category, as do the vapors from some cleaning solvents. Any draining or pouring of such volatile fluids should be done in a well ventilated area.

When using cleaning fluids and solvents, read the instructions on the container carefully. Never use materials from unmarked containers.

Never run the engine in an enclosed space, such as a garage. Exhaust fumes contain carbon monoxide, which is extremely poisonous. If you need to run the engine, always do so in the open air, or at least have the rear of the vehicle outside the work area.

If you are fortunate enough to have the use of an inspection pit, never drain or pour gasoline and never run the engine while the vehicle is over the pit. The fumes, being heavier than air, will concentrate in the pit with possibly lethal results.

The battery

Never create a spark or allow a bare light bulb near a battery. They normally give off a certain amount of hydrogen gas, which is highly explosive.

Always disconnect the battery ground (−) cable *at the battery* before working on the fuel or electrical systems.

If possible, loosen the filler caps or cover when charging the battery from an external source (this does not apply to sealed or maintenance-free batteries). Do not charge at an excessive rate or the battery may burst.

Take care when adding water to a non maintenance-free battery and when carrying a battery. The electrolyte, even when diluted, is very corrosive and should not be allowed to contact clothing or skin.

Always wear eye protection when cleaning the battery to prevent the caustic deposits from entering your eyes.

Mains electricity (household current in the US)

When using an electric power tool, inspection light, etc., which operates on household current, always make sure that the tool is correctly connected to its plug and that, where necessary, it is properly grounded. Do not use such items in damp conditions and, again, do not create a spark or apply excessive heat in the vicinity of fuel or fuel vapor.

Secondary ignition system voltage

A severe electric shock can result from touching certain parts of the ignition system (such as the spark plug wires) when the engine is running or being cranked, particularly if components are damp or the insulation is defective. In the case of an electronic ignition system, the secondary system voltage is much higher and could prove fatal.

Routine maintenance

Maintenance is essential for ensuring safety and desirable for the purpose of getting the best in terms of performance and economy from your car. Over the years the need for periodic lubrication has been greatly reduced if not totally eliminated. This has unfortunately tended to lead some owners to think that because no such action is required, the items either no longer exist, or will last forever. This is certainly not the case; it is essential to carry out regular visual examination as comprehensively as possible in order to spot any possible defects at an early stage, before they develop into major expensive repairs.

Every 250 miles (400 km) or weekly – whichever comes first

Engine
Check the oil level and top up if necessary (photos)
Check coolant level and top up if necessary (photo)
Check battery electrolyte level and top up if necessary (photo)
Check fanbelt, air conditioning compressor belt, and air injection pump belt (as applicable) for tension, and adjust if necessary (photo)

Tyres
Check tyre pressures and adjust if necessary (photo)
Visually examine tyres for wear and damage

Lights, horns and wipers
Check lights and horns for operation
Check windscreen washer fluid level and top up if necessary (photo)

Brakes and clutch
Check brake fluid (and where applicable, clutch fluid) levels and top up if necessary (photo). In the event of regular topping up, check the hydraulic circuit for leakage

First 600 miles (1000 km)

Note that this will normally be carried out by your dealer

Engine
Tighten cylinder head bolts and manifold nuts
Change engine oil (photo)
Adjust valve clearances
Adjust drivebelts
Adjust ignition timing
Adjust idle speed and mixture

Suspension, steering and body
Tighten all nuts and bolts as necessary

Every 6000 miles (10 000 km) or 6 months

Engine
Change engine oil and filter
Adjust valve clearances
Examine drivebelts for wear and adjust as necessary
Clean air cleaner element
Clean and adjust contact breaker points
Clean and adjust spark plugs and examine for wear
Adjust ignition timing
Adjust idle speed and mixture

Brakes
Check disc pads for wear
Check and if necessary adjust handbrake lever

Steering
Check steering wheel free play

Gearbox (manual) and rear axle
Check oil level and top up if necessary – change oil at first 6000 miles (10 000 km) (photos)

Wheels
Rotate wheels as shown in the illustration in Chapter 11

Every 12 000 miles (20 000 km) or 12 months

Engine
Check cooling system hoses and components for deterioration and leakage
Check fuel lines and components for deterioration and leakage
Renew fuel filter
Lubricate carburettor and choke linkages
Check antifreeze strength and adjust if necessary
Examine exhaust system for corrosion and leakage

Brakes
Examine brake lines, hoses, and connections for deterioration and leakage
Check rear brake shoes for wear and adjust
Check servo unit for operation and examine vacuum hose for deterioration

Steering
Check steering gear oil level and top up if necessary (photo)

Automatic transmission
Check fluid level and top up if necessary

Removing engine oil level dipstick

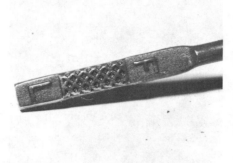
Engine oil level dipstick markings

Topping up engine oil level

Coolant level markings on expansion tank

Topping up battery electrolyte level

Checking fanbelt tension

Checking tyre pressures

Topping up windscreen washer fluid level

Brake fluid level markings on the reservoir

Engine oil drain plug on sump

Topping up gearbox oil level

Gearbox level and drain plug locations
(4-speed)

Rear axle level and drain plug locations

Steering gear oil level plug location (arrowed)

General
    Tighten all nuts and bolts as necessary
    Check wiper blades and renew if necessary
    Examine seat belts and anchorages for wear and security
    Lubricate all locks and hinges

Every 24 000 miles (40 000 km) or 24 months

Engine
    Tighten cylinder head bolts and manifold nuts as necessary
    Drain, flush and refill cooling system
    Renew air cleaner element

Brakes
    Change brake fluid

Steering
    Examine steering balljoints and idler arm for wear

Suspension and wheels
    Examine front suspension balljoints for wear
    Renew front wheel bearing grease

Body
    Check body for rust and corrosion and repair as necessary

---

Every 30 000 miles (50 000 km) or 30 months

Gearbox (manual) and rear axle
    Change oil

Fault diagnosis

Introduction

The car owner who does his or her own maintenance according to the recommended schedules should not have to use this section of the manual very often. Modern component reliability is such that, provided those items subject to wear or deterioration are inspected or renewed at the specified intervals, sudden failure is comparatively rare. Faults do not usually just happen as a result of sudden failure, but develop over a period of time. Major mechanical failures in particular are usually preceded by characteristic symptoms over hundreds or even thousands of miles. Those components which do occasionally fail without warning are often small and easily carried in the car.

With any fault finding, the first step is to decide where to begin investigations. Sometimes this is obvious, but on other occasions a little detective work will be necessary. The owner who makes half a dozen haphazard adjustments or replacements may be successful in curing a fault (or its symptoms), but he will be none the wiser if the fault recurs and he may well have spent more time and money than was necessary. A calm and logical approach will be found to be more satisfactory in the long run. Always take into account any warning signs or abnormalities that may have been noticed in the period preceding the fault – power loss, high or low gauge readings, unusual noises or smells, etc – and remember that failure of components such as fuses or spark plugs may only be pointers to some underlying fault.

The pages which follow here are intended to help in cases of failure to start or breakdown on the road. There is also a Fault Diagnosis Section at the end of each Chapter which should be consulted if the preliminary checks prove unfruitful. Whatever the fault, certain basic principles apply. These are as follows:

Verify the fault. This is simply a matter of being sure that you know what the symptoms are before starting work. This is particularly important if you are investigating a fault for someone else who may not have described it very accurately.

Don't overlook the obvious. For example, if the car won't start, is there petrol in the tank? (Don't take anyone else's word on this particular point, and don't trust the fuel gauge either!) If an electrical fault is indicated, look for loose or broken wires before digging out the test gear.

Cure the disease, not the symptom. Substituting a flat battery with a fully charged one will get you off the hard shoulder, but if the underlying cause is not attended to, the new battery will go the same way. Similarly, changing oil-fouled spark plugs for a new set will get you moving again, but remember that the reason for the fouling (if it wasn't simply an incorrect grade of plug) will have to be established and corrected.

Don't take anything for granted. Particularly, don't forget that a 'new' component may itself be defective (especially if it's been rattling round in the boot for months), and don't leave components out of a fault diagnosis sequence just because they are new or recently fitted. When you do finally diagnose a difficult fault, you'll probably realise that all the evidence was there from the start.

Electrical faults

Electrical faults can be more puzzling than straightforward mechanical failures, but they are no less susceptible to logical analysis if the basic principles of operation are understood. Car electrical wiring exists in extremely unfavourable conditions – heat, vibration and chemical attack – and the first things to look for are loose or corroded connections and broken or chafed wires, especially where the wires pass through holes in the bodywork or are subject to vibration.

All metal-bodied cars in current production have one pole of the battery 'earthed', ie connected to the car bodywork, and in nearly all modern cars it is the negative (–) terminal. The various electrical components' motors, bulb holders etc – are also connected to earth, either by means of a lead or directly by their mountings. Electric current flows through the component and then back to the battery via the car bodywork. If the component mounting is loose or corroded, or if a good path back to the battery is not available, the circuit will be incomplete and malfunction will result. The engine and/or gearbox are also earthed by means of flexible metal straps to the body or subframe; if these straps are loose or missing, starter motor, generator and ignition trouble may result.

Assuming the earth return to be satisfactory, electrical faults will be due either to component malfunction or to defects in the current supply. Individual components are dealt with in Chapter 10. If supply wires are broken or cracked internally this results in an open-circuit, and the easiest way to check for this is to bypass the suspect wire temporarily with a length of wire having a crocodile clip or suitable connector at each end. Alternatively, a 12V test lamp can be used to verify the presence of supply voltage at various points along the wire and the break can be thus isolated.

If a bare portion of a live wire touches the car bodywork or other earthed metal part, the electricity will take the low-resistance path thus formed back to the battery: this is known as a short-circuit. Hopefully a short-circuit will blow a fuse, but otherwise it may cause burning of the insulation (and possibly further short-circuits) or even a fire. This is why it is inadvisable to bypass persistently blowing fuses with silver foil or wire.

Spares and tool kit

Most cars are only supplied with sufficient tools for wheel changing; the *Maintenance and minor repair* tool kit detailed in *Tools and working facilities,* with the addition of a hammer, is probably sufficient for those repairs that most motorists would consider attempting at the roadside. In addition a few items which can be fitted without too much trouble in the event of a breakdown should be carried. Experience and available space will modify the list below, but the following may save having to call on professional assistance:

Spark plugs, clean and correctly gapped
HT lead and plug cap – long enough to reach the plug furthest from the distributor
Distributor rotor, condenser and contact breaker points (as applicable)
Drivebelt – emergency type may suffice
Spare fuses
Set of principal light bulbs
Tin of radiator sealer and hose bandage
Exhaust bandage
Roll of insulating tape
Length of soft iron wire
Length of electrical flex
Torch or inspection lamp (can double as test lamp)
Battery jump leads
Tow-rope
Ignition waterproofing aerosol
Litre of engine oil
Sealed can of hydraulic fluid
Emergency windscreen
Worm drive hose clips
Tube of filler paste

If spare fuel is carried, a can designed for the purpose should be used to minimise risks of leakage and collision damage. A first aid kit and a warning triangle, whilst not at present compulsory in the UK, are obviously sensible items to carry in addition to the above.

When touring abroad it may be advisable to carry additional spares which, even if you cannot fit them yourself, could save having to wait while parts are obtained. The items below may be worth considering:

Clutch and throttle cables (as applicable)
Cylinder head gasket
Alternator brushes
Tyre valve core

One of the motoring organisations will be able to advise on availability of fuel etc in foreign countries.

Engine will not start

Engine fails to turn when starter operated
Flat battery (recharge, use jump leads, or push start)
Battery terminals loose or corroded
Battery earth to body defective
Engine earth strap loose or broken
Starter motor (or solenoid) wiring loose or broken
Automatic transmission selector in wrong position, or inhibitor switch faulty
Ignition/starter switch faulty
Major mechanical failure (seizure) or long disuse (piston rings rusted to bores)
Starter or solenoid internal fault (see Chapter 10)

Starter motor turns engine slowly
Partially discharged battery (recharge, use jump leads, or push start)
Battery terminals loose or corroded
Battery earth to body defective
Engine earth strap loose
Starter motor (or solenoid) wiring loose
Starter motor internal fault (see Chapter 10)

Starter motor spins without turning engine
Flywheel gear teeth damaged or worn

Engine turns normally but fails to start
Damp or dirty HT leads and distributor cap (crank engine and check for spark) (photo)
Dirty or incorrectly gapped CB points (if applicable)
No fuel in tank (check for delivery at carburettor through sight glass)
Excessive choke (hot engine) or insufficient choke (cold engine)
Fouled or incorrectly gapped spark plugs (remove, clean and regap)
Other ignition system fault (see Chapter 4)
Other fuel system fault (see Chapter 3)
Poor compression (see Chapter 1)
Major mechanical failure (eg camshaft drive)

Engine fires but will not run
Insufficient choke (cold engine)
Air leaks at carburettor or inlet manifold
Fuel starvation (see Chapter 3)
Ballast resistor defective, or other ignition fault (see Chapter 4)

Engine cuts out and will not restart

Engine cuts out suddenly – ignition fault
Loose or disconnected LT wires
Wet HT leads or distributor cap (after traversing water splash)
Coil or condenser failure (check for spark)
Other ignition fault (see Chapter 4)

Engine misfires before cutting out – fuel fault
Fuel tank empty
Fuel pump defective or filter blocked (check for delivery)
Fuel tank filler vent blocked on UK models (suction will be evident on releasing cap)
Carburettor needle valve sticking
Carburettor jets bocked (fuel contaminated)
Other fuel system fault (see Chapter 3)

Engine cuts out – other causes
Serious overheating
Major mechanical failure (eg camshaft drive)

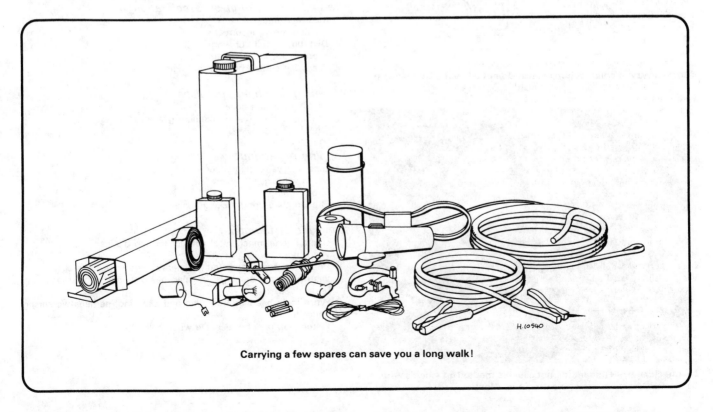

Carrying a few spares can save you a long walk!

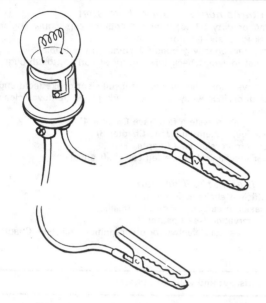

A simple test lamp is useful for tracing electrical faults

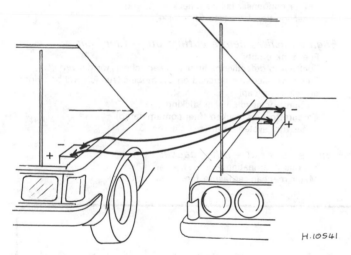

H.10541

Correct way to connect jump leads. Do not allow the car bodies to touch!

Checking for HT spark (do not use this method on models with electronic ignition)

Engine overheats

Ignition (no-charge) warning light illuminated
Slack or broken drivebelt – retension or renew (Chapter 2)

Ignition warning light not illuminated
Coolant loss due to internal or external leakage (see Chapter 2)
Thermostat defective
Low oil level
Brakes binding
Radiator clogged externally or internally
Engine waterways clogged
Ignition timing incorrect or automatic advance malfunctioning
Mixture too weak

Note: *Do not add cold water to an overheated engine or damage may result*

Low engine oil pressure

Warning light illuminated with engine running
Oil level low or incorrect grade
Defective sender unit
Wire to sender unit earthed
Engine overheating
Oil filter clogged or bypass valve defective
Oil pressure relief valve defective
Oil pick-up strainer clogged
Oil pump worn or mountings loose
Worn main or big-end bearings

Note: *Low oil pressure in a high-mileage engine at tickover is not necessarily a cause for concern. Sudden pressure loss at speed is far more significant. In any event, check the warning light sender before condemning the engine!*

Engine noises

Pre-ignition (pinking) on acceleration
Incorrect grade of fuel
Ignition timing incorrect
Distributor faulty or worn
Worn or maladjusted carburettor
Excessive carbon build-up in engine

Whistling or wheezing noises
Leaking vacuum hose
Leaking carburettor or manifold gasket
Blowing head gasket

Tapping or rattling
Incorrect valve clearances
Worn valve gear
Worn timing belt
Broken piston ring (ticking noise)

Knocking or thumping
Unintentional mechanical contact (eg fan blades)
Worn fanbelt
Peripheral component fault (generator, water pump etc)
Worn big-end bearings (regular heavy knocking, perhaps less under load)
Worn main bearings (rumbling and knocking, perhaps worsening under load)
Piston slap (most noticeable when cold)

Chapter 1 Engine

Refer to Chapter 13 for revisions and information related to 1982 models

Contents

Specifications

Engine – general

	1600	2000
Type	Four cylinder in-line, overhead camshaft	Four cylinder in-line, overhead camshaft
Displacement	1586 cc (96.8 cu in)	1970 cc (120.2 cu in)
Bore	78 mm (3.07 in)	80 mm (3.15 in)
Stroke	83 mm (3.27 in)	98 mm (3.86 in)
Compression ratio	8.6 : 1	8.6 : 1
Compression pressure	169 lbf/in² (11.9 kgf/cm²)	171 lbf/in² (12.0 kgf/cm²)
Firing order	1-3-4-2	1-3-4-2

Cylinder head

Type	Aluminium alloy, with hemispherical combustion chambers
Height (minimum)	108.0 ± 0.05 mm (4.28 ± 0.002 in)
Distortion (maximum)	0.15 mm (0.006 in)
Valve seat angle	45°
Valve seat width	1.4 mm (0.055 in)

Valves and valve gear

Valve clearance (warm engine):	
Valve side	0.012 in (0.30 mm)
Cam side	0.009 in (0.22 mm)
Valve face angle	45°
Valve stem-to-guide clearance (maximum)	0.20 mm (0.008 in)
Valve spring free length (minimum):	
Outer spring	36.2 mm (1.425 in)
Inner spring	35.7 mm (1.406 in)
Rocker arm running clearance (maximum)	0.10 mm (0.004 in)
Timing chain tensioner plunger movement (maximum)	17.0 mm (0.67 in)

Valve timing:
    Inlet valve opens .... 10° BTDC
    Inlet valve closes .... 57° ABDC
    Exhaust valve opens .... 54° BBDC
    Exhaust valve closes .... 13° ATDC

Camshaft

Number of bearings 3
Journal diameter (standard):
    Front and rear .... 44.945 to 44.960 mm (1.769 to 1.770 in)
    Centre .... 44.935 to 44.950 mm (1.7690 to 1.7696 in)
Journal wear limit .... 0.05 mm (0.002 in)
Camshaft endplay (maximum) .... 0.20 mm (0.008 in)
Camshaft run-out (maximum) .... 0.03 mm (0.0012 in)
Bearing clearance (maximum) .... 0.15 mm (0.0059 in)
Bearing undersizes .... 0.25, 0.50, 0.75 mm (0.010, 0.020, 0.030 in)

Cylinder block

Material .... Cast iron
Bore diameter (standard):
    1600 .... 78.000 to 78.019 mm (3.0709 to 3.0716 in)
    2000 .... 80.000 to 80.019 mm (3.1497 to 3.1504 in)
Bore wear limit .... 0.15 mm (0.0059 in)
Bore oversizes:
    1600 .... 0.25, 0.50, 0.75, 1.00 mm (0.010, 0.020, 0.030, 0.040 in)
    2000 .... 0.25, 0.50 mm (0.010, 0.020 in)

Pistons

Gudgeon pin type .... Interference fit in connecting rod
Piston ring side clearance:
    Top .... 0.030 to 0.070 mm (0.0012 to 0.0028 in)
    Second .... 0.030 to 0.064 mm (0.0012 to 0.0025 in)
Piston ring end gap:
    Top and second .... 0.2 to 0.4 mm (0.08 to 0.016 in)
    Oil .... 0.3 to 0.9 mm (0.012 to 0.035 in)

Connecting rods

Side clearance on crankshaft .... 0.11 to 0.21 mm (0.004 to 0.008 in)
Big-end bearing clearance (maximum) .... 0.10 mm (0.0039 in)

Crankshaft

Main journal diameter:
    New .... 62.940 to 62.955 mm (2.478 to 2.479 in)
    Wear limit .... 0.05 mm (0.002 in)
Crankpin diameter:
    New .... 52.940 to 52.955 mm (2.084 to 2.085 in)
    Wear limit .... 0.05 mm (0.002 in)
Crankshaft run-out (maximum) .... 0.03 mm (0.0012 in)
Main bearing running clearance (maximum) .... 0.08 mm (0.0031 in)
Crankshaft endplay (maximum) .... 0.30 mm (0.012 in)

Lubrication system

Oil pump type .... Bi-rotor, chain driven from crankshaft
Outer rotor-to-body clearance (maximum) .... 0.30 mm (0.012 in)
Inner rotor-to-outer rotor clearance (maximum) .... 0.25 mm (0.010 in)
Rotor endfloat (maximum) .... 0.15 mm (0.006 in)
Pump shaft running clearance (maximum) .... 0.10 mm (0.004 in)
Oil pressure at idling speed (minimum) .... 4.3 lbf/in² (0.3 kgf/cm²)
Oil pressure at 3000 rpm .... 50 to 64 lbf/in² (3.5 to 4.5 kgf/cm²)
Oil capacity (including filter):
    1600 .... 3.2 Imp qt; 36 litre; 3.8 US qt
    2000 .... 3.4 Imp qt; 3.9 litre; 4.1 US qt

Torque wrench settings

	lbf ft	Nm
Main bearing caps	61 to 65	82 to 88
Big-end caps:		
1600	36 to 40	48 to 54
2000	30 to 33	40 to 44
Oil pump sprocket	24	32
Sump	6	8
Cylinder head bolts:		
1600 – cold	56 to 60	75 to 81
1600 – warm	69 to 72	93 to 97
2000 – cold	65 to 69	88 to 93
2000 – warm	69 to 72	93 to 97

Camshaft sprocket	51 to 58	69 to 78
Distributor drivegear	51 to 58	69 to 78
Valve cover	1.3	1.7
Crankshaft pulley	101 to 108	136 to 146
Oil pressure switch	12	16
Flywheel/driveplate	112 to 118	151 to 159
Engine mountings	29	39

1 General description

The engine is of four-cylinder, in-line overhead camshaft type, and is available in 1600 cc and 2000 cc versions.

The aluminium alloy cylinder head incorporates hemispherical combustion chambers, and the inclined valves are operated by rocker arms from the centrally located camshaft. The camshaft is driven by a double-row timing chain from the front of the crankshaft, and is supported in three bearings. Endfloat is controlled by a thrust plate bolted to the front bearing cap. A hydraulically assisted timing chain tensioner is fitted.

Positive crankcase ventilation is provided by a valve located on the side of the inlet manifold and connected to the valve cover by a hose. A further hose connects the air cleaner to the valve cover.

The lubrication system uses an oil pump, driven by a chain from the front of the crankshaft. The oil is fed from the oil pump to an externally mounted oil filter canister of the full-flow type. It is then fed to the crankshaft, camshaft and rocker shafts. A pressure relief valve is incorporated into the oil pump body.

2 Major operations possible with engine in car

The following operations can be carried out without having to remove the engine from the car:

(a) *Removal and refitting of the camshaft and bearings*
(b) *Removal, servicing and refitting of the cylinder head*
(c) *Removal and refitting of the sump, big-end bearings and pistons*
(d) *Removal and refitting of the timing cover, oil pump and timing chain*
(e) *Renewal of the crankshaft rear oil seal*
(f) *Removal and refitting of the flywheel driveplate*
(g) *Renewal of the engine mountings*

3 Major operations only possible after removal of engine

The following operation can only be carried out after removal of the engine from the car.

Removal and refitting of the crankshaft

4 Methods of engine removal

On manual gearbox models, the engine can be removed complete with the gearbox, or independently, leaving the gearbox in the car. If work is required on both the gearbox and engine, remove both units at the same time and separate them on the bench. If work is only required on the engine, remove the engine separately.

On automatic transmission models, it is recommended that the engine is always removed separately, due to space limitations in the engine compartment and the extra weight of the transmission.

5 Engine – removal without manual gearbox/automatic transmission

1 Remove the bonnet as described in Chapter 12.
2 Disconnect the battery negative lead.
3 Drain the cooling system and remove the radiator as described in Chapter 2.

4 Remove the air cleaner assembly as described in Chapter 3.
5 Note the location of the engine wiring harness (photo), then disconnect it from the following components:

(a) *Distributor – primary and HT*
(b) *Alternator – plug and terminal*
(c) *Oil pressure switch (photo)*
(d) *Water temperature sender unit*
(e) *Fuel-cut solenoid*
(f) *Starter motor*
(g) *Automatic choke (where applicable)*

6 Unbolt the earth cable from the engine (photo).
7 Disconnect the fuel hoses from the carburettor.
8 Disconnect the accelerator and choke cables from the carburettor and engine with reference to Chapter 3.
9 Where applicable on US and Canadian models, disconnect the emission control air and vacuum hoses from the engine.
10 Disconnect the brake servo vacuum hose from the inlet manifold.
11 Disconnect the heater and cooling system hoses from the engine (photo).
12 Unscrew and remove the engine mounting nuts.
13 Where applicable, remove the air conditioner compressor and throttle opener.
14 Jack up the front of the car and support it on axle stands. Apply the handbrake.
15 Remove the engine guard panel (photo).
16 Unscrew the bolt securing the exhaust pipe to the front mounting. Unscrew the manifold-to-downpipe nuts, lower the exhaust pipe and tie it to one side. Recover the gasket.
17 Remove the clutch cable or slave cylinder from the gearbox with reference to Chapter 5 (manual gearbox models only).
18 Unscrew the drain plug and drain the engine oil into a suitable container. Refit and tighten the plug.
19 Prise the two cable fasteners from the left-hand engine mounting.
20 Unbolt and remove the manual gearbox/automatic transmission front cover and brackets.
21 Remove the starter motor as described in Chapter 10.
22 On automatic transmission models unscrew the bolts securing the torque converter to the driveplate. These bolts are accessible through the front cover aperture and it is necessary to turn the engine in order to reach all of them.
23 Connect a chain or sling to the engine lifting hooks and take the weight of the engine with a suitable hoist. If the hoist height is limited, it may be necessary at this point to first lower the car to the ground.
24 Position a trolley jack beneath the gearbox/automatic transmission with a block of wood between the jack and the casing. Take the weight of the gearbox/transmission.
25 Unscrew the gearbox/transmission-to-engine bolts, noting the location of the exhaust mounting bracket, reversing light switch wiring clip, and engine hanger. Reverse the bolt position to reconnect the hanger to the engine.
26 Check that all wires, cables and hoses have been disconnected, then lift the engine until it clears the front mountings.
27 Adjust the trolley jack then pull the engine forward until it clears the input shaft (manual gearbox models) or torque converter (automatic transmission models). On automatic transmission models the torque converter must be held fully engaged with the transmission oil pump. To do this, use a length of wood inserted through a hole in the driveplate, and press the torque converter from the driveplate as the engine is being removed.
28 Lift the engine from the car and lower it into a workbench or large piece of wood.

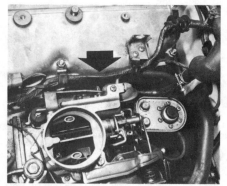

5.5A Engine wiring harness location

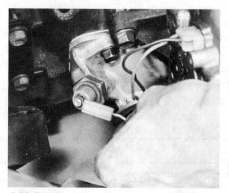

5.5B Disconnecting oil pressure switch wire

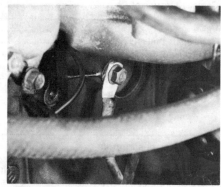

5.6 Engine earth cable location

5.11 Disconnecting a heater hose

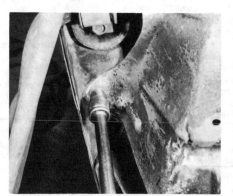

5.15 Removing engine guard panel

6.10A Lifting engine and gearbox from car

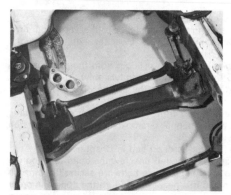

6.10B Engine compartment showing mounting brackets on the crossmember

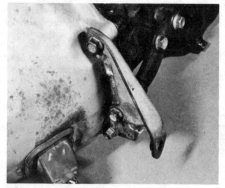

7.3 Exhaust mounting bracket location

7.4 Separating engine from gearbox

6   Engine – removal with manual gearbox

1   Follow the procedure given in Section 5, paragraphs 1 to 19 inclusive.

2   Unscrew the drain plug and drain the gearbox oil into a suitable container. Refit and tighten the plug.

3   Remove the propeller shaft as described in Chapter 7.

4   Working inside the car, prise out the plastic cover, remove the screws and knob, and withdraw the centre console over the handbrake lever.

5   Prise off the rubber boot, unscrew the bolts, and lift the gear lever from the extension housing.

6   Working beneath the car, unscrew the knurled ring and disconnect the speedometer cable.

7   Connect a chain or sling to the engine lifting hooks so that, when lifted, the engine and gearbox will assume a steep angle. Take the weight of the engine and gearbox with a suitable hoist. If the hoist

height is limited, it may be necessary at this point to first lower the car to the ground.

8   Position a trolley jack beneath the gearbox with a block of wood between the jack and the casing. Take the weight of the gearbox.

9   Unscrew the nuts securing the gearbox mounting crossmember to the bodyframe, and remove the washers.

10   Check that all wires, cables and hoses have been disconnected, then lift the engine until it clears the front mountings. Lower the trolley jack and move it forward, at the same time lift the engine and gearbox from the engine compartment. Lower the assembly onto a workbench or large piece of wood (photos).

7   Engine – separation from manual gearbox

1   With the engine and gearbox removed from the car unbolt and remove the gearbox front cover and brackets.

2   Remove the starter motor as described in Chapter 10.

3 Unscrew the gearbox-to-engine bolts, noting the location of the exhaust mounting bracket, reversing light switch wiring clip, and engine hanger (photo).

4 Withdraw the gearbox from the engine, taking care not to allow the weight of the gearbox to hang on the input shaft while the shaft is still engaged with the clutch disc (photo).

8 Engine dismantling – general

1 It is best to mount the engine on a dismantling stand, but if this is not available, stand the engine on a strong bench at a comfortable working height. Failing this, it will have to be stripped down on the floor.

2 During the dismantling process, the greatest care should be taken to keep the exposed parts free from dirt. As an aid to achieving this, thoroughly clean down the outside of the engine, first removing all traces of oil and congealed dirt.

3 A good grease solvent will make the job much easier, for, after the solvent has been applied and allowed to stand for a time, a vigorous jet of water will wash off the solvent and grease with it. If the dirt is thick and deeply embedded, work the solvent into it with a strong stiff brush.

4 Finally, wipe down the exterior of the engine with a rag and only then, when it is quite clean, should the dismantling process begin. As the engine is stripped, clean each part in a bath of paraffin or petrol.

5 Never immerse parts with oilways in paraffin (eg crankshaft). To clean these parts, wipe down carefully with a petrol dampened rag. Oilways can be cleaned out with wire. If an air-line is available, all parts can be blown dry and the oilways blown through as an added precaution.

6 Re-use of old gaskets is false economy. To avoid the possibility of trouble after the engine has been reassembled **always** use new gaskets throughout.

7 Do not throw away the old gaskets, for sometimes it happens that an immediate replacement cannot be found and the old gasket is then very useful as a template. Hang up the gaskets as they are removed.

8 To strip the engine, it is best to work from the top down. When the stage is reached where the crankshaft must be removed, the engine can be turned on its side and all other work carried out with it in this position.

9 Wherever possible, refit nuts, bolts and washers finger tight from wherever they were removed. This helps to avoid loss and muddle. If they cannot be refitted, then arrange them in such a fashion that it is clear from whence they came.

9 Ancillary components – removal

With the engine on the bench, the external ancillary components can be removed. The removal sequence need not necessarily follow the order given:

Clutch assembly (Chapter 5)
Inlet and exhaust manifolds (Chapter 3)
Water pump (Chapter 2)
Distributor (Chapter 4)
Alternator (Chapter 10)
HT leads and spark plugs (Chapter 4)
Engine mountings and brackets (Section 20 of this Chapter)
Oil pressure switch
Emission control components on US and Canadian models (Chapter 3)

10 Camshaft – removal

1 If the engine is still in the car, first carry out the following operations:

(a) Drain the cooling system (Chapter 2)
(b) Remove the air cleaner assembly (Chapter 3)
(c) Disconnect the accelerator and choke cables as applicable from the carburettor and valve cover bracket
(d) Disconnect the crankcase ventilation hose from the valve cover
(e) Remove the distributor (Chapter 4)

2 Unscrew the valve cover nuts and remove the wiring harness clips, noting their location. Remove the valve cover and gasket (photo). Remove the half round rubber oil seals from the front and rear of the cylinder head.

3 Before starting to remove the camshaft check the endplay using a dial gauge as shown in Fig. 1.1 – if it exceeds the specified maximum amount it will be necessary to renew the thrust plate located on the front bearing cap.

4 Flatten the locktab and unscrew the nut from the front of the camshaft (photo). Hold the crankshaft stationary while the nut is being loosened by either engaging top gear (engine in car) or having an assistant hold a wide bladed screwdriver in engagement with the flywheel/driveplate ring gear (engine out of car).

5 Remove the lockwasher and slide the distributor drivegear from the key (photo).

6 If the timing chain is not being subsequently removed, wire the camshaft sprocket to the timing chain in order to retain the valve timing.

7 Flatten the locktab and unscrew the sprocket retaining nut using the method described in paragraph 3. Remove the lockwasher (photos).

8 Unscrew the cylinder head bolts a little at a time in the reverse order to that shown in Fig. 1.11.

9 With all the bolts loose, wire the four corner bolts together and lift the complete valve rocker gear assembly from the cylinder head (photo).

10 During the next operation, the camshaft sprocket must be held in a raised position in order to keep the timing chain taut, so that the tensioner plunger is not allowed to come out of its body. First insert some cloth beneath the sprocket to catch the Woodruff key if it should come out.

11 Lift the rear of the camshaft and slide it from the sprocket (photo). Wire the sprocket and timing chain to the cylinder head to hold the chain in contact with the crankshaft sprocket.

12 Extract the bearing shells from the cylinder head and bearing caps, but keep them identified for position (photo).

13 If only the camshaft is being removed, it is important not to distort the cylinder head gasket, otherwise it will be necessary to remove the complete cylinder head in order to renew the gasket

11 Cylinder head – removal

1 If the engine is still in the car, first carry out the following operations:

(a) Remove the inlet and exhaust manifolds (Chapter 3)
(b) Remove the HT leads and spark plugs (Chapter 4)
(c) Remove the emission control components as necessary on US and Canadian models (Chapter 3)
(d) Disconnect the engine wiring harness from the distributor and water temperature sender unit
(e) Drain the cooling system (Chapter 2) and disconnect the heater and cooling system hoses from the engine
(f) Where applicable, remove the air conditioning compressor and throttle opener

Fig. 1.1 Checking camshaft endplay with a dial gauge (Sec 10)

10.2 Removing the valve cover

10.4 Unscrewing camshaft front nut

10.5 Removing distributor drivegear

10.7A Flatten the locktab ...

10.7B ... and unscrew the camshaft sprocket retaining nut

10.9 Removing valve rocker gear assembly

10.11 Removing the camshaft

10.12 Extracting a camshaft bearing shell from the cylinder head

11.2 Unscrewing cylinder head front bolt

11.4 Removing the cylinder head

12.2A Compressing valve springs to remove the split collets

12.2B Removing valve retainer ...

2   Remove the camshaft as described in Section 10. Unscrew the bolt securing the front to the cylinder head to the timing cover (photo). On some models this bolt is accessible from inside the head casing, on others it is outside.

3   Remove the wire securing the camshaft sprocket to the head, but keep the sprocket raised in order to prevent the timing chain tensioner from coming out.

4   Have an assistant hold the sprocket raised with a length of welding rod, then lift the cylinder head from the block and dowel pins (photo). If it is stuck, tap it free with a wooden mallet. *Do not insert a lever into the gasket joint* – you may damage the mating faces.

5   Remove the cylinder head gasket, and position a block of wood between the sprocket and cylinder block to keep the timing chain tensioned.

12 Cylinder head – dismantling

1   Remove the thermostat and spacer as described in Chapter 2.

2   Using a valve spring compressor, compress the springs in turn until the split collets can be removed. Release the compressor and remove the retainer, springs, and spring seat (photos). If the retainer is difficult to release, do not continue to tighten the compressor, but gently tap the top of the tool with a hammer. Always make sure that the compressor is held firmly over the retainer.

3   Remove each valve from the combustion chambers, keeping all the components in their correct sequence unless they are to be renewed (photo). To identify the valves they can be inserted in holes punched in stiff card with the letters 'I' (inlet) and 'E' (exhaust) adjacent to the valves. Number the cylinders 1 to 4 from the thermostat end of the cylinder head.

4   If necessary, prise the valve seals from the guides (photo).

13 Sump – removal

1   If the engine is still in the car, first carry out the following operations:

(a) *Jack up the front of the car and support it on axle stands*

(b) *Unscrew the drain plug and drain the engine oil into a suitable container. Refit and tighten the plug*

(c) *Remove the engine guard panel*

(d) *Unscrew the engine mounting nuts then, using a suitable hoist, lift the engine approximately 2 inches (50 mm)*

2   Unscrew the bolts and remove the sump from the crankcase (photo). If it is stuck use a sharp knife to release it.

3   Remove the gasket from the crankcase and timing cover.

4   Remove the oil level dipstick.

14 Timing cover, oil pump and timing chain – removal

1   If the engine is still in the car, first carry out the following operations:

(a) *Remove the water pump as described in Chapter 2*

(b) *Remove the alternator as described in Chapter 10*

2   Remove the cylinder head as described in Section 11. Remove the sump as described in Section 13.

3   Unbolt the alternator mounting bracket from the timing cover and cylinder block (photo).

4   Unscrew the crankshaft pulley bolt – to hold the crankshaft stationary position a block of wood between a crankshaft web and the crankcase (photo).

5   Withdraw the pulley from the nose of the crankshaft (photo).

6   Unbolt the timing chain cover from the front of the cylinder block and remove the gasket (photo).

7   Prise the oil seal from the timing chain cover and remove the oil thrower.

8   Remove the camshaft sprocket from the timing chain.

9   Withdraw the oil thrower from the crankshaft noting that its concave side faces outward (photo).

10 Remove the screws and withdraw the timing chain guide and damper.

11 Unbolt the chain tensioner body and plunger from the cylinder block.

12 Flatten the locktab and unscrew the oil pump sprocket nut (photo). Hold the sprocket stationary with a screwdriver inserted through one of the holes.

13 Pull the sprocket from the oil pump, then release the chain from the crankshaft sprocket. Recover the key from the oil pump shaft (photos).

14 Slide the sprockets and timing chain from the crankshaft and remove the Woodruff key.

15 Unbolt the oil pump from the crankcase and remove any shims fitted (photo).

15 Flywheel/driveplate – removal

1   If the engine is still in the car, first carry out the following operations:

(a) *On manual gearbox models, remove the clutch as described in Chapter 5*

(b) *On automatic transmission models, remove the transmission as described in Chapter 5*

2   Unscrew and remove the retaining bolts, noting that the spigot bearing retaining washers are located on opposite bolts. Hold the flywheel/driveplate stationary by placing a piece of angle iron in the teeth of the starter ring gear against a bolt inserted into the cylinder block (photos).

3   Mark the position of the flywheel/driveplate on the crankshaft by putting a dab of paint in one of the bolt hole threads and on the flywheel/driveplate.

4   Lift the flywheel/driveplate from the crankshaft (photo).

16 Crankshaft rear oil seal – renewal

1   Remove the flywheel/driveplate as described in Section 15.

2   Using an awl, punch two diametrically opposite holes in the crankshaft rear oil seal and insert two self-tapping screws.

3   Prise out the seal with a screwdriver, then clean the recess with lint-free cloth.

4   Lubricate the new oil seal with engine oil and drive it squarely into position using a suitable length of metal tube.

5   Refit the flywheel/driveplate as described in Section 34.

17 Big-end bearings and pistons – removal

1   Remove the cylinder head as described in Section 11.

2   Remove the sump as described in Section 13.

3   Unbolt the pick-up pipe and strainer from the oil pump body and remove the O-ring.

4   Check that the big-end caps and connecting rods are identified for location. If not, use a centre punch to mark them.

5   Turn the crankshaft (if necessary with a lever and two bolts inserted on the rear flange) so that No 1 big-end bearing bolts are accessible. Unscrew the bolts and remove the cap with the bearing shell.

6   Using a hammer handle, tap the connecting rod and piston out through the top of the cylinder block, taking care not to damage the bore.

7   Prise the bearing shells from the cap and connecting rod, but leave the components together to ensure correct reassembly.

8   Repeat the procedure given in paragraphs 5 to 7 on piston No 4, then turn the crankshaft through 180° and remove pistons No 2 and 3 (photos).

12.2C ... springs ...

12.2D ... and spring seat

12.3 Removing an exhaust valve

12.4 Valve seal location on the valve guide

13.2 Removing the sump

14.3 Removing the alternator mounting bracket

14.4 Removing the crankshaft pulley bolt

14.5 Withdrawing camshaft pulley

14.6 Removing the timing chain cover

14.9 Crankshaft front oil thrower

14.12 Oil pump sprocket and nut

14.13A Removing oil pump sprocket and chain

14.13B Oil pump shaft and key

14.15 Removing the oil pump

15.2A Method of holding flywheel/driveplate and crankshaft stationary

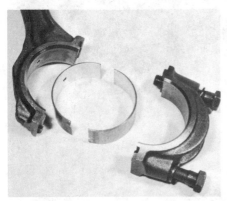

15.2B Flywheel retaining bolts and spigot bearing

15.4 Removing the flywheel

17.8A Removing a big-end bearing cap

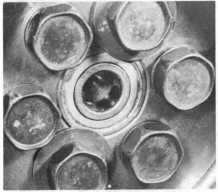

17.8B Big-end bearing shells, cap and connecting rod

18.5 Checking crankshaft endfloat with a feeler gauge

18.6A Removing front main bearing cap on an early model; note that as from September 1980, the timing chain stopper is incorporated into the timing chain cover

18.6B Removing rear main bearing cap

18.7 Lifting out the crankshaft

18.8 Removing a main bearing shell from the crankcase

19.2 Unscrewing the oil filter canister

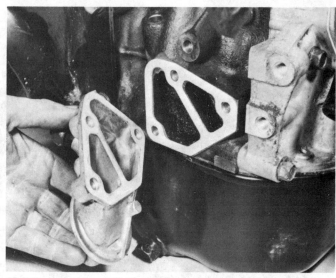

19.3 Removing the oil filter housing

20.4A Removing engine mounting cover ...

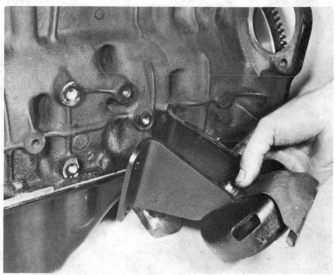

20.4B ... and bracket

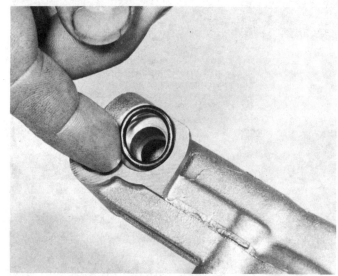

23.1 Oil pump outlet O-ring seal location

23.3 Removing oil pump cover

18 Crankshaft and main bearings – removal

1   Remove the timing cover, oil pump and timing chain as described in Section 14.
2   Remove the flywheel/driveplate as described in Section 15.
3   Remove the big-end bearings and pistons as described in Section 17, but note that if it is only required to remove the crankshaft, it is not necessary to remove the pistons from the cylinder block.
4   Check that the main bearing caps are identified for location. If not, use a centre punch to mark them.
5   Before removing the crankshaft check the endfloat with a feeler blade inserted between the rear crankshaft web and the thrust washer (photo). This will indicate whether new thrust washers are required.
6   Unscrew and remove the main bearing cap bolts and withdraw the caps complete with bearing shells. Prise out the shells, but keep them identified for position. When removing the rear cap, lift the crankshaft to release the side seals (photos).
7   Lift the crankshaft from the crankcase and remove the oil seal from the rear flange (photo).
8   Prise the bearing shells from the crankcase recesses, but keep them identified for location (photo). Remove the thrust washers.

19 Oil filter and housing – removal and refitting

1   If the engine is in the car, jack up the front of the car and support it on axle stands. Apply the handbrake and remove the engine guard panel.
2   Using a strap wrench, unscrew the oil filter canister from the housing and discard it (photo).
3   If it is required to remove the housing, first remove the alternator as described in Chapter 10, then unbolt the alternator mounting bracket from the cylinder block. Unbolt the housing and remove the gasket (photo).
4   Wipe clean the mating faces, then refit the housing to the cylinder block, together with a new gasket, and tighten the bolts. Refit the alternator mounting bracket and alternator with reference to Chapter 10.
5   To fit the new oil filter, wipe clean the mating face on the housing and smear a little engine oil on the filter sealing rubber.
6   Screw the filter onto the housing hand tight only.
7   If the engine is in the car, lower the car to the ground.

20 Engine mountings – removal and refitting

1   Jack up the front of the car and support it with axle stands. Renew the engine guard panel.
2   Unscrew and remove the mounting nuts.
3   Position a trolley jack beneath the sump with a block of wood on the jack, then take the weight of the engine.
4   Unbolt the mounting bracket from the cylinder block and remove the mounting and cover (photos).
5   Refitting is a reversal of removal.

Fig. 1.2 Oil pump relief valve components (Sec 23)

1   Split pin   2   Spring seat   3   Spring

21 Crankcase ventilation system – general

1   The positive crankcase ventilation system is controlled by a valve located in the side of the inlet manifold. To test the valve, first run the engine until it reaches its normal operating temperature.
2   Stop the engine and disconnect the ventilation hose from the valve cover.
3   Start the engine and allow it to idle, then block the hose with the thumb. The engine speed should drop if the valve is working – if this is not the case, renew the valve.
4   Periodically, the crankcase ventilation valve and hoses should be removed and cleaned with paraffin to remove any accumulation of sludge. At the same time check the hoses for deterioration, and if necessary renew them.

22 Examination and renovation – general

With the engine completely stripped, clean all the components and examine them for wear. Each part should be checked and, where necessary, renewed or renovated as described in the following Sections. Renew main and big-end bearing shells as a matter of course, unless you know that they have had little wear and are in perfect condition.

23 Oil pump – examination and renovation

1   Extract the O-ring seal from the oil pump outlet (photo).
2   Unbolt the pick-up pipe and strainer from the oil pump body, and remove the O-ring.
3   Unscrew the bolts and remove the cover (photo).
4   Withdraw the inner rotor and shaft followed by the outer rotor.
5   Remove the split pin and withdraw the spring seat, spring and relief valve plunger from the pump body.
6   Clean the components and examine them for wear and damage.
7   Insert the rotors into the body, making sure that the assembly marks face the same way. Using a feeler blade check that the rotor clearances do not exceed those given in Specifications (photos).
8   Check the condition of the plunger and seat.
9   Renew the oil pump if it is worn excessively.
10 Reassembly of the oil pump is a reversal of dismantling, but make sure that the mating faces are clean.

24 Crankshaft and main bearings – examination and renovation

1   Examine the bearing surfaces of the crankshaft for scratches or scoring and, using a micrometer, check each journal and crankpin for wear and ovality. Where the ovality is in excess of 0.0254 mm (0.001 in) or the wear limit exceeds that given in Specifications, the crankshaft will have to be reground and undersize bearings fitted.
2   Crankshaft regrinding is normally carried out by an engine reconditioning engineering works, who will supply matching undersize main and big-end shell bearings, and also new thrust washers.
3   Check the main bearing shells for wear and scoring. If the shells are matt grey in colour over the bearing surface, they are probably serviceable, but, if the engine has completed in excess of 40 000 miles they should be renewed as a matter of course.

25 Cylinder block and crankcase – examination and renovation

1   The cylinder bores must be examined for taper, ovality, scoring and scratches. Start by carefully examining the top of the cylinder bores. If they are at all worn, a very slight ridge will be found on the thrust side. This marks the top of the piston travel. The owner will have a good indication of the bore wear prior to dismantling the engine, or removing the cylinder head. Excessive oil consumption accompanied by blue smoke from the exhaust is a sure sign of worn cylinder bores and piston rings.
2   Measure the bore diameter just under the ridge with a micrometer and compare it with the diameter at the bottom of the bore, which is not subject to wear. If the difference between the two measurements

23.7A Checking oil pump outer rotor-to-body clearance

23.7B Checking oil pump inner rotor-to-outer rotor clearance

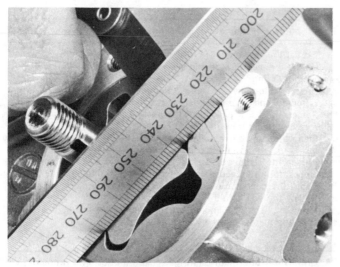

23.7C Add oil pump rotor clearance ...

23.7D ... to cover clearance to calculate rotor endfloat

is more than 0.006 in (0.15 mm) then it will be necessary to fit oversize pistons and rings. If no micrometer is available, remove the rings from a piston and place the piston in each bore in turn about three quarters of an inch below the top of the bore. If a 0.010 in (0.25 mm) feeler gauge can be slid between the piston and the cylinder wall on the thrust side of the bore then oversize pistons must be obtained. These are accurately machined to just below the rebore measurements, so as to provide correct running clearances in bores bored out to the exact oversize dimensions.

3   If the bores are slightly worn, but not so badly worn as to justify reboring them, special oil control rings can be installed to the existing pistons which will help restore compression and stop the engine burning oil. Several different types are available and the manufacturer's instructions concerning their installation must be followed closely.

4   Thoroughly examine the crankcase for damage, and use a piece of wire to probe all oilways and waterways to ensure they are unobstructed.

26 Pistons and connecting tods – examination and renovation

1   If the cylinder block is to be rebored, new pistons must be fitted, and these can usually be supplied by the reboring specialist. However,

for the removal of the old pistons and the fitting of the new pistons to the connecting rods, the components should be taken to a Mazda dealer, as special equipment is necessary to press the gudgeon pins from the connecting rods.

2   If new rings are to be fitted to the original pistons, expand the old rings over the top of the pistons. The use of two or three old feeler blades will prevent the rings dropping into empty grooves. Note that the oil control ring is in three sections.

3   Before fitting the new rings to the pistons, insert them into the bottom of the cylinder bore and use a feeler gauge to check that the ring end gaps are within the specified limits.

4   With the rings fitted, using feeler blades as for removal, use a feeler gauge to check that the side clearances within the grooves are within the specified limits.

5   Arrange the piston ring gaps at equidistant points so that they are not in alignment.

6   Check the connecting rods for wear and damage. If their alignment is uncertain they should be checked by a competent engineering works.

7   Check the big-end bearing shells for wear and scoring. If wear is evident but the crankshaft crankpins are not worn excessively, obtain new shells of the same size – the size is marked on the back of the shells.

27 Flywheel/driveplate – examination and renovation

1   On the flywheel, examine the clutch driven plate mating surface – if this is excessively scored, it must be either refaced or a new flywheel obtained.

2   On the flywheel or driveplate, examine the starter ring gear – if the teeth are chipped or worn, the ring gear must be renewed on the flywheel, or the complete driveplate renewed.

3   To renew the flywheel ring gear, partially drill it from the side, then split it with a cold chisel (taking suitable precautions to avoid injury caused by flying fragments) and remove it. Heat the new ring to 480 to 570°F (250 to 300°C), then quickly fit it to the flywheel with the teeth chamfer facing the engine side. Allow the ring to cool naturally without quenching.

4   Check the gearbox input shaft spigot bearing in the centre of the flywheel for wear. If necessary drive out the old bearing and install a new one.

5   Examine the torque converter locating hole in the centre of the driveplate for damage. If evident, renew the driveplate.

28 Timing cover and chains – examination and renovation

1   Examine the timing cover for damage, and also for corrosion on the water pump location. If evident, renew it.

2   Examine all the teeth on the camshaft, crankshaft, and oil pump sprockets. If these are hooked in appearance, renew the sprockets.

3   Examine the timing and oil pump chains for wear. If they appear deeply bowed when held extended with the rollers vertical, renew them.

4   Examine the chain tensioner, guide and damper for wear and renew them as necessary (photo).

29 Cylinder head – decarbonising and valve grinding

1   This operation will normally only be required at comparatively high mileages. However, if persistent pinking occurs and performance has deteriorated even though the engine adjustments are correct, decarbonising and valve grinding may be required.

2   With the cylinder head off, carefully remove with a wire brush and blunt scraper all traces of carbon deposits from the combustion spaces and ports. The valve stems and valve guides should be also freed from any carbon deposits. Wash the combustion spaces and ports down with paraffin (kerosene) and scrape the cylinder head surface of any foreign matter with the side of a steel rule or a similar article. Take care not to scratch the surface.

3   Using a straight edge and feeler gauge, check the cylinder head surface for distortion. If this is in excess of the specified maximum, the head will have to be resurfaced within limits by a specialist engineering works.

28.4 Timing chain tensioner components

4   If the engine is still in the car, clean the piston crowns and upper edges of the bores. Make sure that no carbon finds its way between the pistons and bores otherwise damage may occur. To avoid this first turn the crankshaft so that two of the pistons are on top of the bores. Place a clean lint-free cloth into the other two bores or seal them off with paper and masking tape. Press a little grease between the two pistons and bores, then clean away the carbon. Lower the two pistons and wipe away the grease, which will now contain carbon particles.

5   The remaining piston crowns should be cleaned in a similar manner. To prevent carbon build-up, polish the piston crowns with metal polish, removing all traces afterwards.

6   Check the valve guides for wear. To do this insert each valve into its matching guide and check for side movement. If available use a dial gauge and compare the side clearance with the maximum given in the Specifications. If excessive, drive out the guide with a soft metal drift inserted through the combustion chamber, then drive in the new guide until the location ring touches the head. Note that inlet and exhaust guides are different (see Fig. 1.5).

7   Examine the heads of the valves for pitting and burning, especially the heads of the exhaust valves. The valve seatings should be examined at the same time. If the pitting on the valve and seats is very slight, the marks can be removed by grinding the seats and valves together with coarse, and then fine, valve grinding paste. Where bad pitting has occurred to the valve seats, it will be necessary to recut them to install new valves, and this work should be entrusted to a suitably equipped engineering works.

Fig. 1.3 Starter ring gear removed from the flywheel (Sec 27)

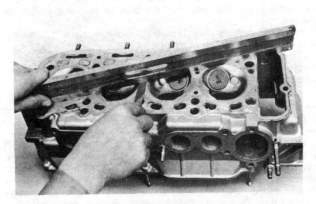

Fig. 1.4 Checking cylinder head surfaces for distortion (Sec 29)

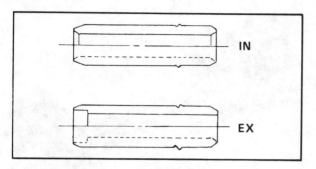

**Fig. 1.5 Cross-sectional diagram of inlet and exhaust valve guides
(Sec 29)**

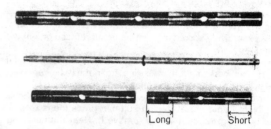

Fig. 1.6 Rocker shafts and oil distribution tube (Sec 30)

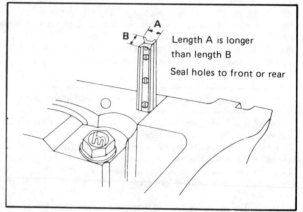

**Fig. 1.7 Correct installation of rear main bearing side seals
(Sec 32)**

8   Valve grinding is carried out for each valve as follows: Place the
cylinder head upside down on a bench with a block of wood at each
end to give clearance for the valve stems. Alternatively, place the head
at 45 degrees to a wall with the combustion chambers away from the
wall.
9   Smear a trace of coarse carborundum paste on the seat face and
apply a suction grinder tool to the valve head. With a semi-rotary
action, grind the valve head to its seat, lifting the valve occasionally to
redistribute the grinding parts. When a dull matt surface finish is
produced on both the valve seat and the valve, wipe off the paste and
repeat the process with fine carborundum paste, lifting and turning the
valve to redistribute the paste as before. A light spring placed under
the valve head will greatly ease this operation. When a smooth
unbroken ring of light grey matt finish is produced, on both valve and
the valve seat faces, the grinding operation is complete.
10   Scrape away all carbon from the valve head and the valve stem.
Carefully clean away every trace of grinding compound, taking great
care to leave none in the ports or in the valve guides. Clean the valves
and valve seats with a paraffin (kerosene) soaked rag, then with a
clean rag. Finally, if an air line is available, blow the valves, valve
guides and valve ports clean.
11   Check each valve spring free length, and if any are less than the
specified minimum, renew them as a set.
12   Make sure that the cylinder head oil and waterways are clear by
probing them with a piece of wire.

30 Camshaft and rocker gear – examination and renovation

1   Examine the camshaft bearing journals for scratches or scoring,
and using a micrometer check each journal for wear.
2   Check the bearing shells for wear and scoring. If evident, but the
camshaft journals are good, renew the shells.
2   If the camshaft journals are worn, they should be reground by an
engineering works provided that the cam lobes are still in good
condition.
4   If the camshaft endplay, as previously checked, is more than the
specified maximum, obtain a new thrust plate.
5   Check the rocker gear components for wear and renew them as
necessary. Make sure that the oil holes in the rocker shafts, oil
distribution pipe, and bearing caps are unobstructed (photos).

31 Engine reassembly – general

1   To ensure maximum life with minimum trouble from a rebuilt
engine, not only must every part be correctly assembled, but everything must be spotlessly clean, all the oilways must be clear, locking
washers and spring washers must always be fitted where indicated,
and all bearings and other working surfaces must be thoroughly
lubricated during assembly. Before assembly begins, renew any bolts
or studs with damaged threads.
2   Gather together a torque wrench, oil can, clean rag, and a set of
engine gaskets and oil seals, together with a new oil filter canister.

32 Crankshaft and main bearings – refitting

1   Clean the backs of the bearing shells and the bearing recesses in
both the crankcase and the caps.
2   Press the main bearing shells into the crankcase and caps and oil
them liberally. Note that there are different types of shell, and make
sure that they are located in the correct position (photos).
3   Stick the thrust washers on each side of the rear bearing shells
using a little grease. Make sure that the oil grooves face away from the
shells (photo).
4   Lower the crankshaft into position and locate the new oil seal on
the rear flange (photo).
5   Smear the rear main bearing side seals with sealing compound
and stick them into the grooves in the cap with the holes facing to the
front or rear of the engine (photo).
6   Lower the main bearing caps into position. Note that on early
models the manufacturers have only marked cap No 4 – the front, rear,
and centre caps can only be fitted in one position, but caps 2 and 4 are
identical (photo).
7   Insert and tighten the main bearing cap bolts to the specified
torque (photo).
8   Check that the crankshaft rotates smoothly and that the endplay
is less that the specified maximum.
9   Refit the big-end bearings and pistons as necessary as described
in Section 33.
10   Refit the flywheel/driveplate as described in Section 34.
11   Refit the timing cover, oil pump and timing chain as described in
Section 35.

33 Big-end bearings and pistons – refitting

1   Clean the backs of the bearing shells and the recesses in the
connecting rods and big-end caps.
2   Press the big-end bearing shells into the connecting rods and caps
in their correct positions, then apply engine oil liberally to the pistons,
bores and bearing shells.
3   Fit a ring compressor to No 1 piston, then insert the piston in No
1 bore with the 'F' mark on the side of the piston facing the front of
the engine (photo).

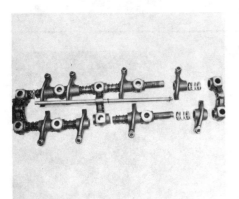
30.5A Valve rocker gear components

30.5B Valve rocker arms and camshaft end bearing cap

30.5C Camshaft oil distribution pipe

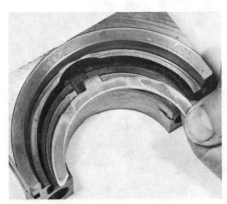
32.2A Crankshaft main bearing shells fitted into the crankcase

32.2B Lubricating main bearing shells

32.2C Inserting a main bearing shell into the rear cap

32.3 Installing the crankshaft thrust washers

32.4 Installing the crankshaft rear oil seal

32.5 Installing rear main bearing cap side seals

32.6 Number 4 crankshaft main bearing cap; note that the arrow on all caps must face the front of the engine

32.7 Tightening main bearing cap bolts

33.3 Piston showing 'F' mark which must face the front of the engine

33.4 Inserting a piston into the cylinder block

33.5 Tightening big-end bearing cap bolts

34.2 Tightening flywheel retaining bolts

4   Using the wooden handle of a hammer, drive the piston into the bore, and at the same time guide the connecting rod onto the crankshaft (photo).
5   Fit the correct big-end bearing cap to the connecting rod, then insert the bolts. Turn the crankshaft so that the bolts are accessible, then tighten them evenly to the specified torque (photo).
6   Check that the crankshaft turns smoothly.
7   Repeat the procedure given in paragraphs 3 to 6 on the remaining pistons.
8   As necessary, refit the pick-up pipe and strainer to the oil pump body, refit the sump as described in Section 36, and refit the cylinder head as described in Section 37.

34 Flywheel/driveplate – refitting

1   Locate the flywheel/driveplate on the rear of the crankshaft with the previously made marks aligned.
2   Insert the bolts, with the spigot bearing retaining washers located on opposite bolts, then tighten them evenly in diametrical sequence to the specified torque – hold the flywheel/driveplate stationary using the method described in Section 15, and remove the bolt and angle iron when completed (photo).
3   If the engine is in the car, reverse the preliminary procedure given in Section 15.

35 Timing cover, oil pump and timing chain – refitting

1   Locate any shims removed on the crankcase oil pump location.
2   Check that the O-ring is located in the oil pump outlet, then position the oil pump on the crankcase dowels. Insert and tighten the bolts.
3   Turn the crankshaft so that No 1 and 4 pistons are at the top of their bores, then position the engine upside down.
4   Engage the crankshaft and camshaft sprockets with the timing chain as shown in Fig. 1.8 and wire the camshaft sprocket as shown. Note that on some models only one bright link is provided for the crankshaft sprocket (photo).
5   Refit the Woodruff key, then slide the sprocket onto the camshaft.
6   Engage the oil pump and crankshaft sprockets with the oil pump chain, with the key grooves aligned in relation to each other.
7   Fit the key on the oil pump shaft with the flat facing outward, then slide the two sprockets into position. Locate the locktab and tighten the nut while holding the sprocket stationary with a screwdriver inserted through one of the holes.
8   Check the oil pump chain slack; if it exceeds 4.0 mm (0.157 in), install shims beneath the oil pump after temporarily removing the sprocket (photo). When correct, bend the locktab over the nut to lock it.
9   Fully compress the timing chain tensioner and retain it in this position with a length of welding rod bent to engage the plunger and body – this will prevent the plunger from coming out before the camshaft sprocket is fitted to the camshaft. Attach a piece of adhesive

tape to the rod to prevent it subsequently dropping into the sump (photo).
10   Locate the timing chain tensioner on the cylinder block and insert and tighten the bolts (photo).
11   Locate the timing chain guide and damper on the cylinder block and insert the screws. Tighten the damper (flat) screws but leave the guide (curved) screws finger tight (photo).
12   Fit the oil thrower on the crankshaft with its concave side outward.
13   Using a block of wood and a hammer, fit the oil thrower and new oil seal into the timing chain cover with its sealing lip facing inward (photos). Smear a little grease on the seal lip.
14   Smear the timing chain cover gaskets with sealing compound and stick them onto the front of the cylinder block (photo).
15   Locate the timing chain cover onto the dowel pins, then insert and tighten the bolts evenly.

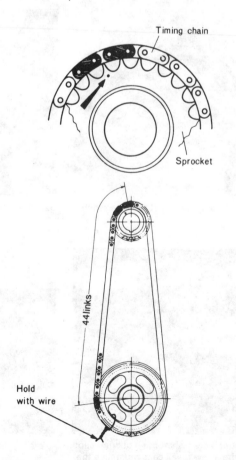

Fig. 1.8 Installation of timing gears in timing chain (Sec 35)

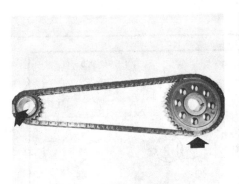

35.4 Crankshaft and camshaft sprockets positioned in timing chain; note the bright links (arrowed)

35.8 Checking oil pump chain tension

35.9 Using welding rod to retain plunger in timing chain tensioner

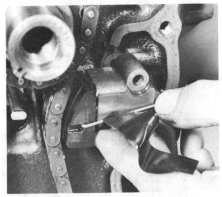

35.10 Installing timing chain tensioner

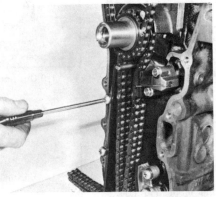

35.11 Tightening timing chain damper screws

35.13A Installing oil thrower ...

35.13B ... and oil seal to timing chain cover

35.14 Installing timing chain cover gaskets

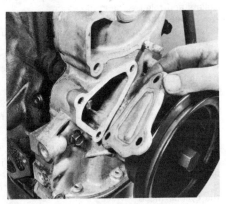

35.16A Removing access cover ...

35.16B ... to remove adhesive tape on timing chain tensioner

35.18 Tightening crankshaft pulley bolt

37.7 Installing cylinder head gasket

16 Unbolt the access cover from the timing chain cover and hook the adhesive tape out – use additional tape to stick it to the cover but do not disengage the welding rod (photos).

17 If necessary trim off the excess gasket from the sump and cylinder head mating surfaces.

18 Slide the pulley onto the front of the crankshaft and engage it with the key. Smear sealing compound onto the front face of the pulley, then insert the bolt and tighten it to the specified torque while holding the crankshaft stationary with a block of wood positioned between the crankshaft web and the crankcase (photo).

19 Locate the alternator mounting bracket on the timing cover and cylinder block, then insert and tighten the bolts to the specified torque.

20 Refit the sump as described in Section 36 and the cylinder head as described in Section 37.

21 If the engine is in the car, reverse the preliminary procedure given in Section 14.

36 Sump – refitting

1 Clean the mating faces of the sump, crankcase, timing cover and rear main bearing cap, then smear jointing compound on them.

2 Stick the gasket into position on the crankcase.

3 Locate the sump on the crankcase, insert the bolts, and tighten them in diagonal sequence.

4 If the engine is in the car, reverse the preliminary procedure given in Section 13, then refit the oil level dipstick.

37 Cylinder head – reassembly and refitting

1 Press the new valve seals onto the valve guides if the original seals were removed. Take care not to damage the seal lips.

2 Locate the valves in their correct positions after lubricating their stems with engine oil.

3 Fit the spring seat, springs and retainer over the first valve. Compress the springs with the valve spring compressor, insert the split collets and release the compressor.

4 Repeat the procedure given in paragraph 3 on the remaining valves. Tap the end of each valve stem with a non-metallic mallet to settle the collets.

5 Refit the thermostat and spacer as described in Chapter 2.

6 Make sure that the faces of the cylinder head and block are perfectly clean. If the engine is out of the car, position it upright and rest the camshaft sprocket between the timing chain guide and damper. If the engine is in the car and the timing chain has not been removed, have an assistant hold the sprocket raised with the welding rod and remove the wooden block.

7 Place the new gasket on the cylinder block (it will only locate in one position) (photo).

8 Lower the cylinder head into position on the dowels, then insert and tighten the bolt securing the front of the head to the timing cover.

9 While keeping the timing chain taut, wire the camshaft sprocket to the cylinder head.

10 Refit the camshaft as described in Section 38.

11 If the engine is in the car, reverse the preliminary procedure given in Section 11.

38 Camshaft – refitting

1 Clean the backs of the bearing shells and the bearing recess in both the cylinder head and caps.

2 Press the camshaft bearing shells into the cylinder head and caps, and oil them liberally (photo). Lubricate the camshaft with molybdenum disulfide grease.

3 Remove the wires from the camshaft sprocket but hold it in a raised position.

4 With the key and pin on the front of the camshaft uppermost (photo), insert the camshaft into engagement with the sprocket, then lower it into the bearings. Take care not to displace the Woodruff key.

5 Lower the complete valve rocker gear assembly onto the cylinder head, making sure that the central oil pipe holes are facing the camshaft, the centre bearing cap oil hole is on the left-hand side, and the anti-vibration O-ring is located in the centre bearing cap (photo). Remove the wire from the rocker gear assembly.

6 Align the rocker shafts and insert the cylinder head bolts, then

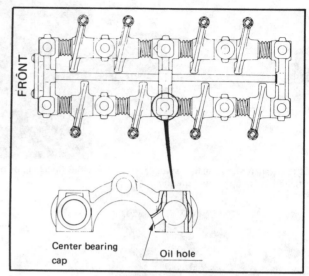

Fig. 1.9 Correct installation of camshaft centre bearing cap (Sec 38)

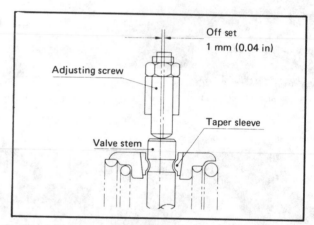

Fig. 1.10 Rocker arm-to-valve stem alignment (Sec 38)

Fig. 1.11 Cylinder head bolt tightening sequence (Sec 38)

screw them in finger tight (photo).

7 Move the caps and pedestals so that the centres of the rocker arm adjusting screws are offset to the centres of the valve stems by 1.0 mm (0.4 in) as shown in Fig. 1.10.

8 Tighten the cylinder head bolts in two stages to the specified torque using the sequence shown in Fig. 1.11 (photo).

9 Check the tightness of the bolt securing the front of the head to the timing cover.

38.2 Camshaft bearing shells installed in cylinder head

38.4 Camshaft key and pin location

38.5 Oil hole location in camshaft centre bearing cap

38.6 Cylinder head bolts inserted through valve gear

38.8 Tightening cylinder head bolts

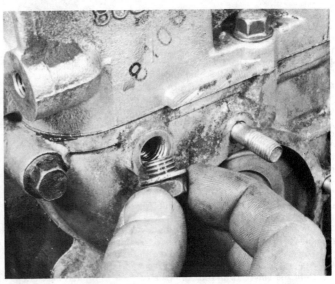

38.11A Removing access plug ...

38.11B ... in order to adjust the timing chain guide

38.14 Cylinder head rubber seal location

42.5A Adjusting valve clearances using feeler blade at valve side

42.5B Adjusting valve clearances using feeler blades at camshaft side

10   Locate the lockwasher on the front of the camshaft, and fit the sprocket retaining nut. If the timing chain *has not* been removed, tighten the nut and bend over the locktab.

11   If the timing chain *has* been removed, remove the two plugs located on the timing cover just above the water pump position. Turn the crankshaft slightly clockwise to tension the left-hand side of the timing chain. Insert a screwdriver through the right-hand side of the timing cover and depress the chain guide in order to tension the chain. Tighten the guide screws (cross-head) through the holes in the timing cover, then insert and tighten the plugs (photos).

12   Where applicable remove the adhesive tape and welding rod from the timing chain tensioner, and refit the access cover together with a new gasket. Tighten the camshaft sprocket nut and bend over the locktab.

13   Locate the distributor drivegear on the front of the camshaft, together with the lockwasher and nut. Tighten the nut and bend over the locktab.

14   Locate the half round rubber oil seals to the front and rear of the cylinder head with the 'OUT' marks facing outward (photo).

15   Lower the new valve cover gasket onto the cylinder head studs.

16   Adjust the valve clearances as described in Section 42.

17   Refit the valve cover and wiring harness clips. Tighten the nuts in diagonal sequence.

18   If the engine is in the car, reverse the preliminary procedure given in Section 10.

39   Auxiliary components – refitting

Refer to Section 9, and refit the listed components

40   Engine – refitting

1   Reverse the removal procedure given in Section 5, 6 and 7, as applicable.

2   Refill the engine and gearbox, as applicable, with oil.

3   Refill the automatic transmission, as applicable, with the correct fluid with reference to Chapter 6.

4   Refill the cooling system with reference to Chapter 2.

41   Engine – adjustment after major overhaul

1   With the engine refitted to the car, make a final check to make sure that everything has been reconnected and that no rags or tools have been left in the engine compartment.

2   Turn the carburettor slow running screw in about half a turn – this will be necessary to compensate for the tightness of any new engine components.

3   Pull the choke fully out on manual choke models.

4   Start the engine – this will take a little longer than usual if the carburettor float chamber is empty.

5   As soon as the engine starts, adjust the choke, as applicable, until the engine runs at a fast tickover. Check that the oil pressure light goes out.

6   Check the oil filter, fuse hoses, and water hoses for leaks.

7   Run the engine to normal operating temperature, then adjust the slow running as described in Chapter 3.

8   After the engine has run for approximately ten minutes, switch off the ignition and readjust the valve clearances as described in Section 42 after retightening the cylinder head bolts.

9   When new internal components have been fitted, the engine speed should be restricted for the first 600 miles (1000 km). At this mileage, renew the engine oil, tighten the cylinder head bolts to the specified torque, and adjust the valve clearances.

42 Valve clearances – adjustment

1   If the engine is in the car, run it to normal operating temperature, then switch if off. Remove the air cleaner assembly as described in Chapter 3, and disconnect the accelerator and choke cables, as applicable, from the valve cover bracket.

2   Disconnect the crankcase ventilation hose from the valve cover.

3   Unscrew the valve cover nuts and remove the wiring harness clips, noting their location. Remove the valve cover.

4   Turn the engine with a spanner on the crankshaft pulley bolt until No 1 piston (nearest radiator) is at TDC (top dead centre) on its compression stroke. Check that the engine is at the correct point by removing the distributor cap – the rotor arm should be pointing downwards. The mark on the crankshaft pulley should also be aligned with the pin on the timing cover.

5   The clearances for No 1 cylinder valves can now be adjusted. To do this insert a feeler blade of the specified thickness between the end of the valve stem and the rocker arm adjusting screw, or alternatively between the rocker arm and the camshaft – the feeler blade should be a firm sliding fit. If necessary loosen the locknut with a ring spanner and turn the adjusting screw with a screwdriver until the clearance is correct. Tighten the locknut and recheck the adjustment (photos).

6   Turn the crankshaft through 180° and adjust the valve clearances on No 3 cylinder.

7   Turn the crankshaft through a further 180° and adjust the valve clearances on No 4 cylinder.

8   Finally, turn the crankshaft through a further 180° and adjust the valve clearances on No 2 cylinder.

9   Refit the valve cover together with the wiring harness clips, then install and tighten the nuts.

10 Connect the crankcase ventilation hose to the valve cover.

11 If the engine is in the car refit the accelerator and choke cables as applicable, and refit the air cleaner assembly.

43 Fault diagnosis – engine

Note: *Use this Section in conjunction with the Fault Diagnosis Section at the beginning of this manual*

Symptom	Reason(s)
Engine idles erratically	Intake manifold air leak Cylinder head gasket leaking Worn timing sprockets Worn camshaft lobes Incorrect valve clearances Poor compression due to worn valves or piston rings
Excessive oil consumption	Worn pistons, rings and bores Oil leak from timing cover or crankshaft rear oil seal Valve guides and valve stem seals worn

Chapter 2 Cooling system

Contents

Specifications

Type of system .... Pressurised, with centrifugal pump, thermostat, fan, and radiator with expansion tank

Thermostat
Opens at .... 82°C (180°F)
Fully open at .... 95°C (203°F)
Minimum lift .... 8 mm (0.315 in)

Fanbelt tension
New belt .... 9 to 11 mm (0.35 to 0.43 in) deflection
Used belt .... 12 to 14 mm (0.47 to 0.55 in) deflection

Viscous fan speed at engine speed of 4000 rpm (US and Canadian models)
1979 models .... 2250 to 2550 rpm
1980 models .... 2750 to 3050 rpm

Radiator
Type .... Corrugated fin
Pressure cap opens at .... 0.9 kgf/cm² (13 lbf/in²)

System capacity
With heater .... 6.6 Imp quart; 7.9 US quart; 7.5 litre
Without heater (except US models 1980 on) .... 6.2 Imp quart; 7.4 US quart; 7.0 litre
Without heater (US models 1980 on) .... 6.1 Imp quart; 7.3 US quart; 6.9 litre

Torque wrench settings

	lbf ft	Nm
Temperature gauge sender unit	6	8
Radiator	17	23

1 Cooling system – general description

The cooling system comprises a radiator and expansion tank, fan, thermostat, pressure cap and centrifugal water pump. The fan and water pump are driven by a V-belt from the crankshaft pulley. This belt also drives the alternator.

When the engine is cold, coolant circulates in the engine through the bypass hose, since the thermostat is closed. As the engine warms up, the thermostat starts to open the outlet to the radiator, which provides additional cooling for the engine. Coolant now circulates through the radiator, and into the cylinder and block water jackets and then to the outside surfaces of the combustion chambers, which are the hottest parts of the engine. After cooling the combustion chambers, the coolant circulates through the thermostat and back into the radiator.

Fig. 2.1 Cooling system components on a US model equipped with an air injection pump (Sec 1)

1 Expansion tank hose	*3 Viscous fan unit*
2 Radiator top and bottom	*4 Radiator shroud*
hoses	*5 Radiator*

The coolant is cooled in the radiator by the combined effects of the cooling fan and the forward motion of the vehicle as air passes the cooling fins.

An internal combustion engine runs most efficiently when hot, and in order to increase the temperature above the boiling point of water, but at the same time control the temperature within suitable limits, a pressurized system is used. This is accomplished by the use of a radiator pressure cap which contains two valves. The main valve will relieve the system pressure when it increases to 0.9 kgf/cm² (13 lbf/in²), which occurs as the temperature rises to the maximum permitted for the vehicle. The excess coolant will then flow into the expansion tank. When the system cools down, the coolant contracts and a further relief valve allows the excess coolant to return to the radiator. The radiator thus remains full at all times.

Water temperature is measured by a sender unit located on the left-hand side of the cylinder head, on top of the thermostat housing spacer.

US and Canadian models are fitted with a viscous fan unit which has a governed maximum speed. The unit eliminates unnecessary loads on the engine (and thus power loss) at high engine speeds.

2 Cooling system – routine maintenance

1   The cooling system requires very little routine maintenance, but in view of its important nature, this maintenance must not be neglected.

2   The maintenance intervals are given in the Routine Maintenance Section at the beginning of this manual.

3   Apart from regular checking of the coolant level, and inspection for leaks and deterioration of hose connections, the only other items of major importance are the use of antifreeze solutions or rust inhibitors suitable for engines with aluminium components, and renewal of the coolant. These items are covered separately in this Chapter.

4   It must be remembered that the cooling system is pressurized. This means that when the engine is hot, the coolant will be at a temperature in excess of 212°F (100°C). Great care must therefore be taken if the radiator pressure cap has to be removed when the engine is hot, since steam and boiling water will be ejected. If possible, let the engine cool down before removing the pressure cap. If this is not possible, place a cloth on the cap and turn it slowly anti-clockwise to the first notch. Keep it in this position until all the steam has escaped, then turn it further until it can be removed.

3 Cooling system – draining

1   Place the vehicle on level ground. If the coolant is to be re-used, place suitable containers under the drain plugs for its collection.

2   Remove the radiator cap. If the engine is hot see paragraph 4, of the previous Section.

3   Open the radiator and engine block drain plugs and drain off all the coolant (photo). Ensure that the heater water valve is in the 'hot' position to permit the coolant to be drained from the heater matrix.

4   When coolant ceases to flow from the drain plugs, probe them with a piece of stiff wire to ensure that there is no sediment blocking the drain orifices.

5   On completion, refer to Section 4 or 5, as appropriate.

4 Cooling system – flushing

1   With the passage of time, deposits can build up in an engine which will lead to engine overheating and possibly serious damage.

2   It is a good policy, whenever the cooling system is drained, to flush the system with cold water from a hosepipe. This can conveniently be done by leaving a hosepipe in the radiator filler orifice for about 15 minutes while water is allowed to run through. This will usually be sufficient to clear any sediment which may be present.

3   In extreme cases of contamination it will be necessary to reverse flush the cooling system. To do this, remove the radiator as described in Section 7, then invert it and insert a hosepipe in the radiator outlet to flush it. Also remove the thermostat as described in Section 9 and insert the hosepipe into the cylinder head outlet to flush the system.

4   If the radiator flow is restricted by something other than loose sediment, then no amount of flushing will shift it and it is then that a proprietary chemical cleaner, suitable for aluminium component en-

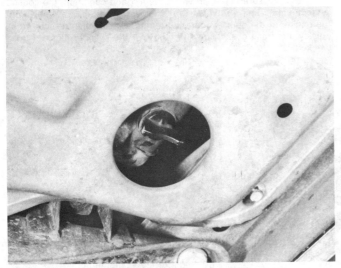

3.3 Radiator drain plug location

5.1 Filling radiator with coolant

gines, is needed. Use this according to the manufacturer's directions and make sure that the residue is fully flushed out afterwards. If leaks develop after using a chemical cleaner, a proprietary radiator sealer may cure them, but the signs are that the radiator has suffered considerable chemical corrosion and that the metal is obviously getting very thin in places.

5 Cooling system – filling

1   When draining (and flushing if applicable) has been accomplished, close the drain plugs and top up the cooling system with water which contains the correct proportion of antifreeze or inhibitor (see Section 6). Ensure that the heater water valve is open to prevent airlocks from occurring in the heater matrix (photo).
2   When the radiator is full, run the engine for 5 to 10 minutes at a fast idle. As the water circulates, and then as the thermostat opens, the coolant level will be seen to fall. Top up the radiator until it is full, install the cap, then run the engine for a few more minutes and check carefully for water leaks. Make sure that the expansion tank is $\frac{1}{3}$ to $\frac{1}{2}$ full with coolant.
3   Allow the system to cool, then remove the cap and if necessary top up the radiator until full, then install the cap firmly.

6 Antifreeze mixture

1   Tap water alone should not be used in an engine with aluminium components except in an emergency. If it has to be used, it should be drained off at the earliest opportunity and the correct coolant mixture used instead.
2   Generally speaking, the basis of the coolant mixture can be tap water, except where this has a high alkali content or is exceptionally hard. If these conditions exist, clean rainwater or distilled water should be used.
3   Antifreeze must be of a type suitable for use with aluminium component engines (ethylene glycol based antifreeze is suitable) and many proprietary products will be available for use. The fact that all products tend to be expensive should not deter you from using them, since they are a good insurance against freezing and corrosion.
4   The following table gives suitable concentrations of antifreeze. Do not use concentrations of antifreeze. Do not use concentrations in excess of 55% except where protection to below -40°C (-40°F) is required.

Coolant freezing water point	Mixture percentage (volume)		Specific gravity of mixture at 68° (20°C)
	Anti-freeze	Water	
-26°C (-15°F)	45	55	1.066
-40°C (-40°F)	55	45	1.078

5   Antifreeze mixtures are normally suitable for use for a period of two years (even so-called permanent antifreeze) after which they should be discarded and a fresh mixture used.
6   Antifreeze normally contains suitable corrosion inhibitors for

protection of the engine. However, if antifreeze is not used for some reason, the vehicle manufacturers market suitable inhibitors which will give satisfactory protection to the engine. Any inhibitors which are used must be mixed in accordance with the instructions on the container.
7   Where the cooling system contains antifreeze, always top it up with a solution made up to the original concentration to avoid dilution.

7 Radiator – removal, inspection, cleaning and refitting

1   Drain the cooling system as described in Section 3.
2   Disconnect the expansion tank hose from the radiator, and the top and bottom hoses from the radiator.
3   On automatic transmission models disconnect the hoses from the cooler and drain the fluid into a suitable container.
4   On UK models remove the retaining screws and withdraw the radiator shroud.
5   On US and Canadian models loosen the pivot and adjustment bolts and swivel the alternator and air injection pump (where fitted to US models) towards the engine. Unscrew the bolts and withdraw the radiator shroud and unbolt the viscous fan unit at the same time.
6   On all models unscrew the mounting bolts and lift out the radiator, taking care not to damage the cooling fins (photos). Do not allow antifreeze to drop onto the bodywork otherwise damage to the paintwork will result.
7   Radiator repair is best left to a specialist; applying heat with a soldering iron is not always successful and may easily result in further leaks. Filler paste can sometimes be used for emergency repairs.
8   Clean the radiator matrix of flies by brushing with a soft brush or hosing with water.
9   Flush the radiator as described in Section 4 and check it thoroughly for signs of leakage or damage. Renew any hoses or clips which are unserviceable.
10 Refitting is a reversal of the removal procedure, but fill the cooling system as described in Section 5. Where applicable, adjust the alternator and air injection pump drivebelts with reference to Section 12, and Chapter 3. Top up the automatic transmission fluid (where applicable) as described in Chapter 6.

8 Radiator pressure cap – description and testing

1   The cooling system is pressurised by a spring-tensioned valve in the radiator pressure cap. If escaping pressure can be heard from the cap, or if the system requires constant topping up, and no other leaks are located, the cap may be faulty and should be checked.
2   Most garages are equipped to test pressure caps, and if the valve does not operate at the specified pressure, the cap should be renewed with one of the correct rating.
3   If the pressure cap is proved to be in good condition, the cooling system should be pressurised to the release pressure, preferably with the engine at the normal operating temperature. If the pressure drops quickly, the head gasket may be faulty, or the cylinder block or head cracked.

7.6A Unscrewing a radiator mounting bolt

7.6B Removing the radiator

7.6C Radiator lower mounting

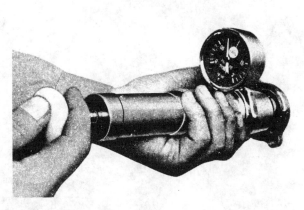

Fig. 2.2 Testing the radiator pressure cap (Sec 8)

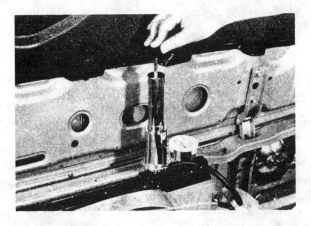

Fig. 2.3 Pressure testing the radiator and cooling system (Sec 8)

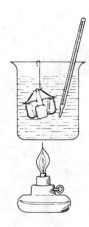

Fig. 2.4 Checking the thermostat opening temperature (Sec 9)

Fig. 2.5 Water pump and hose connections (Sec 10)

1	Radiator bottom hose	3	Bypass hose
2	Heater hose (where fitted)	4	Water pump

9 Thermostat – removal, testing and refitting

1   A faulty thermostat can cause overheating or slow engine warm up, and can also affect the performance of the heater.
2   Drain off approximately half of the coolant so that the level is below the thermostat housing – refer to Section 3 as necessary.
3   Where applicable on US models, remove the air injection pump assembly with reference to Chapter 3.
4   Loosen the clip and disconnect the top hose from the thermostat outlet.
5   Where applicable on US models, remove the air injection hoses for better access.
6   Unscrew the thermostat outlet bolts and nut as applicable, and on UK models remove the front engine lifting hook by unscrewing the nut.
7   Withdraw the outlet and gasket and lift out the thermostat (photos).
8   If required, disconnect the bypass hose and the water temperature sender unit wire, and withdraw the thermostat housing spacer from the cylinder head.
9   To test whether the thermostat is serviceable, suspend it by a piece of string in a pan of cold water, which is then heated. Using a thermometer, check that the thermostat commences to open at the specified temperature, and that it is fully open by the specified amount at the specified fully-open temperature. Remove the thermostat and check that it closes completely after cooling. Renew the thermostat if it fails to open or close correctly.

10 Refitting is a reversal of removal, but check that the mating surfaces are clean and always fit new gaskets. Note that the thermostat jiggle pin must be positioned upwards. Refill the system as described in Section 5. Where applicable adjust the air injection pump drivebelt with reference to Chapter 3.

10 Water pump – removal and refitting

1   Drain the cooling system as described in Section 3.
2   Disconnect the battery negative terminal.
3   Loosen the alternator pivot and adjustment bolts and swivel the alternator towards the engine.
4   Where applicable on US models, loosen the pivot and adjustment bolts and swivel the air injection pump towards the engine.
5   Remove the drivebelt(s) over the fan blades.
6   Unscrew the bolts and place the radiator shroud over the fan blades.
7   Unscrew the fan bolts and withdraw the fan, pulley and radiator shroud (photos).
8   Disconnect the bottom hose and bypass hose from the water pump. When fitted, disconnect the heater hose from the water pump.
9   Note where the alternator adjustment strap is located, then unscrew the retaining nuts and bolts in diagonal sequence and withdraw the water pump from the front of the cylinder block (photos). Remove the gasket.

9.7A Removing thermostat outlet

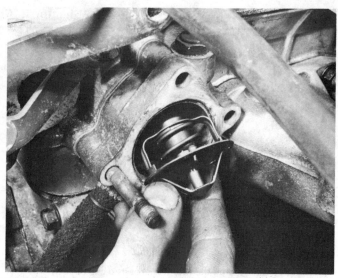

9.7B Removing thermostat

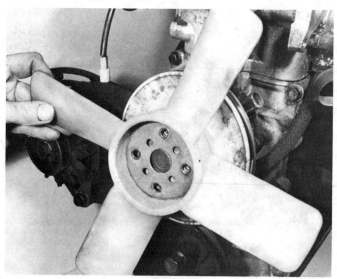

10.7A Removing the fan ...

10.7B ... and pulley from the water pump

10.9A Removing the alternator strap from the water pump

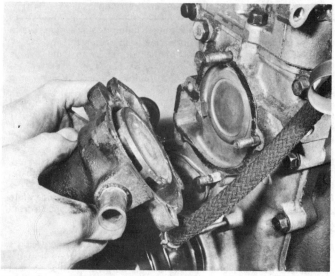

10.9B Removing water pump

Fig. 2.6 Pressing the water pump shaft through the pulley boss (Sec 11)

METAL TUBING

Fig. 2.7 Pressing the water pump shaft and bearing assembly through the impeller and body (Sec 11)

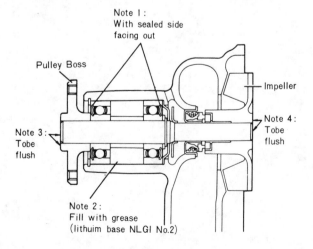

Note I :
With sealed side facing out

Pulley Boss

Impeller

Note 4 :
Tobe flush

Note 3 :
Tobe flush

Note 2 :
Fill with grease
(lithuim base NLGI No.2)

Fig. 2.8 Cross-section of water pump showing reassembly notes (Sec 11)

10 Refitting is a reversal of removal, but check that the mating surfaces are clean, and always fit a new gasket. Adjust the fanbelt tension as described in Section 12, and refill the cooling system as described in Section 5. Where applicable, on US models adjust the drivebelt tension for the air injection pump with reference to Chapter 3.

11 Water pump – overhaul

Note: *Check that spare parts are available before commencing work; if not, a replacement unit must be fitted.*
1 Using a puller or press, remove the pulley boss from the shaft.
2 Extract the circlip from the front of the water pump.
3 Support the front of the water pump body on a length of metal tubing, and press the shaft and bearing assembly out of the body until the impeller can be withdrawn.
4 Continue to press the shaft and bearing assembly out of the body.
5 Drive out the seal assembly.
6 Clean all components in paraffin, dry them, and examine them for wear and damage. Check the bearings for roughness and excessive wear. Renew the seal assembly whenever the water pump is dismantled, and renew all other components as necessary.
7 Reassembly of the water pump is a reversal of dismantling, but refer to Fig. 2.8 and note that the sealed ends of the bearings must face outwards, and that the space between them must be fitted with a lithium-based grease. Also the outer faces of the impeller and pulley boss must be flush with the ends of the shaft.

12 Fan/alternator drivebelt – renewal and adjustment

1 To remove the drivebelt, first loosen the alternator pivot and adjustment bolts and swivel the alternator towards the engine.
2 Where an air injection pump is fitted on US models, remove the drivebelt with reference to Chapter 3.
3 Release the fan/alternator drivebelt from the crankshaft, water pump and alternator pulleys, and withdraw it over the fan blades.
4 Fit the new drivebelt over the pulleys and swivel the alternator away from the engine. Tighten the adjustment bolt sufficiently to hold the alternator but still allow movement of the alternator using a lever.
5 Using a lever at the pulley end of the alternator, tension the drivebelt until, with a pressure of 22 lbf (10 kgf) applied midway between the water pump and alternator pulleys, the drivebelt deflects by the amount given in the Specifications (for practical purposes, firm thumb pressure is sufficient) (photo).
6 Tighten the adjustment and pivot bolts.
7 Adjust the air injection pump drivebelt, where fitted to US models, with reference to Chapter 3.

13 Viscous fan – testing

1 US and Canadian models are fitted with a viscous fan unit in which the drive from the water pump pulley boss is transmitted to the fan blades through a fluid film. The unit effectively governs the maximum speed of the fan blades to approximately either 2400 or 2900 rpm (see Specifications).
2 Testing of the unit is best left to a suitably equipped garage, as it entails the use of a tachometer and stroboscopic lamp. The fan blades are first marked with a light coloured mark on one of the blades. A tachometer is connected to the engine and the engine speed held at 4000 rpm. Using the stroboscopic lamp, the speed of the fan is then determined; if it is not within the specified tolerance the unit is faulty and should be renewed.

14 Temperature gauge sender unit – removal and refitting

1 Drain off approximately half of the coolant so that the level is below the sender unit – refer to Section 3 as necessary.
2 Disconnect the temperature gauge sender unit supply wire, and unscrew the unit from the thermostat housing spacer (photo).
3 Refitting is a reversal of removal, but refill the cooling system as described in Section 5.

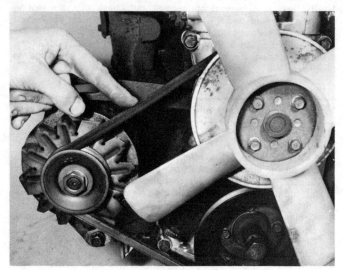

12.5 Checking fan/alternator drivebelt tension

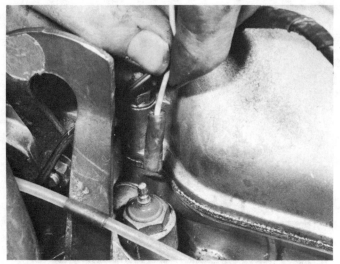

14.2 Disconnecting temperature gauge sender unit wire

15 Fault diagnosis – cooling system

Symptom	Reason(s)
Overheating	Insufficient water in cooling system
	Fanbelt slipping
	Radiator core blocked or radiator grille restricted
	Thermostat faulty
	Viscous fan faulty (where applicable)
	Radiator pressure cap faulty
	Incorrect ignition timing
Overcooling	Thermostat faulty or not fitted
	Temperature gauge or sender unit faulty
Loss of coolant	Hose or radiator leaking
	Water pump seal or gasket leaking
	Blown cylinder head gasket

Chapter 3 Fuel, exhaust and emission control systems

Refer to Chapter 13 for revisions and information related to 1982 models

Contents

Specifications

Fuel pump

Type	Electric
Operating pressure	0.20 to 0.25 kgf/cm^2 (2.8 to 3.6 lbf/in^2)

Carburettor

Type .... Nikki downdraught, dual barrel

UK models

	Primary	Secondary
Barrel diameter	28 mm	32 mm
Venturi	23 mm	28 mm
Main nozzle	2.1 mm	2.5 mm
Main jet:		
1600	105	140
2000 (without air injection or with automatic transmission)	104	150
2000 (with air injection)	106	150
Main air bleed	50	60
Idle jet:		
1600	48	80
2000	46	90
Idle air bleed:		
1600	140 (No 1); 210 (No 2)	160
2000	140 (No 1); 170 (No 2)	140
Power jet (accelerator pump):		
1600	70	
2000	60	
Fast idle adjustment	1.80 mm (0.071 in)	
Float level:		
1600	6.0 ± 0.5 mm (0.236 ± 0.020 in)	
2000	11.0 mm (0.433 in)	
Float drop:		
1600	1.2 mm (0.047 in)	
2000	2.0 mm (0.079 in)	
Idle speed:		
1600 (manual transmission)	750 to 800 rpm	
2000 (manual transmission)	700 to 750 rpm	
2000 (automatic transmission)	650 to 700 rpm (selector in 'D')	
CO at idle	2.5 ± 0.5%	

US and Canadian models	Primary	Secondary
Barrel diameter	32 mm	34 mm
Venturi:		
1980 US models	23 mm	29 mm
Except 1980 US models	24 mm	29 mm
Main nozzle	2.6 mm	2.8 mm
Main jet:		
1980 US models	100	155
Except 1980 US models	112	155
Main air bleed:		
1980 US models	55	50
Except 1980 US models	50	50
Idle jet:		
1980 US models	50	90
Except 1980 US models	46	90
Idle air bleed	100 (No 1); 170 (No 2)	50 (No 1); 120 (No 2)
Power jet (accelerator pump)	35	
Fast idle adjustment:		
1979 models	1.0 mm (0.039 in)	
1980 models	0.5 to 0.65 mm (0.019 to 0.026 in)	
Float level	11.0 mm (0.433 in)	
Float drop	46.0 mm (1.811 in)	
Idle speed:		
Manual transmission models	600 to 700 rpm	
Automatic transmission models	600 to 700 rpm (selector in 'D')	
CO at idle (without air injection):		
1979 models	2.0 ± 1.0%	
1980 US models	3.0 ± 1.0%	
1980 Canadian models	2.0 ± 1.0%	

Air pump drivebelt tension (1980 US models):

New belt	11 to 14 mm (0.4 to 0.6 in) deflection
Used belt	15 to 18 mm (0.6 to 0.7 in) deflection

Fuel tank capacity

12.1 Imp gal; 14.5 US gal; 55 litre

Torque wrench settings

	lbf ft	Nm
Inlet manifold	17	23
Exhaust manifold	19	26

1　General description

The fuel tank is mounted beneath the rear luggage compartment. An in-line filter and the electric fuel pump are also mounted beneath the underbody on the left-hand side.

The carburettor is of downdraught, dual barrel construction with each throttle valve mounted on a separate shaft. Throttle valve opening is of progressive type – idling and normal running functions are through the primary choke, but under full throttle operation both throttle valves are opened.

The air cleaner incorporates a renewable paper element, and on some models the intake air temperature is controlled automatically.

The exhaust system is in three sections, incorporating a front pipe and silencer with twin downpipes, a centre pipe and silencer, and a tailpipe. It is supported by rubber mountings.

2　Air cleaner element and body – removal, servicing and refitting

1　The air cleaner element should be removed and cleaned every 6000 miles (10 000 km) and renewed every 24 000 miles (40 000 km). More frequent cleaning may be required if the car is operated in very dusty conditions.

2　To remove the element, unscrew the control wing nut, lift off the cover, and withdraw the element (photo).

3　Wipe clean the interior of the air cleaner body with a slightly damp cloth and allow to dry. Tap the element to release any accumulations of dust.

4　To remove the body, unscrew the wire rod located beneath the body and the mounting bolt (photo). Lift the body, and on UK models release the intake tube from the bracket.

5　Disconnect the hot air hose, crankcase ventilation hose, and where applicable on US models, the idle compensator, evaporation shutter, and evaporation feed hoses. Withdraw the body (photos).

6　Refitting is a reversal of removal, but on UK models, check that the intake temperature lever is set correctly – if the ambient temperature is above 15°C (60°F) the lever should be in the 'S' position; at lower temperatures it should be in the 'W' position (photo). On US and Canadian models, check that the bi-metal temperature control valve moves freely against the spring tension, and where applicable on US models, the evaporation shutter valve and vacuum diaphragm operate correctly.

3　Fuel pump – removal and refitting

1　Jack up the rear of the car and support on axle stands. Chock the front wheels.

2　Disconnect the battery negative lead.

3　Working in the luggage compartment, disconnect the fuel pump supply wire.

4　Working beneath the car unbolt the fuel pump bracket from the underbody and unclip the fuel filter (photo).

5　Disconnect and plug the fuel inlet and outlet hoses.

6　Unscrew the mounting nuts and withdraw the fuel pump and wire.

7　Refitting is a reversal of the removal procedure.

4　Fuel filter – renewal

1　The fuel filter should be renewed every 12 000 miles (20 000 km). To do this, first jack up the rear of the car and support on axle stands. Chock the front wheels.

2　Note which way round the filter is fitted, then disconnect the inlet and outlet hoses and unclip the filter (photo). If the outlet hose clip is

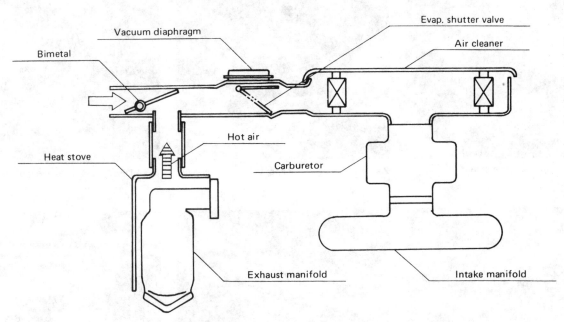

Fig. 3.1 Cross-sectional diagram of air cleaner incorporating intake air temperature control and evaporative shutter valve (Sec 1)

Fig. 3.2 Air cleaner showing air temperature control valve (Sec 2)

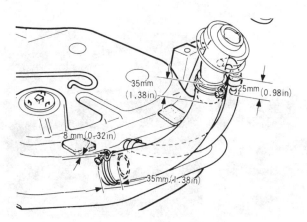

Fig. 3.3 Fuel tank hose installation dimensions (Sec 5)

difficult to release, unbolt the fuel pump bracket.

3   Install the new filter using a reversal of the removal procedure.

5   Fuel tank – removal, servicing and refitting

1   Remove the fuel tank filler cap and syphon all the fuel from the fuel tank.

2   Jack up the rear of the car and support on axle stands. Chock the front wheels.

3   Working in the luggage compartment, remove the cover and disconnect the wires from the fuel gauge level unit (photo).

4   Support the fuel tank, then unscrew the mounting bolts and strap (photo).

5   Disconnect the inlet, vent, outlet, and return hoses from the fuel tank and withdraw it from under the car.

6   If the tank is leaking, it should be repaired by a specialist, or alternatively a new tank fitted. *Never be tempted to solder or weld a leaking fuel tank.*

7   If the tank is contaminated with sediment or water, it can be swilled out using several changes of fuel, but if any vigorous shaking is required to dislodge accumulations of dirt, the fuel gauge sender unit should first be removed.

8   Refitting is a reversal of the removal procedure, but refer to Fig. 3.3 for the hose installation dimensions.

6   Accelerator and choke cables – removal, refitting and adjustment

Accelerator cable

1   Remove the air cleaner as described in Section 2.

2   Turn the throttle lever on the carburettor and unhook the inner cable.

3   On right-hand drive models release the inner cable from the accelerator pedal.

4   On left-hand drive models release the inner cable from the linkage.

5   On all models, unscrew the locknuts and remove the outer cable from the bracket on the valve cover (photo).

6   Withdraw the cable from the bulkhead.

7   Refitting is a reversal of the removal procedure, but adjust the linkage as follows. First check the accelerator pedal height – it should be lower than the brake pedal by 45 $\pm$ 5 mm (1.7 $\pm$ 0.2 in). If not, adjust the upper stop as necessary. Check that the inner cable free play is 1 to 3 mm (0.04 to 0.12 in). If not, loosen the outer cable locknuts,

2.2 Removing air cleaner element

2.4 Unscrewing air cleaner body mounting bolt

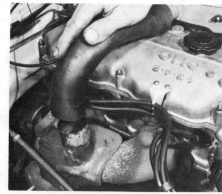

2.5A Disconnecting air cleaner hot air hose

2.5B Removing air cleaner body

2.6 Air cleaner intake temperature setting wing nut

3.4 Fuel pump and bracket

4.2 Fuel filter location

5.3 Fuel gauge level unit location in luggage compartment

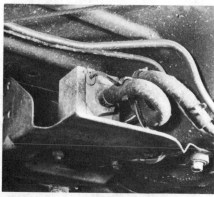

5.4 Fuel tank mounting strap

6.5 Removing accelerator outer cable

6.9 Removing choke inner cable from clamp pin

9.1 Carburettor fuel level sight glass

reposition them, and retighten them. Have an assistant fully depress the accelerator pedal and check that the carburettor throttle valves are fully open. If not, loosen the locknut and adjust the position of the stop bolt on the pedal bracket.

Choke cable (where applicable)

8   Remove the air cleaner as described in Section 2.
9   Unscrew the clamp pin and cable bracket, and release the cable from the carburettor (photo).
10 Unclip the outer cable from the valve cover.
11 Working inside the car, unscrew the mounting nut and withdraw the cable from the facia.
12 Refitting is a reversal of the removal procedure, but before tightening the clamp pin, fully depress the choke knob then pull it out approximately 3.2 mm (0.125 in).

7   Fuel cut and check valves – description, removal and refitting

Fuel cut valve

1   The fuel cut valve is fitted to US and Canadian models and is located by the fuel pump. If, as the result of an accident, the car is inclined more than 60° laterally, one of two balls within the valve will block the fuel supply.
2   To return the balls to their original positions, disconnect the hoses and blow in air through the outlet then inlet ports.
3   To remove the fuel cut valve, jack up the rear of the car and support on axle stands.
4   Unbolt the mounting bracket, then unbolt the valve from the bracket. Disconnect the hoses and withdraw the valve.

5   Refitting is a reversal of the removal procedure, but take care not to incline the valve more than 60° otherwise the balls will be displaced.

Fuel check valve

6   The fuel check valve is fitted to US and Canadian models and is located by the carburettor in the fuel return line.
7   To remove the valve, first note that the arrow points to the carburettor connection and has the word 'CARB' stamped on it.
8   Disconnect the hoses and withdraw the valve.
9   Refitting is a reversal of the removal procedure.

8   Throttle opener system – description and adjustment

1   The throttle opener system is fitted to US and Canadian models equipped with air conditioning, and its function is to maintain normal idling speed when the air conditioning compressor is operating.
2   To adjust the throttle spacer, first connect a tachometer to the engine.
3   Run the engine at idling speed to normal operating temperature.
4   Stop the engine and remove the air cleaner as described in Section 2.
5   Disconnect the vacuum sensing tube (Fig. 3.6) at the capsule, and where fitted, the evaporative shutter valve vacuum sensing tube at the inlet manifold.
6   Connect a further tube between the inlet manifold and the capsule.
7   On all models except 1980 US models, disconnect the EGR valve first stage vacuum sensing tube, and the distributor vacuum sensing tube.

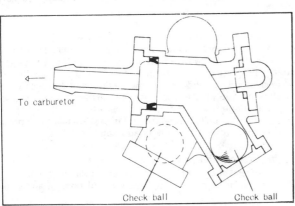

Fig. 3.4 Cross-section of the fuel cut valve fitted to US and Canadian models (Sec 7)

To carburetor

Check ball   Check ball

Fig. 3.5 Fuel check valve installation (Sec 7)

From carburetor   To fuel tank

Fig. 3.6 Throttle opener (air conditioning) vacuum sensing tube 'A' and temporary testing tube 'B' (Sec 8)

Fig. 3.7 Fuel level sight glass on US and Canadian models (Sec 9)

10.6 Disconnecting fuel inlet and return hoses

11.15 Choke vacuum break (pull-off) diaphragm control

8   On all models, run the engine at approximately 2000 rpm, then release the accelerator pedal and check that the engine speed is between 1150 and 1200 rpm. If not, adjust the screw on the throttle opener as necessary.

9   Stop the engine, reconnect the tubes, install the air cleaner, and remove the tachometer.

9   Carburettor – general description

The carburettor is of downdraught, dual barrel construction, and the throttle valve opening is of the progressive type.

The carburettor fitted to UK models incorporates a manual choke with automatic vacuum controlled pull-off. US and Canadian models incorporate an electrically controlled automatic choke.

All carburettors are equipped with a fuel cut solenoid which blocks the idling fuel supply when the ignition is switched off. A sight glass is provided on the side of the carburettor for checking the fuel level and supply (photo).

The mixture adjustment screw on the side of the carburettor is sealed with a plastic 'tamperproof' plug. If adjustment is necessary, the cap can be prised out to reveal the screw, but before doing this it is advisable to check that local legislation permits this action.

10   Carburettor – removal and refitting

1   Disconnect the battery negative lead.
2   Remove the air cleaner assembly as described in Section 2.
3   Disconnect the accelerator cable and, where applicable, the choke cable from the carburettor.
4   Disconnect the wiring from the fuel cut solenoid and automatic choke as applicable.
5   Disconnect the vacuum sensing hoses after noting their location.
6   Disconnect the fuel inlet and return hoses (photo).
7   Unscrew the mounting nuts and withdraw the carburettor from the inlet manifold.
8   Refitting is a reversal of the removal procedure, but always use a new gasket. Adjust the idling, mixture, and fast idling as described in Sections 14 and 16.

11   Carburettor – dismantling and reassembly

1   Clean the exterior of the carburettor with paraffin.

Automatic choke models

2   Disconnect the vacuum tube, throttle return spring, accelerator pump rod and arm, and the choke operating arm.

3   Remove the screws and withdraw the air horn, automatic choke, and gasket.

Manual choke models

4   Disconnect the throttle return spring, accelerator pump rod and arm, and the fast idle rod.
5   Remove the screws and withdraw the air horn, brackets, and gasket.

All models

6   Unscrew the bolt and remove the inlet/return union and washers.
7   From the main body remove the accelerator pump plunger, then extract the strainer retaining clip.
8   Invert the body and remove the strainer and pump check ball.
9   Unscrew the plug and washer, and extract the pump discharge weight or spring (as applicable) and check ball.
10   Remove the fuel cut solenoid and gasket/washer by removing the screws or unscrewing the unit as applicable.

US and Canadian models

11   Disconnect the throttle link and vacuum diaphragm rod.
12   Remove the screws and withdraw the diaphragm and gasket.

All models

13   Unbolt the main body from the throttle body – note that one bolt is located under the throttle body.
14   Unscrew and remove the various jets from the main body noting their location (Figs 3.11 and 3.12).

UK models

15   From the throttle body remove the vacuum break (pull-off) diaphragm and throttle link (photo), diaphragm cover and spring, the cover and diaphragm.
16   Remove the screws and withdraw the sight glass cover, gasket, glass and rubber.
17   Remove the float and collar, and the needle valve assembly.

US and Canadian models

18   Remove the float and collar, and the needle valve assembly from the air horn.

All models

19   If necessary remove the levers from the throttle shafts, but do not attempt to remove the shafts or throttle valves.
20   With the carburettor dismantled, examine all the components for wear and damage after washing them in clean paraffin. Clear the internal passageways with compressed air from a tyre footpump. *Do not probe the jets or passageways with wire.*

Fig. 3.8 Carburettor components on UK models (Sec 11)

1 Accelerator pump plunger
2 Clip
3 Strainer and check ball
4 Plug
5 Discharge weight and check ball
6 Fuel cut solenoid

Fig. 3.9 Accelerator pump and fuel cut solenoid components on US and Canadian models (Sec 11)

Fig. 3.10 Carburettor main body-to-lower body bolt location (Sec 11)

Fig. 3.11 Jet locations on UK models (Sec 11)

1 Secondary main air bleed
2 Secondary slow jet
3 Secondary slow air bleed
4 Primary main air bleed
5 Primary slow jet
6 Primary slow air bleed
7 Power valve

Fig. 3.12 Jet locations on US and Canadian models (Sec 11)

1 Progression fuel jet
2 Primary progression air bleed
3 Secondary progression air bleed
4 Secondary main air bleed
5 Power valve
6 Secondary main jet
7 Primary main jet
8 Primary main air bleed
9 Idling jet
10 Primary idling air bleed
11 Secondary idling air bleed

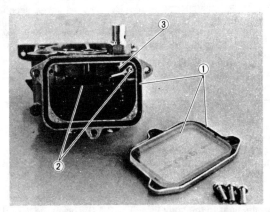

Fig. 3.13 Carburettor components on UK models (Sec 11)

1 Sight glass
2 Float
3 Needle valve

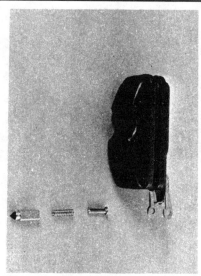

Fig. 3.14 Float and needle valve on US and Canadian models
(Sec 11)

Fig. 3.15 Carburettor main body, air horn and automatic choke,
and throttle body on US and Canadian models (Sec 11)

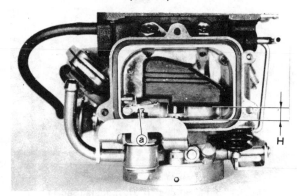

Fig. 3.16 Checking float level dimension 'H' on UK models
(Sec 12)
a   Adjustment arm

Fig. 3.17 Checking float drop dimension 'L' on UK models
(Sec 12)
b   Adjustment arm

21 Renew the components as necessary and obtain a set of new gaskets.

22 Check the operation of the fuel cut solenoid by connecting a 12 volt supply across it – the negative supply should be connected to the body and the positive supply to the supply lead. When energised the stem should move into the solenoid – renew it if it is defective.

23 Reassembly is a reversal of dismantling, but lubricate all moving surfaces with a little engine oil. Adjust the float level, secondary throttle valve, and fast idle (manual choke models only) *before* refitting the carburettor to the engine, and adjust the automatic choke (where applicable) *after* refitting the carburettor – refer to Sections 12 to 15 for the procedure.

12 Carburettor – float level adjustment

UK models

1 With the carburettor removed from the engine, remove the sight glass cover, gasket, and sight glass.

2 Invert the carburettor and allow the float to close the needle valve.

3 Using vernier calipers, measure the distance from the float to the body ('H' in Fig. 3.16). If this level is not as given in the Specifications, bend the arm in contact with the needle valve as necessary.

4 Turn the carburettor upright, and measure the distance from the bottom of the float to the body ('L' in Fig. 3.17). This is the float drop, and if not as given in the Specifications, bend the stop arm as necessary.

5 Refit the sight glass.

US and Canadian models

6 With the carburettor removed from the engine and the air horn removed as described in Section 11, invert the air horn and allow the float to close the needle valve. Remove the gasket from the air horn.

7 Using vernier calipers, measure the distance from the float to the air horn ('H' in Fig. 3.18). If this level is not as given in the Specifications, bend the arm in contact with the needle valve as necessary.

8 Turn the air horn upright, and measure the distance from the bottom of the float to the air horn ('L' in Fig. 3.19). This is the float drop, and if not as given in the Specifications, bend the stop arm as necessary.

9 Refit the gasket and air horn.

13 Carburettor – secondary throttle valve adjustment

1 With the carburettor removed from the engine, invert it so that the throttle valves are visible.

2 Turn the primary throttle valve to the point where the secondary throttle valve just commences to move. Using a twist drill, check the distance between the primary throttle valve and the primary barrel as shown in Fig. 3.20. On 1600 models the dimension should be 6.7 mm (0.264 mm); on 2000 models it should be 5.6 mm (0.220 in) for UK models and 6.75 mm (0.266 in) for US and Canadian models.

3 If adjustment is necessary, bend the throttle connecting rod.

14 Carburettor – fast idle adjustment (manual choke)

1 With the carburettor removed from the engine, fully close the choke valve and use feeler blades or a twist drill to check the clearance between the primary throttle valve and the primary barrel as shown in Fig. 3.21.

2 If adjustment is necessary, bend the choke-to-throttle operating rod.

Fig. 3.18 Checking float level dimension 'H' on US and Canadian models (Sec 12)

a   Adjustment arm

Fig. 3.19 Checking float drop dimension 'L' on US and Canadian models (Sec 12)

b   Adjustment arm

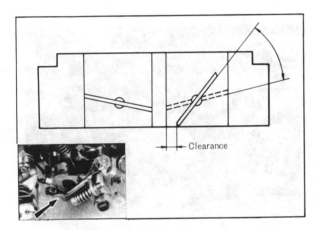

Fig. 3.20 Throttle valve synchronising adjustment (Sec 13)

Arrow shows adjustment point

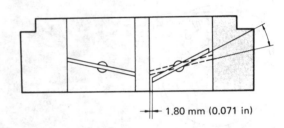

Fig. 3.21 Fast idle adjustment dimension on UK models (Sec 14)

15 Carburettor – automatic choke adjustment

1   An automatic choke is fitted to the carburettor on US and Canadian models. To test the choke, first remove the air cleaner assembly as described in Section 2.

2   With the engine cold, fully depress the accelerator pedal once and check that the choke valve closes fully.

3   Check that the index mark on the choke cover is aligned with the centre index mark on the choke housing.

4   Start the engine and run to normal operating temperature, then check that the choke valve is fully open. If not, make sure that the choke valve is not binding and lubricate if necessary.

Fast idle

Carburettor removed from engine

5   Open the throttle valves, close the choke valve, then release the throttle valves so that the lever rests on the second step of the cam (Fig. 3.23).

6   Using a feeler blade or twist drill, check that the clearance between the primary throttle valve and the primary barrel is between 0.5 and 0.65 mm (0.019 and 0.026 in).

7   If adjustment is necessary, turn the adjusting screw.

Carburettor fitted on engine

8   Adjust the idling speed as described in Section 16.

9   Connect a tachometer to the engine.

10 Run the engine to normal operating temperature, then stop it and remove the air cleaner assembly as described in Section 2.

Fig. 3.22 Automatic choke index mark alignment (Sec 15)

11 Open the throttle valves, fully close the choke valve manually, then release the throttle valves so that it rests on the highest part of the cam.

12 Without touching the accelerator pedal, start the engine and check that its speed is between 3000 and 4000 rpm. If not, turn the fast idle adjustment screw as necessary.

13 Stop the engine and disconnect the tachometer.

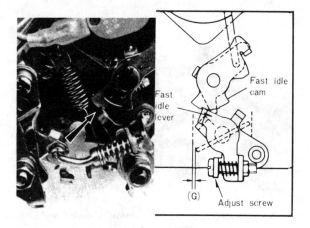

Fig. 3.23 Automatic choke fast idle adjustment (Sec 15)

G   Primary throttle valve clearance

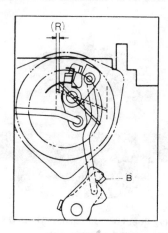

Fig. 3.24 Automatic choke, choke valve opening clearance 'R' and adjustment arm 'B' (Sec 15)

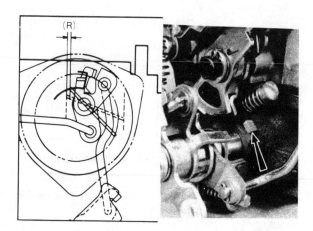

Fig. 3.25 Automatic choke, choke unloader clearance 'R' and adjustment arm arrowed (Sec 15)

Fig. 3.26 Location of carburettor throttle adjusting screw 'A' and mixture screw 'B' (Sec 16)

Choke valve opening

14 With the fast idle adjusted, set the fast idle cam as described in paragraph 5.
15 Using a feeler blade or twist drill, check that the clearance between the choke valve and the air horn centre is between 0.60 and 0.95 mm (0.024 and 0.037 in).
16 If adjustment is necessary, bend the arm shown in Fig. 3.24.

Choke unloader

17 With the air cleaner assembly removed, fully open the throttle valve. If the engine is not cold, close the choke valve until it contacts the unloader arm.
18 Using a feeler blade or twist drill, check that the clearance between the choke valve and the air horn centre is between 2.6 and 3.4 mm (0.102 and 0.134 in).
19 If adjustment is necessary, bend the unloader arm shown in Fig. 3.25.

16 Carburettor – idling speed and mixture adjustment

1   Run the engine to normal operating temperature, and set the transmission in neutral (manual) or 'D' position (automatic). Firmly apply the handbrake, and chock the wheels on automatic transmission models.
2   Make sure that all the lights and electrical components are switched off.

UK models

3   Make sure that the choke is fully open (ie knob returned to facia).
4   Connect a tachometer to the engine, then allow the engine to idle. Turn the throttle adjusting screw until the idling speed is as given in the Specifications (photo).
5   If local legislation permits, prise the cap from the top of the mixture screw.
6   If an exhaust gas analyser is not available, turn the mixture screw in or out as necessary to obtain a smooth idle, then readjust the idling speed if necessary (photo).
7   If an exhaust gas analyser is available, connect it to the exhaust system and turn the mixture screw in or out as necessary to obtain the specified CO percentage. Readjust the idling speed if necessary.
8   Fit a new cap to the top of the mixture screw, and switch off the engine.

US and Canadian models

9   Connect a tachometer to the engine.
10 Except on 1980 US models, disconnect and plug the vacuum hoses at the EGR valve.
11 Temporarily engage neutral on automatic models, and on all models run the engine for approximately 3 minutes at 2000 rpm.
12 Except on 1980 US models, reconnect the EGR valve hoses and disconnect the canister purge hose.
13 On all models turn the throttle adjusting screw until the idling speed is as given in the Specifications.
14 Connect an exhaust gas analyser to the exhaust system.

16.4 Adjusting carburettor throttle adjusting screw

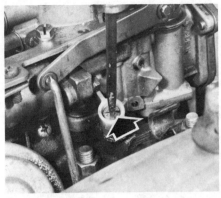
16.6 Adjusting carburettor mixture screw

17.1A Installing inlet manifold

17.1B Inlet manifold hose connections

17.2 Installing exhaust manifold

17.3A Exhaust system front pipe (manifold end)

17.3B Exhaust system front pipe front mounting

17.3C Exhaust system front pipe rear mounting

17.4 Exhaust system rear section rear mounting

17.5A Exhaust system middle section-to-front pipe flange

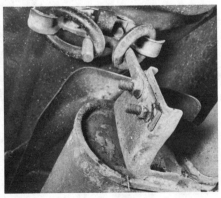
17.5B Exhaust system middle section mounting

18.1A Throttle opener components (UK models), also showing choke vacuum break diaphragm

18.1B Throttle opener vacuum control valve (UK models)

18.1C Throttle opener servo diaphragm (UK models)

18.5 Adjusting throttle opener linkage (UK models)

15　As applicable, disconnect the air hose between the air silencer and reed valve, or air pump and check valve, and plug the port of the reed valve/check valve.

16　Prise the cap from the mixture screw, then turn the screw in or out to obtain the specified CO percentage.

17　Reconnect the air hose and, except on 1980 US models, the canister purge hose.

18　Readjust the idling speed if necessary, and fit the cap to the mixture screw. Switch off the engine.

17 Manifolds and exhaust system – general

1　The inlet manifold is attached to the left-hand side of the cylinder head. Always use a new gasket when installing the manifold and tighten the nuts to the specified torque (photos).

2　The exhaust manifold is attached to the right-hand side of the cylinder head. Always fit new double shims when installing the manifold, and tighten the nuts to the specified torque (photo).

3　To remove the exhaust front pipe and silencer, unscrew the nuts securing it to the manifold, unbolt the two mountings, and unbolt the flange from the rear section (photos). Use new gaskets when installing the pipe.

4　To remove the exhaust rear section, unbolt the clamp, disconnect the rubber mountings, and separate the rear section from the middle section (photo).

5　To remove the exhaust middle section unbolt the centre flange and the rear clamp. Disconnect the rubber mountings and separate the middle section from the rear section (photos). Use a new flange gasket when installing the pipe.

18 Emission control systems (UK) – general

1　On certain UK models, the emission control system takes the form of a throttle opener. The throttle opener system comprises a servo diaphragm (which opens the throttle valve), connected to the intake manifold via a vacuum control valve (photos).

2　The system delays the return of the throttle valve during deceleration and provides more complete combustion of fuel.

3　To adjust the system first connect a tachometer to the engine and adjust the idling speed as described in Section 16.

4　Stop the engine, remove the air cleaner (Section 2), and disconnect the control valve hoses from the intake manifold and diaphragm.

5　Connect a hose between the intake manifold and diaphragm and start the engine. The engine speed should be between 1400 and 1600 rpm – if not, adjust the screw on the diaphragm linkage (photo).

6　Stop the engine, remove the tachometer, and fit the hoses and air cleaner.

19 Emission control systems (US and Canadian models) – general

Air injection system

1　The air injection system provides air to the exhaust manifold in order to promote the burning of any unburnt fuel, and thus reduce hydrocarbon and CO emissions.

2　1980 US models are equipped with an air injection pump driven from the water pump pulley. The air supply is controlled by a bypass valve, and a check valve prevents hot exhaust gases from being forced back into the bypass valve and pump should the pump fail.

3　The air injection pump drivebelt should be tensioned to give the specified deflection when pressed with moderate thumb pressure midway between the two pulleys.

4　On models other than 1980 US models, air injection is provided

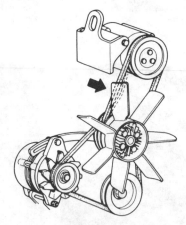

Fig. 3.27 Air injection pump drivebelt tension checking point – arrowed (Sec 19)

Fig. 3.28 Removing an air injection reed valve (Sec 19)

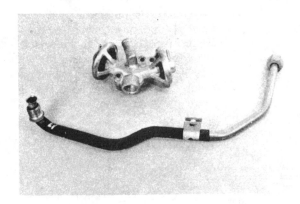

Fig. 3.29 EGR valve and interconnecting pipe (Sec 19)

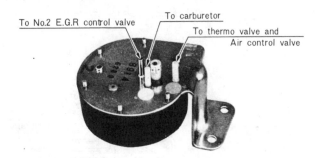

Fig. 3.30 EGR system vacuum amplifier (Sec 19)

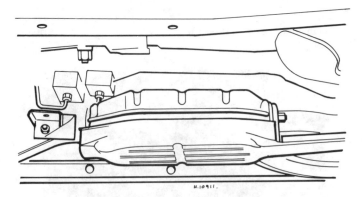

Fig. 3.31 Catalytic converter (Sec 19)

Fig. 3.32 Deceleration control air bypass valve (Sec 19)

Fig. 3.33 Throttle positioner adjusting screw (Sec 19)

by a reed valve which utilises pressure pulses to draw the air into the exhaust manifold.

Exhaust gas recirculation (EGR) system

5   The EGR system introduces a small amount of exhaust gas into the intake manifold during part throttle openings. This has the effect of reducing combustion chamber peak temperatures and pressures, thus reducing nitrous oxide emissions.

6   The EGR valve is located between the exhaust and intake manifolds. The valve and interconnecting pipe should periodically be removed and cleaned of any carbon deposits.

7   A thermo valve ensures that the EGR system does not operate until the engine reaches normal operating temperature.

8   1980 US models are provided with a vacuum amplifier and a vacuum delay valve.

Catalytic converter

9   The catalytic converter is located in the front exhaust pipe, and contains a catalyst which promotes a chemical reaction between any unburnt fuel and oxygen. This reduces hydrocarbon and CO emissions. The unit should periodically be checked for heat damage and deterioration.

Deceleration control system

10   During deceleration a lean mixture will cause a high level of hydrocarbon emission. To counteract this condition, an air bypass valve, which is vacuum operated, is incorporated into the intake system. Under normal running the valve passes air, but during deceleration the valve closes and the mixture is enriched for a short period.

Throttle positioner system

11   The throttle positioner system is similar to the deceleration control system in that it prevents the emission of hydrocarbon during deceleration. However, this system is linked to an engine speed switch and three-way solenoid valve.

12   To adjust the servo diaphragm, first connect a tachometer to the engine.

13   Adjust the idling speed as described in Section 16.

14   Stop the engine and remove the air cleaner, then disconnect the three-way solenoid valve vacuum hose at the servo diaphragm, and the three-way solenoid valve vacuum hose at the intake manifold.

15   Connect a hose between the intake manifold and servo diaphragm.

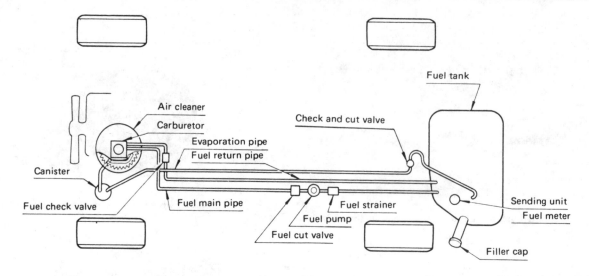

Fig. 3.34 Fuel line and evaporative emission control system (Sec 19)

Fig. 3.35 Evaporative emission control three-way valve location
(Sec 19)

1   Mounting nut   3   Valve
2   Fuel and vent hoses

Fig. 3.37 Checking evaporative shutter valve operation (Sec 19)

16 Start the engine and increase its speed to 2000 rpm. Release the accelerator pedal and check that the engine speed is 1100 to 1300 rpm (1980 US models) or 1000 to 1200 rpm (all other models). If not, turn the throttle positioner adjustment screw as necessary.
17 Stop the engine, reconnect the hoses, and remove the tachometer.

Evaporative emission control system

18 This system is designed to prevent fuel vapour from escaping into the atmosphere by collecting it in a storage tank, consisting of a canister containing activated carbon. When the engine is running, the vapour is drawn from the canister into the air cleaner, and is then drawn into the engine and burnt in the normal manner.
19 A three-way valve located near the fuel tank ensures that excessive pressure or vacuum does not build up in the fuel tank. This is necessary as the filler cap is of non-vented type.
20 1980 US models are equipped with a purge control valve and an evaporative shutter valve in the air cleaner intake.
21 To test the evaporative shutter valve, first remove the air cleaner as described in Section 2 and check that the shutter valve (visible through the intake) is closed.
22 Start the engine and check that the shutter valve opens. Remove the vacuum hose from the diaphragm unit several times and check that the valve operates correctly.
23 Stop the engine and fit the air cleaner.

Heat hazard warning system

24 Cars equipped with a catalytic converter are fitted with a heat sensor on the floor above the unit. If the converter overheats, the sensor will switch on a warning lamp on the instrument panel. Access to the sensor is gained by lifting the right-hand floor mat.

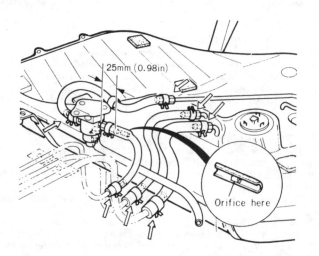

Fig. 3.36 Hose installation on evaporative emission control three-way valve and fuel tank (Sec 19)

20 Fault diagnosis – fuel, exhaust and emission control systems

Symptom	Reason(s)
Difficult starting from cold	Manual or automatic choke inoperative Float chamber fuel level too low Fuel pump faulty Fault in ignition system (Chapter 4)
Insufficient fuel delivery	Clogged fuel filter Fuel pump faulty
Difficulty starting from hot	Float chamber fuel level too high Needle valve sticking open Choked air filter
Excessive fuel consumption	Choked air filter Float chamber fuel level too high Excessively worn carburettor Leak in fuel circuit Needle valve sticking open Mixture adjustment incorrect Fault in ignition system (Chapter 4)

Chapter 4 Ignition system

Contents

Specifications

System type
UK .... Coil and contact breaker
US and Canada .... Electronic; breakerless, with reluctor and pick-up coil

Firing order .... 1-3-4-2 (No 1 nearest radiator)

Distributor
Direction of rotation .... Clockwise (viewed from cap end)

UK models
Contact breaker points gap .... 0.45 to 0.55 mm (0.018 to 0.022 in)
Dwell angle .... 49° to 55°
Condenser capacity .... 0.20 to 0.24 mfd

US and Canadian models
Star type reluctor-to-pick-up coil air gap .... 0.20 mm (0.008 in) minimum
Pick-up coil resistance:
    With star reluctor .... 1050 ohm ± 10% at 20°C (68°F)
    With four-post reluctor .... 800 ohm ± 10% at 20°C (68 °F)

Ignition timing
UK models .... 8° ± 1° BTDC at idling speed
US models – 1979 .... 8° ± 1° BTDC at idling speed, and 16°
BTDC at idling speed with ignition water temperature switch disconnected
US models – 1980/81 .... 5° ± 1° BTDC at idling speed
Canadian models .... 8° ± 1° BTDC at idling speed, and 16° BTDC at idling speed with ignition water temperature switch disconnected

Spark plugs
Type:
    NGK BP5ES, BPR5ES, BP6ES, BPR6ES
    Nippon Denso W16EX-U, W16EXR-U, W20EX-U, W20EXR-U
    Hitachi L45-PW, L46-PW
Gap .... 0.75 to 0.85 mm (0.029 to 0.033 in)

Coil
Type:
    UK models .... Conventional with external ballast resistor
    US and Canadian models .... Conventional, but with electronic module attached to coil or distributor

Ballast resistor resistance .... 1.6 ohm when at 20°C (68°F)

HT lead resistance .... 16 k ohm/metre (39.4 in)

Torque wrench setting

	lbf ft	Nm
Spark plugs	14	19

1 General description

The ignition system fitted to UK models is conventional and comprises a 12-volt battery, coil with external ballast resistor, contact breaker points, distributor, and spark plugs. On US and Canadian models, an electronic system is fitted comprising a 12-volt battery high output coil, a transistorised module, distributor with magnetic impulse generator, and spark plugs.

In order to enable the engine to run correctly at different speeds and under varying loads, an electrical spark must be produced at each spark plug in turn at exactly the right time. In the conventional system, low tension (LT) voltage is fed from the battery to the coil primary windings and then to the distributor contact breaker points. With the points closed, an electromagnetic field is produced around the secondary high tension (HT) windings in the coil. When the points open, a high tension current is induced in the coil secondary windings, which is then fed via the distributor cap and rotor arm to each spark plug. The capacitor or condenser serves as a buffer for the surge of low tension current, and prevents excessive arcing across the points; it also aids the collapse of the primary winding electromagnetic field. The ballast resistor is incorporated in the ignition circuit as an aid to better starting; under normal running, current to the coil primary windings passes through the resistor but during starting the resistor is bypassed to ensure that a strong spark is maintained at the spark plugs.

In the electronic system, the high tension (HT) circuit operates in an identical way to the conventional system. However the low tension (LT) circuit is operated electronically instead of by the contact breaker points. The distributor contains a reluctor with four arms or posts which pass close to a sensor, comprising a permanent magnet and coil. Each time an arm or post passes the sensor, an electrical impulse is created in the coil and is passed to the transistorised module, which switches off the coil primary circuit for a predetermined length of time.

Both conventional and electronic systems incorporate centrifugal and vacuum advance mechanisms at the distributor.

2 Contact breaker points – checking and adjustment

1 Prise the clips away and remove the distributor cap. Remove the rotor arm (photos).
2 Turn the engine with a spanner on the crankshaft pulley bolt, until the heel of the moving contact is on a high point of the cam.
3 Prise the contacts apart and check them for condition. If they are discoloured or pitted, renovate or renew them with reference to Section 3. If they are serviceable, adjust them as follows.
4 Insert a feeler blade of the correct thickness (see Specifications) between the two points; the blade should be a firm sliding fit without forcing the points apart. If adjustment is necessary, loosen the fixed contact screws and move the set with a screwdriver. Always recheck

2.1A Removing distributor cap

2.1B Removing rotor arm

2.4A Checking the points gap with a feeler blade

2.4B Adjusting contact breaker points gap with a screwdriver the gap after retightening the retaining screws (photos).

5   Smear a *small* amount of multi-purpose grease on the cam lobes to lubricate the heel of the moving contact. Lubrication should be carried out sparingly, to avoid contamination of the points' surfaces.

6   Refit the rotor arm and distributor cap.

7   Connect a dwell meter to the engine in accordance with the manufacturer's instructions, start the engine, and check that the dwell angle is as given in the Specifications. If not, reduce the points gap to increase the dwell angle, and vice versa.

8   Check the ignition timing as described in Section 8.

3   Contact breaker points – renovation or renewal

1   Prise the clips away and remove the distributor cap. Remove the rotor arm.

2   Loosen the terminal screw on the fixed contact, and slide out the low tension lead (photo).

3   Note the location of the earth lead, then remove the fixed contact retaining screws and washers and withdraw the contact points set (photos).

4   Extract the circlip and remove the moving contact from its pivot on the fixed contact.

5   If the faces of the contacts are not badly pitted, dress them smooth and square on an oilstone, but if refacing will make the tungsten points very thin, renew them.

6   Refit the moving contact and circlip.

7   Wipe clean the distributor baseplate, then refit the points assembly in reverse order to removal.

8   Apply only one drop of oil to the moving contact pivot. Adjust the points gap as described in Section 2, and also check the ignition timing as described in Section 8.

4   Condenser – testing, removal and refitting

1   Both conventional and electronic systems are fitted with a condenser (capacitor) located on the side of the distributor. A faulty condenser may cause total failure of the ignition system or, on the conventional system, rapid burning of the contact breaker points.

2   Without special test equipment a faulty condenser cannot be readily diagnosed, but where there is an indication of a malfunction, it is best to renew it in view of its very moderate cost. Normal symptoms are difficult starting and misfiring with the engine under load.

3   To remove the condenser on the conventional system, remove the distributor cap, loosen the terminal screw on the fixed contact, and slide out the low tension lead. Remove the condenser mounting screw, slide out the terminal block, and disconnect the lead (photo). On the electronic system remove the mounting screw and disconnect the lead.

4   Refitting is the reversal of removal.

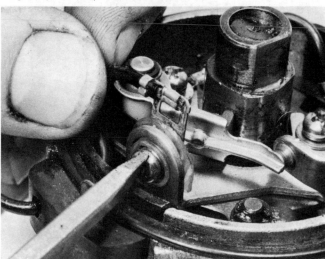
3.2 Removing contact breaker points low tension lead

3.3A Removing contact breaker points earth lead

3.3B Removing contact breaker points

4.3 Removing low tension terminal block

Measuring plug gap. A feeler gauge of the correct size (see ignition system specifications) should have a slight 'drag' when slid between the electrodes. Adjust gap if necessary

Adjusting plug gap. The plug gap is adjusted by bending the ground electrode inwards, or outwards, as necessary until the correct clearance is obtained. Note the use of the correct tool

Normal. Gray brown deposits, lightly coated core nose. Gap increasing by around 0.001 in (0.025 mm) per 1000 miles (1600 km). Plugs ideally suited to engine, and engine in good condition

Carbon fouling. Dry, black, sooty deposits. Will cause weak spark and eventually misfire. Fault: over-rich fuel mixture. Check: carburetor mixture settings, float level and jet sizes; choke operation and cleanliness of air filter. Plugs can be re-used after cleaning

Oil fouling. Wet, oily deposits. Will cause weak spark and eventually misfire. Fault: worn bores/piston rings or valve guides; sometimes occurs (temporarily) during running-in period. Plugs can be re-used after thorough cleaning

Overheating. Electrodes have glazed appearance, core nose very white – few deposits. Fault: plug overheating. Check: plug value, ignition timing, fuel octane rating (too low) and fuel mixture (too weak). Discard plugs and cure fault immediately

Electrode damage. Electrodes burned away; core nose has burned, glazed appearance. Fault: pre-ignition. Check: as for 'Overheating' but may be more severe. Discard plugs and remedy fault before piston or valve damage occurs

Split core nose (may appear initially as a crack). Damage is self-evident, but cracks will only show after cleaning. Fault: pre-ignition or wrong gap-setting technique. Check: ignition timing, cooling system, fuel octane rating (too low) and fuel mixture (too weak). Discard plugs, rectify fault immediately

5 Electronic ignition – star-to-sensor air gap adjustment

1   On distributors fitted with a star type reluctor, the air gap should be adjusted after dismantling and reassembling the distributor.
2   Turn the reluctor until one of the arms is aligned with the pick-up coil.
3   Using a non-magnetic feeler blade, check that the air gap between the arm and coil is as given in Specifications. If not, loosen the three pick-up coil base screws and move the base as necessary. Recheck the adjustment after tightening the screws.

6 Distributor – removal and refitting

1   Remove No 1 spark plug, and turn the engine with a spanner on the crankshaft pulley bolt until pressure at the plug hole can be felt with the thumb, indicating that No 1 piston is on its compression stroke. Continue timing the engine until the timing mark on the crankshaft pulley is aligned with the pin on the timing cover.
2   Remove the distributor cap and place it to one side; according to model either clips or screws retain it in position.
3   Mark the distributor body in line with the rotor arm. Mark the clamp plate in line with the clamp nut.
4   Pull the vacuum hose from the vacuum advance capsule.
5   Unscrew and remove the distributor clamp nut and washer.
6   On UK models disconnect the low tension (LT) wire at the distributor.
7   On US and Canadian models remove the condenser as described in Section 4, then disconnect the wiring to the pick-up coil or module

as applicable.
8   On all models, withdraw the distributor from the cylinder head (photo).
9   Before refitting the distributor, check that the timing mark on the crankshaft pulley is still aligned with the pin on the timing cover.
10   Turn the drivegear on the end of the distributor until the marks on the gear and housing are aligned (see Fig. 4.2).
11   Position the distributor over its location hole with the clamp slot aligned with the clamp stud, then slide it into engagement with the crankshaft skew gear. As it engages, the rotor arm will turn clockwise approximately 30°.
12   Make sure that the distributor body is aligned with the previously made marks. Refit the clamp nut and washer and tighten the nut. If a new distributor is being fitted, position the body so that the contact points just start to separate on the conventional system, or the reluctor arm or post is aligned with the pick-up coil on the electronic system.
13   Refit the distributor cap and No 1 spark plug, and reconnect the wiring and condenser as applicable. Reconnect the vacuum hose.
14   Adjust the ignition timing as described in Section 8.

7 Distributor – overhaul

Note: *Before dismantling the distributor check that spare parts are available.*

Contact breaker type.
1   Remove the contact breaker points as described in Section 3.
2   Remove the condenser as described in Section 4.
3   Remove the retaining screws and C-clip, and withdraw the

Fig. 4.1 Electronic ignition star-to-sensor air gap (Sec 5)

4.2 Distributor drivegear alignment marks (Sec 6)

4.3 Plastic cover (1) and rubber seal and grommet (2) on star reluctor electronic distributor (Sec 7)

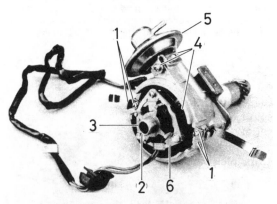

4.4 Star reluctor electronic distributor (Sec 7)

1 Cap retaining clips and screws	4 Vacuum capsule retaining screws and clip
2 Reluctor retaining pin	5 Vacuum capsule
3 Reluctor	6 Pick-up coil assembly

6.8 Withdrawing distributor from the engine

7.22 Distributor oil seal location

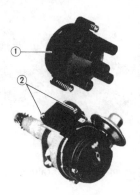

Fig. 4.5 Post reluctor electronic distributor (Sec 7)

1 Cap
2 Screws

3 Module

Fig. 4.6 Post reluctor electronic distributor (Sec 7)

1 Screws

2 Rotor

Fig. 4.7 Removing the centrifugal advance mechanism on the post reluctor electronic distributor (Sec 7)

Fig. 4.8 Post reluctor electronic distributor (Sec 7)

1 Pick-up coil assembly
2 Clip and screws

3 Vacuum capsule

Fig. 4.9 Removing the reluctor on the post reluctor electronic distributor (Sec 7)

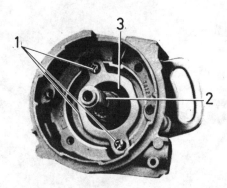

Fig. 4.10 Post reluctor electronic distributor (Sec 7)

1 Thrust plate and screws   3 Oil seal
2 Driveshaft

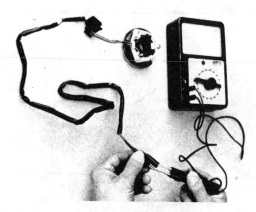

Fig. 4.11 Checking pick-up coil resistance – star reluctor type (Sec 7)

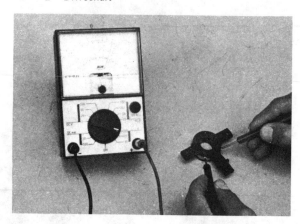

Fig. 4.12 Checking pick-up coil resistance – post reluctor type (Sec 7)

vacuum advance capsule.

4   Remove the distributor cap retaining clips. Remove the screws and withdraw the contact breaker baseplate.

5   Note the position of the cam in relation to the mark on the driving gear. Prise out the lubrication pad, remove the screws, and withdraw the cam.

6   Using a suitable punch, drive out the roll pin and remove the drivegear. Withdraw the driveshaft.

Star reluctor electronic type.

7   With the distributor cap and rotor removed, unclip and remove the plastic cover.

8   Remove the rubber seal and disengage the wiring grommet from the body.

9   Remove the screws and withdraw the cap retaining clips.

10 Remove the retaining pin and withdraw the reluctor star plate.

11 Remove the retaining screws and C-clip, and withdraw the vacuum advance capsule.

12 Remove the screws and withdraw the pick-up coil assembly.

13 Using a suitable punch, drive out the roll pin and remove the drivegear. Withdraw the driveshaft assembly.

Post reluctor electronic type

14 Remove the two screws and withdraw the module carefully from the side of the distributor.

15 With the distributor cap removed, mark the rotor and driveshaft in relation to each other. Remove the cross-head screws and withdraw the rotor.

16 Unscrew the bolt and withdraw the centrifugal advance mechanism.

17 Unscrew the two bolts and remove the pick-up coil assembly.

18 Remove the retaining screws and C-clip, and withdraw the vacuum advance capsule.

19 Remove the two screws and withdraw the reluctor assembly.

20 Using a suitable punch, drive out the roll pin and remove the drivegear from the driveshaft.

21 Remove the two screws, withdraw the thrust plate, and lift the driveshaft assembly from the distributor.

All types

22 Extract the oil seal from the distributor body (photo).

23 Clean the distributor cap and rotor with a dry cloth and examine them for cracks and carbon traces, indicating HT arcing. Check the metal segments and carbon brush in the cap for wear; also check the metal strip on the rotor arm. If necessary, renew the components.

24 Clean the remaining components in paraffin and wipe dry. Examine them for wear and damage and renew them as necessary.

25 On US and Canadian models, use an ohmmeter to check the resistance of the pick-up coil; renew it if the resistance is not as given in the Specifications.

26 Reassemble the distributor using a reversal of the dismantling procedure.

---

8   Ignition timing – adjustment

Note: *For accurate setting of the ignition timing it is essential to use a stroboscopic timing light, although where a conventional contact breaker points system is fitted, the ignition timing may be temporarily set using a test lamp and leads.*

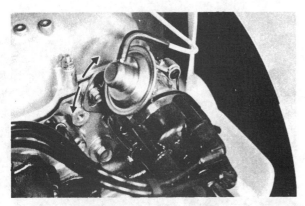

Fig. 4.13 Adjusting the ignition timing (Sec 8)

Fig. 4.14 Connecting the ignition module water temperature switch wiring to check the ignition advance timing (Sec 8)

Stroboscopic timing light method.

1   Run the engine until it reaches the normal operating temperature; this will allow it to idle evenly.
2   Stop the engine and connect a tachometer and stroboscopic timing light in accordance with the manufacturer's instructions.
3   Start the engine and allow it to idle at the specified idling speed given in Chapter 3. On automatic transmission models apply the handbrake and chock the wheels, then place the selector lever in position 'D'.
4   Point the timing light at the timing pin and crankshaft pulley, and check that the timing marks are in alignment (refer to the Specifications for the correct timing). Keep clear of the fan blades. **Note:** *On models fitted with a two-notch pulley, the notches represent TDC, and the relevant mark for ignition timing at idling speed, noting that the pulley rotates clockwise when viewed from the front of the vehicle. 1979 US and 1980/81 Canadian models may have a three-notch pulley, the notches representing TDC, the first ignition timing mark for use with water temperature switch connected, and the second ignition timing mark (if present) for use with the switch disconnected – see paragraph 6. If the latter notch is not present, its position must be estimated using the TDC mark and timing mark.*
5   If adjustment is necessary, loosen the distributor locknut, turn the distributor as necessary, then tighten the locknut.
6   Where the star reluctor electronic ignition is fitted (ie 1979 US models and 1980/81 Canadian models), disconnect the wires from the ignition module water temperature switch and connect them together with a bridging wire. With the engine idling, check that the advance timing is as given in the Specifications, then reconnect the wires.
7   With the timing light still connected, gradually increase the engine speed and check that the ignition timing advances by a minimum of 7° at 2000 rpm. If not, a check should be made in the centrifugal weight mechanism and vacuum advance capsule.
8   Stop the engine and remove the tachometer and timing light.

Test lamp and leads method (contact breaker points system only)

9   Unclip and remove the distributor cap, then turn the engine with a spanner on the crankshaft pulley bolt until the rotor arm is pointing downwards.
10 Continue turning the engine in a forward direction until the timing mark on the crankshaft pulley is aligned with the pin on the timing cover (see paragraph 4).
11 Connect the 12 volt test lamp and leads between the moving contact terminal and a suitable earth.
12 Disconnect the HT lead from the centre of the coil and switch on the ignition. Loosen the distributor locknut.
13 If the test lamp is already glowing, turn the distributor body clockwise until the lamp goes out.
14 Turn the distributor body anti-clockwise until the test lamp just lights up; this indicates that the contact points have just separated.
15 Tighten the locknut then turn the engine through two revolutions and check that the test lamp comes on when the timing mark and pin are in alignment.
16 Switch off the ignition, refit the coil HT lead, disconnect the test lamp, and refit the distributor cap.

9   Coil – description and testing

1   The coil is located on the right-hand side of the engine compartment (photo). On UK models an externally mounted ballast resistor is fitted, but on US and Canadian models the coil either has an externally mounted electronic module, or is conventional without any attachment.
2   Always make sure that the coil leads are fitted to the correct terminals. If they are reversed, misfiring and loss of power will result.
3   Testing of the coil requires an ohmmeter and special equipment, and is best left to a suitably equipped automobile electrician. However, if a coil is suspected of being faulty, substitution with a known good unit will determine whether a fault is present.

10 Spark plugs and HT leads – general

1   The correct functioning of the spark plugs is vital for the proper

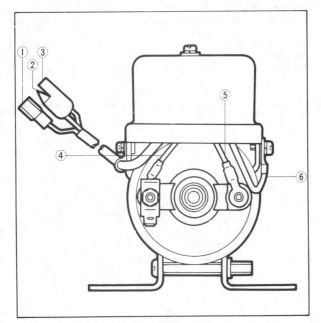

Fig. 4.15 Coil with externally mounted electronic module (Sec 9)

1	To water temperature switch	4	To ignition coil (-)
2	To distributor (+)	5	To fuse and ignition coil (+)
3	To distributor (-)	6	Earth

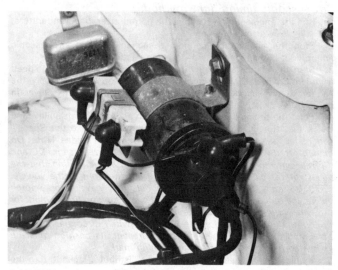

9.1A Coil location on a UK model

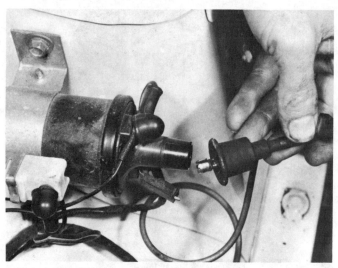

9.1B Inserting HT lead into coil

running and efficient operation of the engine.

2   At the intervals specified (see Routine Maintenance), the plugs should be removed, examined, cleaned, and if worn excessively, renewed. The condition of the spark plug can also tell much about the general condition of the engine – refer to the illustrations.

3   If the insulator nose of the spark plug is clean and white, with no deposits, this is indicative of a weak mixture, or too hot a plug (a hot plug transfers heat away from the electrode slowly – a cold plug transfers heat away quickly).

4   If the insulator nose is covered with hard black deposits, then this is indicative that the mixture is too rich. Should the plug be black and oily then it is likely that the engine is fairly worn, as well as the mixture being too rich.

5   If the insulator nose is covered with light tan to greyish brown deposits, then the mixture is correct, and it is likely that the engine is in good condition.

6   If there are any traces of long brown tapering stains on the outside of the white portion of the plug, then the plug will have to be renewed, as this shows that there is a faulty joint between the plug body and the insulator, and compression is being allowed to leak away.

7   Plugs should be cleaned by a sand blasting machine, which will free them from carbon more than by cleaning by hand. The machine will also test the condition of the plugs under compression. Any plug that fails to spark at the recommended pressure should be renewed.

8   The spark plug gap is of considerable importance as, if it is too large or too small, the size of the spark and its efficiency will be seriously impaired. The spark plug gap is given in the Specifications Section.

9   To set it, measure the gap with a feeler gauge, and then bend open, or close, the outer plug electrode until the correct gap is achieved. the centre electrode should never be bent as this may crack the insulation and cause plug failure, if nothing worse.

10 When installing the plugs, remember to connect the leads from the distributor cap in the correct firing order which is 1, 3, 4, 2, No 1 cylinder being the one nearest the radiator.

11 The plug leads require no maintenance other than being kept clean and wiped over regularly. The leads used are of the carbon cored type which are used to suppress high frequency radio interference from the ignition system. Although these leads can give trouble-free performance for many years, they can sometimes cause starting problems after a considerable period of usage. A procedure is given for checking them in Section 11, paragraph 8, but if they are found to be faulty, consideration should be given to replacing them with the copper cored conductor type and using the suppressor-type plug caps. Your automobile electrical specialist will be able to help with the supply of approved types.

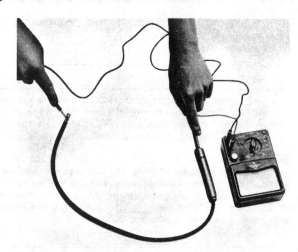

Fig. 4.16 Checking an HT lead with an ohmmeter (Sec 11)

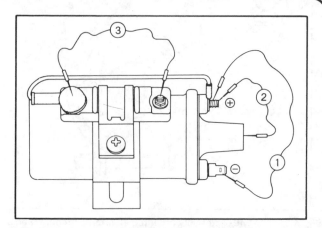

Fig. 4.17 Ohmmeter connections for checking the coil primary windings (1), coil secondary windings (2), and ballast resistor (3) (Sec 11)

11 Fault diagnosis – ignition system

1   With the exception of incorrect ignition timing or a faulty advance-retard mechanism, both of which will be evident as lack of performance and possibly pinking (pre-ignition) or overheating, ignition faults can be divided into two types; total failure (engine fails to start or cuts out completely), and partial failure (misfiring, regular or otherwise, on one or more cylinders).

2   Electronic ignition, where fitted, is normally very reliable. Fault diagnosis should be confined to checking the security and continuity of leads, and insulation and dryness of the HT circuit components. It is not advisable to remove HT leads when the engine is running as the voltage is considerably higher than that in a conventional ignition system, and there is a risk of personal injury and of damage to the coil insulation.

3   On both conventional and electronic systems the commonest cause of difficult starting, especially in winter, is a slow engine cranking speed combined with a poor spark at the plugs. Before commencing any involved checks, always ensure that the battery is fully charged, the HT leads and distributor cap are clean and dry, and the plugs and points (where fitted) are in good condition and correctly gapped. Also make sure that the battery terminals and LT connections are clean and tight.

Engine fails to start.

4   If the engine fails to start and it was running normally when it was last used, first check that there is fuel in the tank. If the engine turns over normally on the starter motor and the battery is evidently well charged, then the fault may be in either the high or low tension circuits. First check the HT circuit. **Note:** *If the battery is known to be fully charged, the ignition light comes on, and the starter motor fails to turn the engine, check the tightness of the leads on the battery terminals and also the secureness of the earth lead connection to the body. If one of the battery terminal posts gets very hot when trying to operate the starter motor, this is a sure indication of a faulty connection to that terminal. For further information on the battery, refer to Chapter 10.*

5   One of the commonest reasons for bad starting is wet or damp spark plugs and distributor leads. Remove the distributor cap. If the condensation is visible internally, dry the cap with a rag and also wipe over the leads, or alternatively use a proprietary water dispersant.

6   If the engine still fails to start, check that the voltage is reaching the plugs. On a conventional contact breaker points ignition system, disconnect each plug lead in turn at the spark plug end, and hold the end of the cable about $\frac{3}{16}$ in (5 mm) away from the cylinder head. Where electronic ignition is fitted, remove each spark plug in turn, and using insulated pliers, hold it firmly against the cylinder head with the HT lead attached. Have an assistant spin the engine by turning the ignition key. A regular strong blue spark indicates that HT voltage is reaching the spark plugs.

7   If no voltage is reaching the plugs, the distributor cap may be cracked, the carbon brush worn or sticking, the rotor arm may be cracked, or the HT leads or coil faulty.

8   Check each HT lead with an ohmmeter, and if the resistance is in excess of that specified, renew the leads as necessary.

9   Using an ohmmeter check the coil primary winding resistance by connecting the meter between the positive and negative LT terminals. On the conventional ignition the resistance should be 1.5 ohm – on electronic ignition it should be 0.9 ohm.

10 Check the coil secondary winding resistance by connecting the meter between the positive LT terminal and the HT tower terminal. On the conventional ignition the resistance should be 9000 ohm – on electronic ignition it should be 7000 ohm.

11 On the conventional ignition connect the ohmmeter between the two ballast resistor terminals – the resistance should be 1.6 ohm.

12 Renew the coil and/or ballast resistor as necessary if the tests described in paragraphs 9 to 11 give incorrect results.

13 To check the LT circuit, switch on the ignition and check that there is voltage at the coil positive terminal, using a voltmeter or test lamp and leads. If not, the ignition switch may be faulty.

14 On the conventional ignition, connect up a test lamp and leads as described in Section 8, then spin the engine with the starter. The test lamp should flash on and off. If it stays on permanently, the contact points are not conducting the current to earth. If it stays off permanently, either there is an open circuit between the coil and the distributor, or the condenser has a short circuit and should be renewed.

Engine fires but will not run.

15 On the conventional ignition, if the coil ballast resistor is defective the ignition system will function normally whilst the starter motor is operating, but will cut out as soon as the ignition key is returned to its normal position. This condition is confirmed if voltage is present at the supply (ignition switch) side of the resistor but not at the coil side. It is inadvisable to bypass the resistor, as this could lead to overheating of the coil and subsequent damage.

Engine misfires.

16 Uneven running and misfiring should first be checked by making sure that all leads, particularly HT, are dry and connected properly. Make sure that they are not shorting to earth through broken or cracked insulation. If this is the case you will normally be able to see and hear the spark.

17 Check the plugs and, on conventional ignition, the contact points and condenser. A regular misfire can be isolated by fitting a metal extension between the plug and HT lead cap using an insulated screwdriver to short out the plug terminal to the cylinder head. Shorting out a plug which is firing normally will accentuate the misfire, but shorting out the misfiring plug will make no difference.

18 Misfiring can also result from mechanical faults, loss of compression etc, or incorrect adjustment of the carburettor.

Chapter 5 Clutch

Contents

Specifications

Type .... Single dry plate, diaphragm spring

Actuation
1.6 right-hand drive models .... Cable
All other models .... Hydraulic

Clutch disc
Maximum run-out .... 1.0 mm (0.039 in)
Minimum rivet head depth .... 0.3 mm (0.012 in)

Clutch pedal free play
Cable type .... 5 to 15 mm (0.20 to 0.59 in)
Hydraulic type .... 1 to 3 mm (0.04 to 0.12 in)

Clutch pedal height .... 193 to 198 mm (7.6 to 7.8 in)

Release fork free play (cable type) .... 3.5 to 4.0 mm (0.14 to 0.16 in)

Maximum clearance between piston and bore of master cylinder or slave cylinder .... 0.15 mm (0.006 in)

Torque wrench settings

	lbf ft	Nm
Clutch-to-flywheel bolts	17	23

1 General description

The clutch is of single dry plate type and incorporates a diaphragm spring. Actuation for 1.6 right-hand drive models is by cable, but for all other models is by a hydraulic system incorporating a master cylinder and slave cylinder. A pendant mounted clutch pedal is fitted.

The cover unit, which is bolted to the flywheel, incorporates a pressure plate, diaphragm spring, and fulcrum rings. The clutch disc is splined to the gearbox input shaft, and is held in position between the flywheel and the pressure plate by the diaphragm spring. Friction lining material is rivetted to the clutch disc, and the disc hub incorporates cushion springs to absorb transmission shocks and assist in smooth clutch engagement.

When the clutch pedal is depressed, the release arm presses the release bearing against the centre of the diaphragm spring. This causes the spring periphery to release the pressure plate from the disc, and drive between the engine and gearbox ceases.

When the clutch pedal is released, the diaphragm spring forces the pressure plate into contact with the disc, which is then firmly sandwiched between the pressure plate and the flywheel, and drive between the engine and gearbox is reconnected.

As the disc friction linings wear, the pressure plate will gradually move closer to the flywheel. On hydraulically actuated models this wear is automatically taken up, but on cable actuated models it will be necessary to adjust the release fork free play.

2 Clutch (cable actuated type) – adjustment

1 The release fork free play should be checked, and if necessary adjusted, every 12 000 miles (20 000 km).

2   Jack up the front of the car and support it on axle stands. Apply the handbrake.
3   Push the release fork forward as far as possible against the tension of the return spring, then release it and check the total movement, which should be within the limits given in the Specifications.
4   If adjustment is necessary, loosen the outer cable locknut on the bulkhead in the engine compartment, and adjust the length of the outer cable until the release fork free play is correct (photo). Tighten the locknut.
5   Lower the car to the ground.

3   Clutch cable – renewal

1   Jack up the front of the car and support it on axle stands. Apply the handbrake.
2   Working inside the car, disconnect the inner cable from the clutch pedal by extracting the clip and removing the clevis pin and bush.
3   Working under the car, unhook the return spring from the release fork, and extract the clip from the outer cable after unbolting the heat shield (photos).
4   Disconnect the clutch cable from the gearbox casing and release fork.
5   Unbolt the bracket from the bulkhead and withdraw the complete clutch cable.
6   Install the new cable using a reversal of the removal procedure, but adjust the release fork free play as described in Section 2.

4   Clutch pedal – removal, refitting and adjustment

Cable actuated models
1   Working inside the car, disconnect the inner cable from the clutch pedal by extracting the clip and removing the clevis pin and bush.

Hydraulically actuated models
2   Working inside the car, unhook the return spring from the pedal.
3   Extract the split pin, remove the clevis pin, and disconnect the master cylinder pushrod from the pedal.

All models
4   Unscrew the pivot nut and slide the clutch pedal, sleeves and bushes from the pivot shaft.
5   Remove the foot pad and return stop from the pedal, and clean the non-rubber components in paraffin.
6   Examine all components for wear and damage, and renew them as necessary.
7   Refitting is a reversal of removal, but first lubricate the pedal and bushes with a little multi-purpose grease. When installed, the pedal free height must be adjusted as follows.
8   Refer to Figs. 5.4 and 5.5 and check that the pedal height is as given in the Specifications. If not, loosen the pedal stop locknut, adjust the bolt as necessary, then tighten the locknut.

Fig. 5.1 Clutch release fork free play on cable actuated models (Sec 2)

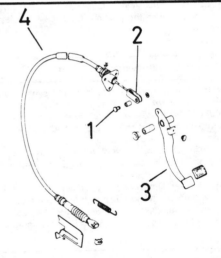

Fig. 5.2 Exploded view of clutch cable and pedal (Sec 3)

1   Clevis pin   2   Inner cable   3   Pedal   4   Outer cable

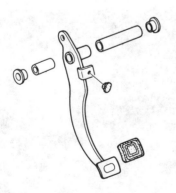

Fig. 5.3 Exploded view of the clutch pedal (Sec 4)

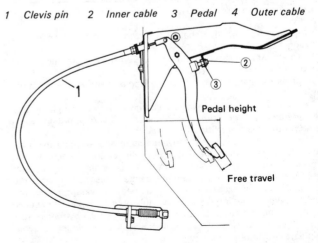

Fig. 5.4 Clutch pedal adjustment on cable actuated models (Sec 4)

1   Cable   3   Locknut
2   Stop adjustment bolt

2.4 Clutch cable adjustment locknuts

3.3A Removing clutch cable heat shield

3.3B Clutch cable and return spring attachment

Cable actuated models

9   Adjust the release fork free play as described in Section 2 – this will automatically bring the clutch pedal free play within the limits given in the Specifications.

Hydraulically actuated models

10 Check that the clutch pedal free play at the pad is within the limits given in the Specifications. If not, loosen the locknut on the master cylinder pushrod, and turn the pushrod until the free play is correct. Tighten the locknut.

5   Master cylinder – removal and refitting

1   Remove the clutch fluid reservoir cap and syphon out the fluid using a pipette. *Note that the fluid is poisonous, and will damage paintwork if spilt – rinse off immediately with cold water if necessary.*
2   Place some cloth under the master cylinder, then unscrew the union nut and remove the outlet pipe.
3   Working inside the car, unscrew the mounting nuts.
4   Withdraw the clutch master cylinder from within the engine compartment.
5   Refitting is a reversal of removal, but insert the pedal pushrod into the piston as the master cylinder is positioned on the bulkhead. Bleed the hydraulic system as described in Section 9, then adjust the pedal height and free play as described in Section 4, paragraphs 8 and 10.

6   Master cylinder – overhaul

1   Clean the exterior of the master cylinder with methylated spirit and wipe dry.
2   With the cap and fluid baffle removed, drain and discard any remaining fluid.
3   Unscrew and remove the bolt and washers from inside the reservoir, and remove the reservoir.
4   Depress the piston, then extract the stop ring and washer from the mouth of the cylinder.
5   Tap the cylinder on the workbench and withdraw the piston and secondary seal, spacer, primary seal, and return spring, noting which way round the seals are fitted.
6   Clean all components in methylated spirit and examine them for wear and damage. Check the piston and cylinder bore for scoring and corrosion. Temporarily refit the piston to the bore and, using a feeler blade, check that the maximum clearance does not exceed the specified amount. If excessive wear or damage is evident, renew the complete cylinder, but if it is still serviceable obtain a repair kit of seals.
7   Discard the old seals. Dip the new seals in clean hydraulic fluid and fit the secondary seal to the piston, using the fingers only to manipulate it into position.
8   Make sure that the cylinder inlet port is unobstructed, then refit the components in the reverse order to removal with reference to Fig. 5.7 if necessary. Make sure that the seal lips face into the cylinder.
9   Half fill the reservoir with clean hydraulic fluid, then, while keeping

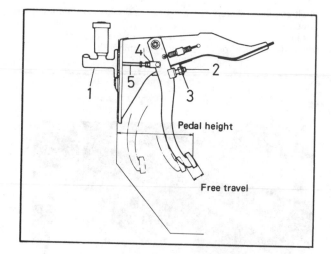

Fig. 5.5 Clutch pedal adjustment on hydraulically actuated models (Sec 4)

1 Master cylinder   4 Locknut
2 Pedal stop adjustment bolt   5 Pushrod
3 Locknut

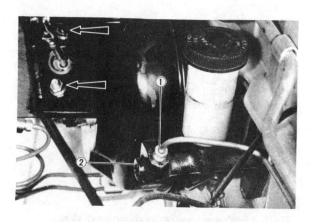

Fig. 5.6 Clutch master cylinder (2) and outlet union (1) (Sec 5)
Inset shows mounting nuts

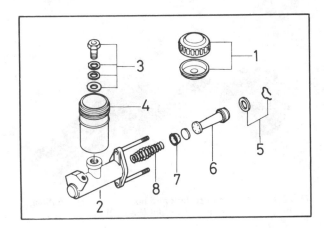

Fig. 5.7 Exploded view of the clutch master cylinder (Sec 6)

1 Filler cap and fluid baffle	5 Stop ring and washer
2 Body	6 Piston
3 Bolt and sealing washers	7 Primary seal
4 Reservoir	8 Spring

Fig. 5.8 Checking clutch master cylinder bore/piston wear with a feeler blade (Sec 6)

Fig. 5.9 Clutch slave cylinder (3), hydraulic hose (1) and mounting bolts (2) (Sec 7)

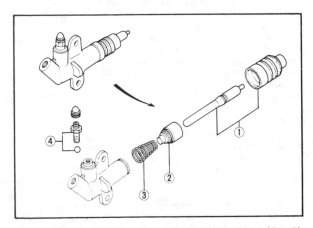

Fig. 5.10 Exploded view of the clutch slave cylinder (Sec 8)

1 Rubber boot and pushrod	3 Spring
2 Piston	4 Bleed screw and ball

the reservoir upright, operate the piston slowly until fluid emerges from the outlet. The master cylinder is now ready to be refitted to the car, but must be kept upright to avoid loss of fluid.

7 Slave cylinder – removal and refitting

1 Jack up the front of the car and support it on axle stands. Apply the handbrake.
2 Working under the car, loosen, but do not remove, the hydraulic hose union from the slave cylinder.
3 Unscrew the mounting bolts, withdraw the slave cylinder from the gearbox casing, and disengage the pushrod from the release fork.
4 Unscrew the slave cylinder from the hydraulic hose, and plug the hose to prevent loss of fluid.
5 Refitting is a reversal of removal, but bleed the hydraulic system as described in Section 9. Make sure that the hydraulic hose is not twisted after the union has been tightened.

8 Slave cylinder – overhaul

1 Clean the exterior of the slave cylinder with methylated spirit and wipe dry.
2 Prise off the rubber boot and remove the pushrod.
3 Tap out the piston and seal and extract the spring.
4 Unscrew the bleed nipple and remove the steel ball from its seat.
5 Clean all components in methylated spirit and examine them for wear and damage. Check the piston and cylinder bore for scoring and

corrosion. Temporarily refit the piston to the bore and, using a feeler blade, check that the maximum clearance does not exceed the specified amount. If excessive wear or damage is evident, renew the complete cylinder, but if it is still serviceable obtain a repair kit of seals.
6 Discard the old seal, then dip the new seal in clean hydraulic fluid and fit it to the piston using the fingers only to manipulate it into position.
7 Refit the components in the reverse order to removal, with reference to Fig. 5.10 if necessary. Make sure that the seal lip faces into the cylinder.

9 Hydraulic system – bleeding

1 The clutch hydraulic system must be bled after work involving the disconnection of any component has taken place, otherwise air will be trapped and the system will not function correctly.
2 Before commencing work, gather together a clean jar and a suitable length of clear plastic tubing which is a tight fit over the bleed screw on the slave cylinder. Also engage the help of an assistant.
3 Jack up the front of the car and support it on axle stands. Apply the handbrake.
4 Remove the filler cap and top up the clutch fluid reservoir with clean hydraulic fluid (brake fluid to the specifications given in Chapter 9 should be used). Take care not to spill fluid onto the paintwork, otherwise damage will result – swill off immediately with cold water if necessary.
5 Clean the area around the bleed screw, then remove the cap and fit the plastic tubing. Put the free end of the tubing in the glass jar.

Fig. 5.11 Bleeding the clutch hydraulic system (Sec 9)

Fig. 5.12 Clutch release fork and bearing on a hydraulically actuated model (Sec 12)

6   Unscrew the bleed screw half a turn, and have the assistant fully depress the clutch pedal and allow it to return slowly. The bleed screw incorporates a one-way valve so there is no need to tighten it after each downstroke of the pedal. As the fluid is pumped into the glass jar it will initially contain air bubbles.

7   Have the clutch pedal depressed two more times, then top up the fluid level in the reservoir. During bleeding, the reservoir must be at least ¾ full.

8   Repeat the bleeding operation until the fluid entering the jar is free of air bubbles, then tighten the bleed screw, remove the plastic tubing, and fit the cap.

9   Top up the fluid level in the reservoir and fit the filler cap. Always discard the fluid drained from the hydraulic system.

10 Lower the car to the ground.

10 Clutch – removal

1   Access to the clutch can be gained by removing the engine or removing the gearbox. Unless additional work on the engine is necessary, it is recommended that the gearbox is removed as described in Chapter 6. Removal of the engine is described in Chapter 1.

2   Mark the clutch cover in relation to the flywheel in order to ensure correct refitting should the original clutch be serviceable.

3   Hold the flywheel stationary with a screwdriver engaged in the teeth of the ring gear, then unscrew the cover bolts a turn at a time until the pressure of the diaphragm spring is relieved. Note that the two painted dowel bolts are located opposite each other, and one has a small marker hole next to it.

4   With all the bolts removed, withdraw the cover assembly and disc from the flywheel (photo).

11 Clutch – inspection

1   Examine the cover assembly and disc for wear and damage. If the disc friction linings are contaminated with oil, the gearbox input shaft oil seal or crankshaft rear oil seal may be faulty, requiring renewal.

2   Light scoring of the pressure plate or flywheel is normal, but if the scoring is very deep, the components must be renewed. In the case of the flywheel it may be possible to regrind the surface, but this should only be carried out by a specialist engineering firm.

3   Check the pressure plate for signs of racking; if evident, renew the assembly.

4   Using vernier calipers, check the depth of the rivet heads below the disc friction linings (photo). If any are less than the minimum depth given in the Specifications, or if the splines, hub, and cushion springs show signs of wear, renew the disc.

5   With the clutch removed from the flywheel, check the condition of the pilot bearing in the flywheel. If the bearing feels rough when the centre track is turned, it should be renewed with reference to Chapter 1.

12 Release bearing and fork – removal and refitting

1   The release bearing is of ball-bearing, grease-sealed type, and although it is designed for long life, it is worth renewing it whenever the clutch requires renewal. If the bearing is excessively worn, there will be signs of grease leakage and the bearing will sound rough when spun.

2   To remove the bearing, the gearbox must be separated from the engine.

3   Remove the rubber grommet surrounding the release fork, then pull the fork from the ball pivot – prise the spring clip apart with a screwdriver if necessary (photo).

4   Slide the release bearing and fork from the input shaft, then unclip the bearing from the fork (photo).

5   The bearing must not be cleaned with any liquid solvent otherwise the pre-packed grease may be contaminated.

6   Examine the bearing, fork and ball pivot for wear and damage and renew them if necessary. To remove the ball pivot, unscrew it from the gearbox front cover housing or casing as applicable.

7   Refitting is a reversal of removal, but lubricate the ball pivot, hub location sleeve, and input shaft splines with a little lithium based grease before assembly. Make sure that the release fork is fully and correctly engaged with the ball pivot before refitting the gearbox (photo).

13 Clutch – refitting

1   In order to centralise the clutch disc, it will be necessary to obtain either an old input shaft, or a suitable length of dowel with a step at one end to engage the pilot bearing in the flywheel. The tool may be made out of metal or wood – the disc spline diameter should be 0.875 in (22.23 mm) and the bearing diameter 0.587 in (14.91 mm).

2   Locate the clutch disc against the face of the flywheel with the projecting hub facing outward (ie away from the flywheel).

3   Temporarily hold the disc in position, then locate the clutch cover over it and align the dowel bolt holes in the cover and flywheel (photo). Align the previously made marks if the original unit is being refitted.

4   Insert the two dowel bolts opposite each other, then insert the remaining bolts and tighten them all finger tight.

5   Insert the guide tool through the splined hub of the clutch disc and into the pilot bearing. Move the tool as necessary until the disc is central.

6   Hold the flywheel stationary with a screwdriver engaged in the teeth of the ring gear, then tighten the cover bolts evenly in diagonal sequence to the specified torque.

7   Remove the guide tool and refit the gearbox or engine as described in Chapters 6 or 1 respectively.

8   On 1.6 right-hand drive models adjust the clutch cable as described in Section 2.

10.4 Removing clutch cover and disc

11.4 Checking clutch disc friction lining wear

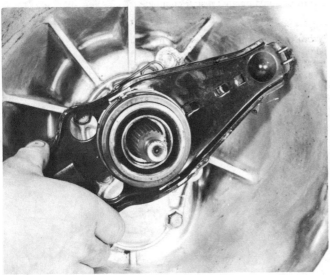

12.3 Removing clutch release bearing and fork

12.4 Removing clutch release bearing from fork

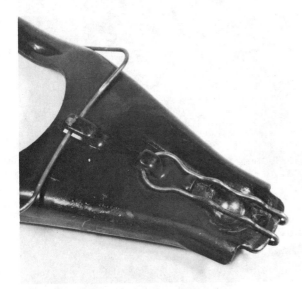

12.7 Ball pivot spring clip on the release fork

13.3 Inserting a clutch cover dowel bolt

14 Fault diagnosis – clutch

Symptom	Reason(s)
Hydraulically actuated clutch	
Spongy pedal and difficult engagement of gears	Air in hydraulic system
	Hydraulic fluid leak
	Faulty master or slave cylinder
Excessive pedal travel	Air in hydraulic system
	Faulty master cylinder
Cable actuated clutch	
Excessive pedal travel	Clutch cable out of adjustment
All clutches	
Excessive pedal travel	Excessive crankshaft endfloat
Clutch will not fully disengage	Disc sticking on input shaft splines
	Disc friction linings distorted or contaminated with oil
	Flywheel pilot bearing seized
Clutch slip	Worn or contaminated disc friction linings
Clutch judder	Disc friction linings contaminated with oil
	Worn or loose engine or gearbox mountings
	Worn input shaft splines or disc hub
Noise when depressing clutch pedal	Worn release bearing
	Worn flywheel pilot bearing

Chapter 6 Manual
gearbox and automatic transmission
Refer to Chapter 13 for revisions and information related to 1982 models

Contents

Specifications

Manual gearbox
Type
1600 models .... Four forward speeds with synchromesh, and one reverse
2000 models .... Four (US and Canada) or five (UK, US and Canada) forward speeds with synchromesh, and one reverse

Ratios
1600 models:

1st	3.403 : 1
2nd	1.925 : 1
3rd	1.373 : 1
4th	1.000 : 1
Reverse	3.665 : 1

2000 models:

	4-speed	5-speed
1st	3.214 : 1	3.214 : 1
2nd	1.818 : 1	1.818 : 1
3rd	1.296 : 1	1.296 : 1
4th	1.000 : 1	1.000 : 1
5th	–	0.860 : 1
Reverse	3.461 : 1	3.461 : 1

Mainshaft maximum run-out .... 0.03 mm (0.0012 in)

Mainshaft-to-gear or bush running clearance (max) .... 0.15 mm (0.006 in)

Reverse idler gear running clearance (max) .... 0.15 mm (0.006 in)

Selector fork-to-synchro sleeve side clearance (max) .... 0.5 mm (0.020 in)

Selector finger-to-gate clearance (max) .... 0.8 mm (0.031 in)

Selector lever-to-reverse idler gear clearance (max) – except 5-speed .... 0.5 mm (0.020 in)

Synchro ring-to-gear clearance (min) .... 0.8 mm (0.031 in)

Oil capacity
4-speed .... 1.2 Imp qt; 1.4 litre; 1.5 US qt
5-speed .... 1.5 Imp qt; 1.7 litre; 1.8 US qt

Torque wrench settings

	lbf ft	Nm
Detent plug	9	12
Interlock plug	9	12
Gear lever socket to control rail	23	31
Selector fork bolts	10	13
Mainshaft nut:		
4-speed	116 to 174	157 to 235
5-speed	94 to 152	127 to 206
Reverse lamp switch	26	35

Automatic transmission

Type
Three-speed, epicyclic gear train, automatic hydraulic control, with three-element torque converter

Ratios
Low	2.458 : 1
2nd	1.458 : 1
Top	1.000 : 1
Reverse	2.181 : 1

Torque converter stall ratio
2.0 : 1

Driveplate run-out (max)
0.5 mm (0.020 in)

Engine stall speed
1600	1950 to 2200 rpm
2000 (UK)	1750 to 2000 rpm
2000 (US and Canada)	2000 to 2250 rpm

Fluid capacity
5.5 Imp qt; 6.2 litre; 6.6 US qt

Torque wrench settings

	lbf ft	Nm
Driveplate to crankshaft	115	155
Driveplate to torque converter	30	40
Transmission to engine	29	39
Inhibitor switch	4	5

1 Manual gearbox – general description

The manual gearbox has synchromesh engagement on all forward gears and is available with four or five speeds according to model.

Gear selection is by means of a floor mounted gear lever in direct contact with the gearbox control rail located in the extension housing.

The gears and selector shafts are attached to the central bearing housing which is sandwiched between the main (four-speed) or intermediate (five-speed) casing and the extension housing.

A combined filler/level plug is screwed into the left-hand side of the gearbox, and a drain plug is located in the extension housing.

2 Manual gearbox – removal and refitting

Method 1
1   If work is necessary on both the engine and the gearbox, remove the engine complete with gearbox as described in Chapter 1, then separate the engine from the gearbox as also described in Chapter 1.
2   Refitting is fully described in Chapter 1. Do not forget to fill the gearbox with oil.

Method 2
3   To remove the gearbox leaving the engine in situ, first jack up the front and rear of the car and support with axle stands. Alternatively, position the car over a pit or on car ramps.
4   Disconnect the battery negative lead.
5   Working inside the car, remove the screws and prise out the plastic cover, remove the screws and knob, and withdraw the centre console over the handbrake lever (photos).
6   Remove the surround and packing, prise off the rubber boot, unscrew the bolts, and lift the gear lever from the extension housing (photos).

7   Unscrew the drain plug and drain the gearbox oil into a suitable container. Refit and tighten the plug.
8   Remove the propeller shaft as described in Chapter 7.
9   Unbolt and remove the gearbox front cover and stays (photo).
10   Unscrew the bolts securing the exhaust pipe clips to the mounting brackets, then unscrew the manifold flange nuts, lower the front of the exhaust system, and tie it to one side.
11   Remove the clutch cable or slave cylinder (as applicable) from the gearbox with reference to Chapter 5.
12   Remove the starter motor as described in Chapter 10.

Fig. 6.1 Gear lever tower (1) and extension housing (2) on a five-speed gearbox (Sec 3)

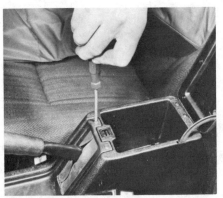
2.5A Removing the screws ...

2.5B ... and plastic cover from the console

2.5C Removing the front screws ...

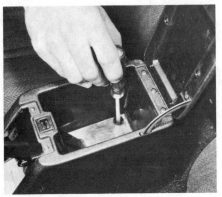
2.5D ... rear screws ...

2.5E ... and then the console

2.6A Removing the surround ...

2.6B ... gear lever retainer bolts ...

2.6C ... and gear lever

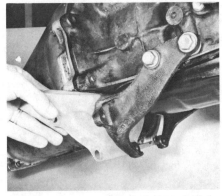
2.9 Removing manual gearbox front cover

2.13A Reversing light switch location

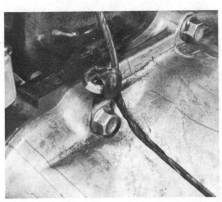
2.13B Reversing light switch wiring clip location

2.16 Gearbox mounting crossmember

2.17 Engine hanger location

2.18 Removing the gearbox

3.2A Removing gearbox front cover ...

3.2B ... and shims

3.4 Removing gear lever tower

3.5 Reversing light switch wiring clip location on bearing housing (four-speed)

3.6 Removing extension housing (four-speed)

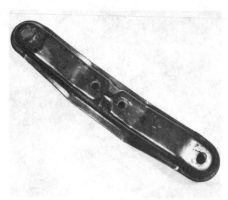
3.7 Gearbox mounting crossmember

3.8A Removing the circlip ...

3.8B ... and speedometer drivegear

3.20 Unscrewing the detent plugs

3.21A Removing the nut ...

13 Pull the wiring connectors from the reversing light switch and release the wiring from the two clips. Note the location of the clips (photos).
14 Unscrew the knurled ring and disconnect the speedometer cable.
15 Place a jack beneath the rear of the sump with a block of wood between the jack and the sump, then support the weight of the engine.
16 Unscrew the bolts securing the gearbox mounting crossmember to the bodyframe, and remove the washers (photo).
17 Unscrew the gearbox-to-engine bolts, noting the location of the exhaust mounting bracket, reversing light switch wiring clip, and engine hanger (photo).
18 Lower the jack until the gearbox can be withdrawn from the engine (photo). Take care not to allow the weight of the gearbox to hang on the input shaft while the shaft is still engaged with the clutch disc.
19 Refitting is a reversal of removal, but smear a small quantity of grease onto the input shaft splines, and on 1.6 right-hand drive models adjust the clutch cable as described in Chapter 5. Refill the gearbox with oil.

3 Manual gearbox – dismantling

1 Remove the clutch release bearing and fork as described in Chapter 5, then clean the gearbox with paraffin and wipe dry.
2 Unbolt the front cover and oil seal from the casing together with the shim(s) (photos). Remove the gasket.
3 Extract the small bearing retaining circlip from the input shaft.
4 Unscrew the four bolts and remove the gear lever tower (photo). Remove the gasket.
5 Unscrew the extension housing bolts, noting the location of the reversing light switch wiring clip (photo).
6 Turn the selector control rail fully to the left and withdraw the extension housing, if necessary using a wooden or plastic mallet (photo).
7 Unbolt the mounting crossmember from the extension housing. Note the left-hand (LH) arrow (photo).
8 Extract the circlip and withdraw the speedometer drivegear from the mainshaft. Recover the steel ball (photos).

Five-speed models

9 Extract the remaining speedometer drivegear retaining circlip from the mainshaft.
10 Identify the selector rod ends for position then unscrew the bolts and remove them.
11 Using a wooden or plastic mallet, tap the intermediate housing from the rear bearings and withdraw it over the mainshaft.
12 Extract the circlip, remove the washer, and use a puller to remove the rear bearing from the mainshaft.
13 Extract the circlip, remove the washer, and use a puller to remove the rear bearing from the countershaft.
14 Slide the counter 5th gear from the countershaft splines, followed

Fig. 6.2 Intermediate housing components on a five-speed gearbox (Sec 3)

1 Circlip
2 Speedometer drivegear
3 Selector rod ends
4 Intermediate housing

Fig. 6.3 5th gear components on a five-speed gearbox (Sec 3)

1 Circlip
2 Mainshaft rear bearing
3 Circlip
4 Countershaft rear bearing
5 Counter 5th gear
6 Spacer
7 Thrust washer
8 5th gear

Fig. 6.4 Gears and bearing housing on a five-speed gearbox (Sec 3)

1 Detent plugs
2 5th/reverse selector rod
3 5th/reverse selector fork
4 Selector rods
5 Selector forks

Fig. 6.5 Using a socket (1) to unscrew the mainshaft rear nut (2) on a five-speed gearbox (Sec 3)

Fig. 6.6 Bearing housing rear components on a five-speed gearbox (Sec 3)

1	5th/reverse synchro unit	5	Reverse idler gear
2	Reverse gear	6	Bearing retainer
3	Counter reverse gear	7	Bearing housing
4	Circlip		

by the spacer.

15 Extract the circlip from the mainshaft and remove the thrust washer. Recover the steel ball.

16 Remove the 5th gear and 5th synchro ring.

Four- and five-speed models

17 Drain the input shaft and countershaft complete with bearing housing from the gearbox casing. Alternatively, the mounting crossmember may be bolted to the casing with long bolts and used together with a spacer as an extractor.

18 Drive the mainshaft front bearing from the casing with a soft metal drift.

19 Using a suitable puller, remove the front bearing from the countershaft.

20 Unscrew the detent plugs and extract the springs and detent balls (photo). Note the location of the springs as they are of different lengths.

Four-speed models

21 Unscrew the nut and remove the reverse idler gear lever (photos).

22 Withdraw the reverse selector rod and fork, but cover the detent hole with a cloth in order to recover the ball. Extract the spring.

23 Remove the reverse idler gear, noting which way round it is fitted to the shaft.

24 Unscrew the bolts securing the selector forks to the selector rods, then withdraw the 1st/2nd and 3rd/4th selector rods and extract the interlock pins (photo). Identify the selector forks for position, then remove them from the synchro units.

25 Grip the mainshaft in a soft-jawed vice. Flatten the locktab and unscrew the mainshaft rear nut. Remove the lockwasher (photos).

26 Identify the reverse gear for position, then remove it and extract the Woodruff key (photos).

27 Extract the circlip and pull the counter reverse gear from the splines on the rear of the countershaft (photos).

28 Unbolt the bearing retainer from the housing.

29 Using a wooden or plastic mallet, drive the mainshaft and countershaft from the bearing housing (photo).

30 Separate the countershaft from the mainshaft and input shaft.

31 Using a soft metal drift, drive the mainshaft rear bearing, countershaft rear bearing, and reverse idler shaft from the bearing housing and remove the shims.

Five-speed models

32 Unscrew the bolt securing the 5th/reverse selector fork to the selector rod, then remove the rod, but cover the detent hole with a cloth in order to recover the ball. Extract the spring.

33 Identify the 5th/reverse fork for position then remove it from the synchro unit.

34 Unscrew the bolts securing the 1st/2nd and 3rd/4th selector forks

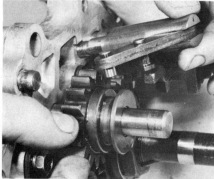

3.21B ... and the reverse idler gear lever (four-speed)

3.24 Removing selector fork retaining bolt

3.25A Removing mainshaft rear nut ...

3.25B ... and lockwasher (four-speed)

3.26A Removing reverse gear ...

3.26B ... and Woodruff key (four-speed)

3.27A Removing circlip ...

3.27B ... and counter reverse gear (four-speed)

3.29 Withdrawing the mainshaft and countershaft from the bearing housing (four-speed)

3.45A Separating the input shaft from the mainshaft (four-speed)

3.45B Removing 4th synchro ring (four-speed)

3.45C Removing the needle bearing (four-speed)

3.46A Removing the circlip ...

3.46B ... and using a puller to remove 3rd/4th synchro unit (four-speed)

3.48A Removing the thrust washer ...

3.48B ... 1st gear and synchro ring ...

3.48C ... and sleeve from the mainshaft (four-speed)

3.49 Using a puller to remove 1st/2nd synchro unit and 2nd gear (four-speed)

3.50A Gear lever socket location in extension housing

3.50B Selector rail location in extension housing

to the selector rods, then withdraw the rods and extract the interlock pins from the bearing housing.
35 Identify the 1st/2nd and 3rd/4th selector forks for position then remove them from the synchro units.
36 Move the synchro sleeves to engage 2nd and reverse gear. Straighten the locking shoulder and unscrew the mainshaft rear nut. Move the sleeves to neutral.
37 Identify the 5th/reverse synchro unit for position, then pull the hub from the mainshaft.
38 Identify the reverse gear for position, then remove it from the mainshaft together with the needle bearing, sleeve and thrust washer.
39 Pull the counter reverse gear from the splines on the rear of the countershaft.
40 Extract the circlip, then remove the thrust washer, reverse idler gear, and inner thrust washer from the idler gear shaft.
41 Unbolt the bearing retainer from the housing.
42 Using a wooden or plastic mallet, drive the mainshaft and countershaft from the bearing housing.
43 Separate the countershaft from the mainshaft and input shaft.
44 Using a soft metal drift, drive the mainshaft centre bearing, countershaft centre bearing, and reverse idler shaft from the bearing housing, and remove the shims.

Four- and five-speed models

45 Separate the input shaft from the mainshaft and remove the 4th synchro ring. Extract the needle bearing from the input shaft or mainshaft (photos).

46 Extract the circlip and use a suitable puller to remove the 3rd/4th synchro unit and hub. Note that the small sleeve groove faces rearward (photos).
47 Remove the synchro ring and 3rd gear.
48 Remove the thrust washer from the rear of the mainshaft, followed by the 1st gear, 1st synchro ring, and 1st gear sleeve (photos).
49 Using a suitable puller, remove the 1st/2nd synchro unit and 2nd gear, then separate the two components and remove the 2nd synchro ring (photo).
50 If necessary the extension housing may be dismantled. Unscrew the bolt and remove the gear lever socket from the end of the selector rail. Withdraw the selector rail from the extension housing (photos). Unscrew the bolt and drive the speedometer driven gear assembly from the housing. Extract the oil seal from the rear of the housing.

4 Manual gearbox – inspection

1   Clean all components with paraffin and wipe dry.
2   Examine the gears for worn or chipped teeth, and check the bearings for wear by spinning them by hand and checking for excessive play or rough running (photos).
3   Examine the selector rail, selector rods, forks and associated components for wear. Temporarily assemble the selector rail finger to each selector rod gate, and use a feeler gauge to check that the clearance does not exceed the maximum given in the Specifications.
4   Temporarily assemble each synchro ring to its respective gear

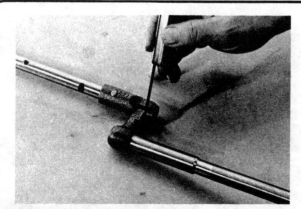

Fig. 6.7 Checking selector rail finger-to-gate clearance with a feeler blade (Sec 4)

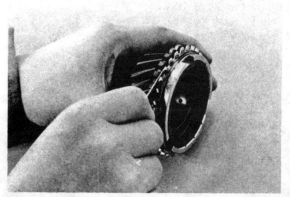

Fig. 6.8 Checking synchro ring wear with a feeler blade (Sec 4)

Fig. 6.9 Checking mainshaft run-out with a dial gauge (Sec 4)

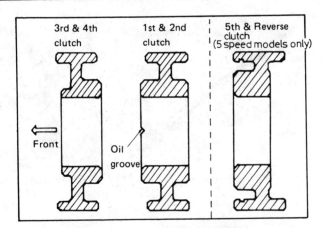

Fig. 6.10 Correct installation of synchro hub (Sec 5)

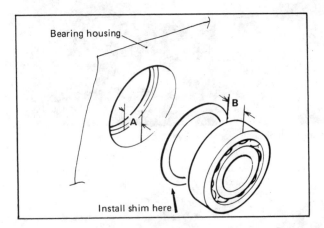

Fig. 6.11 Mainshaft bearing shim calculation (Sec 5)

A – B = shim thickness

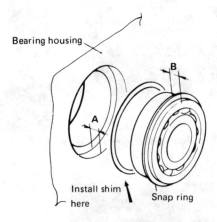

Fig. 6.12 Countershaft bearing shim calculation (Sec 5)

A – B = shim thickness

cone and use a feeler gauge to check that the clearance between the synchro ring and gear is not less than that given in the Specifications (photo).

5   Examine the casing and housings for cracks, wear, and damage (photo).

6   Using a dial gauge, check that the mainshaft run-out does not exceed the maximum given in the Specifications.

7   Temporarily assemble the selector forks to their respective synchro sleeves, and use a feeler gauge to check that the side clearance does not exceed the maximum given in the Specifications.

8   If necessary the synchro units may be dismantled and inspected as follows. Mark the sleeve in relation to the hub and note how the springs are fitted on each side. Slide off the sleeve and remove the keys and springs. Inspect, then reassemble in reverse order (photos).

9   Renew all components as necessary, then obtain a new front cover gasket and seal, and a new rear extension oil seal.

5   Manual gearbox – reassembly

Note: *During reassembly lubricate all moving parts with the recommended gear oil*

1   Install the new oil seal squarely to the rear of the extension housing using a block of wood (photo).

2   Coat the speedometer driven gear assembly with a suitable sealing compound, install the assembly to the housing, and tighten the clamp bolt.

3   Insert the selector rail into the extension housing, install the socket, and tighten the bolt.

4   Install the 2nd synchro ring on the 2nd gear, and engage the 1st/2nd synchro unit into the slots. Using a puller, or alternatively a metal tube, install the 2nd gear and synchro unit fully onto the mainshaft (photos). Make sure that the synchro hub is located as shown in Fig. 6.10 with the small groove on the sliding sleeve facing forward.

5   Install the 1st synchro ring with the slots engaging the sliding keys, followed by the 1st gear sleeve, 1st gear, and the rear thrust washer.

6   Install the 3rd synchro ring on the 3rd gear, and engage the 3rd/4th synchro unit into the slots. Using a puller, or alternatively a metal tube, install the 3rd gear and synchro unit fully onto the front of the mainshaft (photos). Make sure that the synchro hub is located as shown in Fig. 6.10 with the small groove on the sliding sleeve, facing rearward. Install the retaining circlip.

7   Insert the needle bearing into the input shaft. Engage the 4th synchro ring slots with the sliding keys of the 3rd/4th synchro unit, then install the input shaft onto the front of the mainshaft.

Five-speed models

8   Using a depth gauge or vernier calipers, determine the mainshaft centre bearing recess depth in the bearing housing. Deduct the centre bearing outer track width from this dimension and select a shim of the resulting thickness ± 0.05 mm (± 0.002 in).

9   Similarly determine the countershaft centre bearing recess depth in the bearing housing. Deduct the dimension from the inner face of the centre bearing circlip to the rear face of the outer track, and select a shim of the resulting thickness ± 0.05 mm (± 0.002 in).

10 Locate the shims in the bearing housing and drive the centre

4.2A The gearbox mainshaft (four-speed)

4.2B Input shaft and bearing

4.2C Countershaft and gears (four-speed)

4.4 Checking synchro ring wear with a feeler blade

4.5 Rear extension rear bearing with oil seal removed

4.8A Synchro unit sliding key location

4.8B Removing synchro unit sliding key

4.8C Removing a synchro unit spring

4.8D Synchro unit components

5.1 Installing extension housing oil seal

5.4A Installing 2nd gear ...

5.4B ... 2nd synchro ring ...

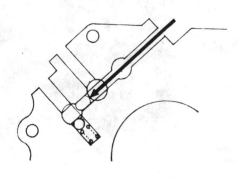

Fig. 6.13 Cross-sectional view of detent ball and pin locations (Sec 5)

Fig. 6.14 Checking 5th gear endplay with a feeler blade (Sec 5)

Fig. 6.15 Checking countershaft rear bearing endplay on a five-speed gearbox (Sec 5)

Fig. 6.16 Checking mainshaft rear bearing endplay on a five-speed gearbox (Sec 5)

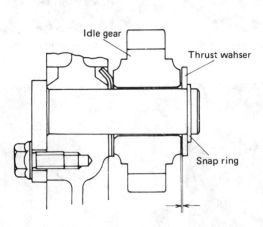

Fig. 6.17 Reverse idler gear endplay (arrowed) on a five-speed gearbox (Sec 5)

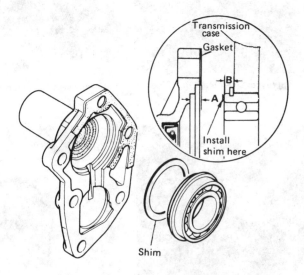

Fig. 6.18 Front cover shim calculation (Sec 5)

$A - B = $ shim thickness

5.4C ... and 1st/2nd synchro unit on the mainshaft (four-speed)

5.4D Using a puller to install 1st/2nd synchro unit on the mainshaft splines (four-speed)

5.6A Installing 3rd gear ...

5.6B ... 3rd synchro ring, and 3rd/4th synchro unit on the mainshaft (four-speed)

5.6C Using a metal tube to install 3rd/4th synchro unit (four-speed)

5.31 Bearings installed in the bearing housing (four-speed)

5.32 Installing reverse idler shaft (four-speed)

5.33 Installing bearing retainer (four-speed)

5.38A Installing mainshaft rear nut (four-speed)

5.38B Locking mainshaft rear nut (four-speed)

5.39A Installing detent spring ...

5.39B ... detent ball ...

5.39C ... and reverse selector rod (four-speed)

5.41A Installing reverse idler gear lever (four-speed)

5.41B Fitted position of reverse idler gear lever (four-speed)

5.42 Installing interlock pin to reverse selector rod (four-speed)

5.43 Installing 3rd/4th selector rod (four-speed)

5.45 Installing interlock pin to 3rd/4th selector rod (four-speed)

5.46 Installing 1st/2nd selector rod (four-speed)

5.48A Inserting detent balls ...

5.48B ... and springs into the bearing housing

5.52A Applying sealing compound to the gearbox casing (four-speed)

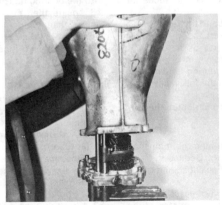

5.52B Lowering the gearbox casing onto the bearing housing (four-speed)

5.64A Gearbox mounting showing left-hand (LH) arrow

5.64B Location of gearbox mounting crossmember left-hand (LH) arrow

5.69A Installing a new oil seal to the front cover

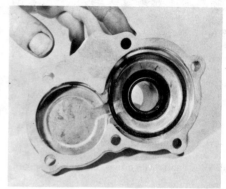

5.69B Oil seal and shim located in front cover

bearings into position, using a metal tube to keep them square.

11 Drive the reverse idler shaft into the bearing housing with the slot facing the retainer location.

12 Locate the bearing retainer on the bearing housing, insert the bolts and tighten them.

13 Mark the countershaft gears with the mainshaft and input shaft gears.

14 Drive the mainshaft and countershaft assembly into the bearing housing using a wooden or plastic mallet, and making sure that the reverse idler shaft faces rearward.

15 Install the inner thrust washer, reverse idler gear, outer thrust washer, and circlip to the idler gear shaft.

16 Using a metal tube, drive the counter reverse gear fully onto the splines on the rear of the countershaft.

17 Install the needle bearing and reverse gear to the mainshaft together with the sleeve and thrust washer.

18 Using a metal tube, drive the 5th/reverse synchro unit and hub fully onto the mainshaft. Make sure that the synchro hub is located as shown in Fig. 6.10.

19 Move the synchro sleeves to engage 2nd and reverse gear, then fit a new rear locknut and tighten it to the specified torque using a box spanner. Peen the locknut shoulder into the hole provided in the mainshaft. Move the sleeves to neutral.

20 Locate the 5th/reverse selector fork into the groove in the synchro sleeve, then insert the selector rod through the fork and enter it a little way into the hole in the bearing housing.

21 Locate the detent spring in the hole in the bearing housing followed by the ball. Using a length of metal rod, depress the detent ball and at the same time push in the 5th/reverse selector rod so that the ball engages the cut-out.

22 Align the holes in the fork and rod, then insert and tighten the bolt.

23 With the 5th/reverse selector rod in neutral, insert the interlock pin into the bearing housing so that it contacts the side of the rod.

24 Locate the 3rd/4th selector fork into the groove in the synchro sleeve, then insert the selector rod through the bearing housing and into the fork. Make sure that the extended part of the fork faces the housing.

25 Align the holes in the fork and rod, then insert and tighten the bolt.

26 With the 3rd/4th selector rod in neutral, insert the interlock pin into the bearing housing so that it contacts the side of the rod.

27 Locate the 1st/2nd selector fork into the groove in the synchro sleeve, then insert the selector rod through the bearing housing and into the fork. Make sure that the extended part of the fork faces away from the housing.

28 Align the holes in the fork and rod, then insert and tighten the bolt.

Four-speed models

29 Using a depth gauge or vernier calipers, determine the mainshaft rear bearing recess depth in the bearing housing. Deduct the rear bearing outer track width from this dimension and select a shim of the resulting thickness ± 0.05 mm (± 0.002 in).

30 Similarly determine the countershaft rear bearing recess depth in the bearing housing. Deduct the dimension from the inner face of the rear bearing circlip to the rear face of the outer track, and select a shim of the resulting thickness ± 0.05 mm (± 0.002 in).

31 Locate the shims in the bearing housing and drive the rear bearings into position, using a metal tube to keep them square (photo).

32 Drive the reverse idler shaft into the bearing housing with the slot facing the retainer location (photo).

33 Locate the bearing retainer on the bearing housing, insert the bolts and tighten them (photo).

34 Mesh the countershaft gears with the mainshaft and input shaft gears.

35 Drive the mainshaft and countershaft assembly into the bearing housing using a wooden or plastic mallet and making sure that the reverse idler shaft faces rearward.

36 Press the counter reverse gear onto the splines on the rear of the countershaft, and fit the circlip.

37 Locate the Woodruff key in the mainshaft groove, then install the reverse gear over the end of the mainshaft, extended side first, and slide it onto the key.

38 Install the lockwasher and nut, then grip the mainshaft in a soft-jawed vice. Tighten the nut to the specified torque, then bend the locktab over one flat of the nut (photos).

39 Insert the detent spring in the hole in the bearing housing followed by the ball. Using a length of metal rod, depress the detent ball and at the same time insert the reverse selector rod until the ball engages the cut-out (photos).

40 Slide the reverse idler gear onto its shaft with the groove rearward.

41 Insert the reverse idler gear lever into the bearing housing and at the same time engage it with the selector fork and the idler gear. Tighten the nut (photos).

42 With the reverse selector rod in neutral, insert the interlock pin into the bearing housing so that it contacts the side of the rod (photo).

43 Locate the 3rd/4th selector fork into the groove in the synchro sleeve, then insert the selector rod through the bearing housing and into the fork. Make sure that the extended part of the fork faces the housing (photo).

44 Align the holes in the fork and rod, then insert and tighten the bolt.

45 With the 3rd/4th selector rod in neutral, insert the interlock pin into the bearing housing so that it contacts the side of the rod (photo).

46 Locate the 1st/2nd selector fork into the groove in the synchro sleeve, then insert the selector rod through the bearing housing and into the fork. Make sure that the extended part of the fork faces away from the housing (photo).

47 Align the holes in the fork and rod, then insert and tighten the bolt.

Four- and five-speed models

48 Insert the detent balls and springs into the bearing housing in their previously noted locations, then screw in and tighten the plugs (photos).

49 Drive the front bearing onto the countershaft using a length of metal tube on the inner track.

50 Drive the mainshaft front bearing into the casing using a length of metal tube on the outer track.

51 Grip the rear of the mainshaft in a soft-jawed vice with the input shaft uppermost.

52 Check that the mating faces of the casing and bearing housing are clean, then smear some suitable sealing compound on them. Lower the casing over the gears and at the same time engage the input shaft

and countershaft front bearing in their respective apertures (photos). use a metal tube on the mainshaft front bearing inner track to ensure that the circlip groove is fully exposed.

Five-speed models

53 Install the 5th synchro ring and engage the slots with the synchro sliding keys.
54 Install the 5th gear, cone end first. Insert the steel ball, install the thrust washer, and insert the circlip. Push the circlip forward as far as possible and use a feeler gauge to check that the endplay is between 0.1 and 0.3 mm (0.004 and 0.012 in). If necessary select a thrust washer of a different thickness to correct the endplay.
55 Install the spacer on the countershaft splines followed by the 5th gear.
56 Drive the rear bearing onto the countershaft using a metal tube on the inner track. Install the washer and circlip. Using a feeler gauge determine the clearance between the washer and circlip – if it is more than 0.1 mm (0.004 in) select a washer of a different thickness.
57 Drive the rear bearing onto the mainshaft using a metal tube on the inner track. Install the washer and circlip and check the clearance as described in paragraph 56.
58 Using a feeler gauge, determine the reverse idler gear endplay as shown in Fig. 6.17 – this should be between 0.1 and 0.3 mm (0.004 and 0.012 in). If not, install a washer of a different thickness.
59 Check that the mating faces of the intermediate housing and bearing housing are clean, then smear some suitable sealing compound on them.
60 Lower the intermediate housing over the mainshaft and onto the dowel pins on the bearing housing.
61 Install the selector rod ends in their previously noted positions, align the holes, and insert and tighten the bolts.
62 Insert the inner speedometer drivegear retaining circlip in the mainshaft groove.

Four- and five-speed models

63 Insert the steel ball, install the speedometer drivegear, and insert the circlip in the mainshaft groove.
64 Bolt the mounting and crossmember to the extension housing noting the 'LH' arrows which must face the left-hand side (photos).
65 Check that the mating faces of the extension housing and gearbox are clean, then smear some suitable sealing compound on them.
66 With the selector control rail turned fully to the left, lower the extension housing over the mainshaft. Insert and tighten the bolts and install the reversing light switch wiring clip in its previously noted location.
67 Install the gear lever tower together with a new gasket and tighten the four bolts.
68 Insert the small circlip to the input shaft.
69 Drive the oil seal from the front cover and install a new seal (photos).
70 Locate the gasket on the front cover, then use a depth gauge to determine the depth of the bearing seat as shown in Fig. 6.18. Deduct from this figure the distance from the bearing outer track to the gearbox case, and select a shim to give an endplay of less than 0.1 mm (0.004 in). Retain the shim in the cover with a little grease, and smear the lip of the oil seal with a little grease.
71 Install the front cover to the casing and tighten the bolts in a diagonal sequence.
72 Install the clutch release bearing and fork as described in Chapter 5.

6 Automatic transmission – description

The automatic transmission is of three-speed hydraulic control type and comprises two main components. The three-element hydrokinetic torque converter transmits drive from the engine to the transmission, and with the car stationary has a torque multiplication of 2 to 1. The torque/speed responsive and hydraulically operated epicyclic transmission comprises planetary gear sets, providing three forward and one reverse ratio. Parking and low gear positions are also provided for the selector lever.

If the automatic transmission develops a fault which cannot be rectified by the procedures given in the following paragraphs, it is essential that it is inspected by a Mazda dealer or automatic transmission specialist *before* removing it from the car.

7 Automatic transmisison – checking fluid level

1 Drive the car for a minimum of five miles in order to bring the engine and transmission to its normal operating temperature.
2 Position the car on level ground and apply the handbrake firmly.
3 With the engine idling, move the selector lever slowly through all the positions, and finally move it to the Park (P) position.
4 Wipe clean with a cloth the dipstick and tube located on the right-hand side of the transmission.
5 Pull out the dipstick, wipe it clean, and reinsert it fully.
6 Pull out the dipstick again and check that the fluid level is between the 'F' and 'L' marks. If necessary top up the transmission with the correct fluid by pouring it through the dipstick tube.
7 Switch off the engine.

8 Automatic transmission – removal and refitting

Note *Removal of the automatic transmission together with the engine is not recommended because of limited room within the engine compartment and the weight of the transmission*
1 Disconnect the battery negative lead.
2 Jack up the front of the car and support it on axle stands. Alternatively, position the car over a pit or on car ramps. Apply the handbrake firmly.

Fig. 6.19 Automatic transmission external components (Sec 8)

1 Front cover   4 Downshift solenoid wire
2 Vacuum hose   5 Speedometer cable
3 Fluid pipes

Fig. 6.20 Torque converter-to-driveplate bolts (1) (Sec 8)

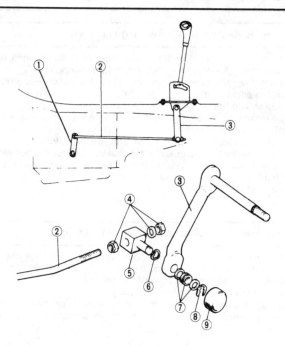

**Fig. 6.21 Automatic transmission control linkage components
(Sec 8)**

1	Manual lever	5	T-joint
2	Shift rod	6	Wave washer
3	Selector lever operating arm	7	Bush and washers
4	Locknuts and washer	8	Retaining clip
		9	Dust cover

Fig. 6.22 Automatic transmission selector lever pushbutton protrusion (A) (Sec 10)

1 Knob	2 Pushbutton	3 Locknut

3　Remove the heat insulator.
4　Disconnect the exhaust bracket, then unscrew the nuts and detach the exhaust system from the manifold. Tie the exhaust system to one side.
5　Remove the propeller shaft as described in Chapter 7.
6　Unscrew the knurled ring and withdraw the speedometer cable from the transmission.
7　Disconnect the selector linkage from the lever on the left-hand side of the transmission.

8　Disconnect the vacuum hose, and the wire to the downshift solenoid.
9　Unscrew the union bolts and disconnect the fluid pipes. Remove the bracket for the upper pipe.
10　Unbolt the front cover from the transmission bellhousing.
11　Unscrew the bolts securing the torque converter to the driveplate. These bolts are accessible through the front cover aperture and it is necessary to turn the engine in order to reach all of them.
12　Remove the starter motor as described in Chapter 10.
13　Position a trolley jack beneath the rear of the engine with a block of wood between the jack and the sump. Take the weight of the engine.
14　Unbolt the transmission rear mounting crossmember from the underbody.
15　Have an assistant support the rear of the transmission, then unscrew the remaining bolts securing it to the engine.
16　Lower the jack a little, then withdraw the transmission from the engine, but take care to keep the torque converter fully engaged with the transmission oil pump – a length of wood inserted through a hole in the driveplate will ensure that the torque converter releases from the driveplate.
17　Refitting is a reversal of removal, but first check that the driveplate run-out does not exceed the maximum given in the Specifications. Tighten the torque converter-to-driveplate bolts to the specified torque. Fill the transmission with the correct fluid and check the level as described in Section 7. Adjust the various components as described in Sections 9, 10 and 13.

9　Automatic transmission control linkage – adjustment

1　Jack up the front of the car and support on axle stands. Apply the handbrake.
2　Place the selector lever in position 'N'.
3　Working beneath the car, remove the cover from the selector lever operating arm and remove the clip, bush and washers from the pin. Note the order of removal.
4　Disconnect the linkage from the arm, then move the selector lever on the transmission to the third detent from the rear which is the 'N' position.
5　Check that the linkage pin enters the operating arm freely. If necessary loosen the locknuts and reposition the pin on the linkage, then tighten the nuts.
6　Refit the linkage to the operating arm and install the washers, bush, clip and cover.
7　Lower the car to the ground.

10　Automatic transmission selector lever knob – adjustment

UK models

1　Move the selector lever to position 'N', then loosen the locknut beneath the knob and turn the knob in or out until the pushbutton protrusion as shown in Fig. 6.22 is between 4.5 and 7.5 mm (0.18 and 0.30 in).
2　Unscrew the knob one complete turn so that the pushbutton faces the driver's side.

US and Canadian models

3　Move the selector lever to position 'N' or 'D', then loosen the locknut beneath the knob and screw in the knob until the pushbutton movement is eliminated.
4　Screw in the knob one complete turn so that the pushbutton faces the driver's side.

All models

5　Depress the pushbutton and check that the selector lever can be moved smoothly to position 'P'. If not, screw in the knob one complete turn at a time until the lever moves correctly.
6　With the pushbutton released, check that it is not possible to move the selector lever from 'N' to 'R' or from 'D' to '2'. If it is possible, unscrew the knob one complete turn at a time until the movement is blocked between the two positions.
7　Tighten the locknut and check that the selector lever functions correctly.

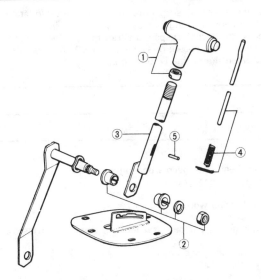

Fig. 6.23 Automatic transmission selector lever components (Sec 11)

1	Knob and locknut	4	Spring
2	Bushes and nut	5	Guide pin
3	Lever		

11 Automatic transmission selector lever – removal and refitting

1 Loosen the locknut on the selector lever and unscrew the knob.
2 Remove the console box. Disconnect the battery negative lead.
3 Working beneath the car, disconnect the linkage from the operating arm with reference to Section 9.
4 Working inside the car, disconnect the multi-plugs then unbolt the mounting plate from the body.
5 Mark the lever in relation to the operating arm, then unscrew the nut and remove the washer, bushes, lever and arm.
6 If necessary remove the rod, spring, split pin and guide pin from the selector lever.
7 Refitting is a reversal of removal, but adjust the control linkage as described in Section 9, and adjust the selector lever knob as described in Section 10.

12 Automatic transmission inhibitor switch – removal, refitting and adjustment

1 Disconnect the battery negative lead.
2 Remove the console box and disconnect the wiring multi-plugs.
3 Remove the screws and withdraw the inhibitor switch.
4 To refit the switch, locate it on the lever bracket and install the screws loosely.
5 Connect the wiring multi-plugs and the battery negative lead.
6 Move the selector lever to position 'N', then align the marks on the inhibitor switch and plate and tighten the screws (see Fig. 6.24).
7 Check that the engine can only be started with the selector lever in positions 'N' and 'P'.
8 Refit the console box.

13 Automatic transmission kickdown switch – removal, refitting and adjustment

1 The kickdown switch is located by the accelerator pedal. It energises the downshift solenoid, on the left-hand side of the transmission, in order to engage a lower gear for improved acceleration when the accelerator is fully depressed.
2 To remove the kickdown switch, disconnect the wiring, loosen the locknut, and unscrew the switch.
3 Before refitting the kickdown switch, adjust the engine idling speed as described in Chapter 3.
4 Screw the kickdown switch onto the bracket to engage a few threads.
5 With the accelerator pedal fully depressed, screw in the switch slowly until the switch contacts can be heard to close, then screw in the switch a further half a turn.
6 Tighten the locknut and reconnect the wiring.

14 Automatic transmission – stall test

1 For a complete test of the automatic transmission, the car should be taken to a Mazda dealer or an automatic transmission specialist who will check the hydraulic pressure and shift speeds of the unit. However, the following stall test procedure will provide the owner with useful information to work on.
2 Run the engine until it attains its normal operating temperature, then check the fluid level as described in Section 7.
3 Connect a tachometer to the engine and position it so that it is visible from the driver's seat.
4 Chock the front and rear wheels, firmly apply the handbrake, and keep the footbrake firmly applied during the test.
5 Start the engine and move the selector lever to position 'D'.
6 Depress the accelerator pedal slowly until the throttle is fully open, then quickly note the engine speed and release the pedal. *The stall test time must not exceed five seconds otherwise the transmission may be damaged.*
7 Move the selector lever to position 'N' and allow the engine to idle

Fig. 6.24 Automatic transmission inhibitor switch alignment (Sec 12)

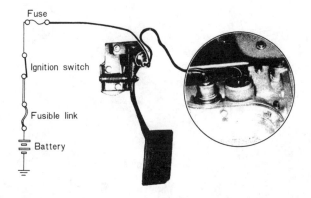

Fuse

Ignition switch

Fusible link

Battery

Fig. 6.25 Kickdown switch, solenoid and circuit (Sec 13)

for at least one minute in order to cool the transmission fluid.

8   Repeat the stall test with the selector lever in positions '2', '1' and 'R'.

9   Compare the engine speeds obtained with the stall speeds given in the Specifications. If the average speed is approximately 500 rpm less than that specified, suspect the torque converter for stator slip. If it is 300 rpm less, the engine may not be developing full power. If it is in excess of 500 rpm, suspect the transmission for an internal fault. Note that the stall speeds may be up to 50 rpm less than those specified when the engine is running-in.

15 Fault diagnosis – manual gearbox and automatic transmission

Symptom	Reason(s)
Manual gearbox	
Gearbox noisy in neutral	Input shaft bearing or needle bearing worn Countershaft bearings worn
Gearbox noisy only when car moving	Mainshaft bearing worn
Gearbox noisy in one particular gear	Worn, damaged or chipped gear teeth or countershaft teeth
Jumps out of gear	Worn synchro units and rings Worn selector forks Weak detent springs
Ineffective synchromesh	Worn synchro units and rings
Difficulty in engaging gears	Clutch faulty (see Chapter 5) Input shaft spigot bearing seized Worn synchro units and rings
Automatic transmission	
Difficulty starting on steep gradients and poor acceleration	Faulty torque converter
Transmission overheats	Faulty torque converter
Poor acceleration on full throttle	Kickdown switch incorrectly adjusted Kickdown switch wiring disconnected or fuse blown
Loss of drive	Low fluid level

Chapter 7 Propeller shaft

Contents

Specifications

Type .... Two-piece, tubular steel with three universal joints, centre ball bearing, and front sliding sleeve

Maximum permissible run-out .... 0.4 mm (0.016 in)

Universal joint journal minimum wear diameter .... 14.595 mm (0.5746 in)

Universal joint turning torque .... 3 to 8 kgf cm (2.6 to 6.9 lbf in)

Torque wrench settings

	lbf ft	Nm
Yoke to rear axle	26	35
Front shaft yoke nut	116 to 130	157 to 176
Centre bearing member and support	33	45

1 General description

The propeller shaft is of two-piece tubular steel construction comprising a front shaft, centre support bearing, and rear shaft. The front shaft has a sliding sleeve at its front end, and its rear end is supported by a rubber mounted centre bearing. A yoke, splined to the rear of the shaft and retained by a nut, is connected to the front of the rear shaft via a universal joint. A further universal joint connects the rear shaft to the companion flange of the rear axle.

The sliding sleeve is necessary due to fore-and-aft movement of the propeller shaft which occurs as a result of deflection of the rear axle on the rear coil springs.

2 Propeller shaft – removal and refitting

1 Jack up the rear of the car and support it on axle stands. Chock the front wheels.

2 Mark the rear axle and propeller shaft flanges in relation to each other.

3 Hold the propeller shaft stationary by inserting a long screwdriver through the rear universal joint, then unscrew the bolts and separate the propeller shaft from the rear axle companion flange (photo).

4 Support the centre bearing crossmember with a trolley jack, then unscrew the crossmember mounting bolts (photo).

5 Lower the jack a few inches and withdraw the propeller shaft from the gearbox or automatic transmission (photo). Some oil may seep from the unit, so place a drip tray beneath it, or alternatively retain a polythene bag in the end housing with an elastic band.

6 Refitting is a reversal of removal, but lubricate the sliding sleeve with fluid or oil (as applicable) and take care not to damage the oil seal in the end housing. Make sure that the flange marks are aligned. Top up the fluid or oil level (as applicable) with the rear wheels on the ground.

3 Universal joints – testing for wear

1 Wear in the needle roller bearings is characterised by vibration in the transmission, 'clonks' on taking up the drive, and in extreme cases of lack of lubrication, metallic squeaking and ultimately grating and shrieking sounds as the bearings break up. If a bearing breaks up at high speed it could be lethal, so they should be changed in good time.

2 It is easy to check whether the needle roller bearings are worn with the propeller shaft in position, by trying to turn the shaft with one hand, the other hand holding the companion flange when the rear universal is being checked, and the front half coupling when the front universal is being checked. Any movement between the shaft and the front and the rear half couplings is indicative of considerable wear. If worn, the old bearings and spiders (trunnions) will have to be discarded and a repair kit, comprising new universal joint trunnions, bearings, seals and circlips purchased. Check also by trying to lift the shaft and noticing any movement in the joints.

3 Examine the propeller shaft splines for wear. If worn it will be necessary to purchase a new front half coupling, or if the yokes are badly worn, an exchange shaft. It is not possible to fit oversize bearings to the trunnion bearing holes.

2.3 Unscrewing the propeller shaft rear yoke bolts

2.4 Propeller shaft centre bearing

2.5 Propeller shaft front universal joint

Fig. 7.1 Removing a universal joint circlip (Sec 4)

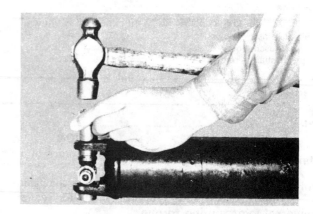

Fig. 7.2 Driving out a trunnion bearing (Sec 4)

Fig. 7.3 Checking a trunnion journal for wear (Sec 4)

Fig. 7.4 Installing a trunnion bearing (Sec 4)

4   Universal joints and centre bearing – overhaul

1   Using a wire brush, clean the propeller shaft and yokes in the area surrounding the universal joint. Mark the yokes in relation to each other in order to retain the propeller shaft balance.

2   Remove the circlips using suitable pliers or a small screwdriver. It does not matter if the circlips are distorted because new ones must be used on reassembly. If they are difficult to remove, a blow with a wooden mallet on the end of the joint may relieve the pressure on them.

3   Using a wooden or hide mallet, tap the base of a yoke until the

trunnion bearing emerges from the same side of the yoke. If the bearing is tight, support the yoke on a length of tubing or a large socket, and drive the trunnion downwards with a suitable socket positioned on the upper bearing (see Fig. 7.2).

4   Ease the bearing from the yoke with a pair of grips.

5   Remove the opposite bearing in a similar way by driving the trunnion in the opposite direction with a drift.

6   Repeat the procedure described in paragraphs 3 to 5 to remove the trunnion from the remaining yoke.

7   Confirmation of how worn the universal joint is will normally be made before its removal, but for accuracy use a micrometer to check the diameter of each trunnion journal. If any one is less than the

Fig. 7.5 Fitting a new circlip to a trunnion bearing cup (Sec 4)

specified minimum diameter, the complete universal joint assembly must be renewed.

8   The centre support bearings and oil seals need not be removed unless damage or wear is evident. If they are to be renewed, hold the centre yoke stationary, remove the nut and washer, and withdraw the front shaft from the centre yoke and bearing. Prise out the oil seals, extract the circlip, and drive the bearing from the support. Pack the new bearing with general purpose grease before installing it into the support, fit the circlip, and drive in the oil seals with their lips towards the bearing. Fit the yoke and front shaft, install the nut and washer, and tighten the nut to the specified torque.

9   To fit the new universal joint, first remove all the bearings from the trunnion and pack the journal holes in the trunnion with general purpose grease. Make sure that the bearing rollers in the cups are well greased.

10 Position the trunnion in the yoke and press in the two opposing cups and seals. To do this, clamp the bearings progressively in a vice while tapping the yoke to relieve any tight spots.

11 Select two new circlips of equal thickness and fit them to the two opposite bearing cups. The circlips are available in thicknesses ranging from 1.22 mm (0.0480 in) to 1.38 mm (0.0543 in) in increments of 0.02 mm (0.0008 in), and they should be selected to give the trunnion a slight drag. If a spring balance is available, check that the turning torque is as given in the Specifications.

12 Repeat the procedure given in paragraphs 10 and 11 for the remaining yoke, but make sure that the previously made marks are aligned.

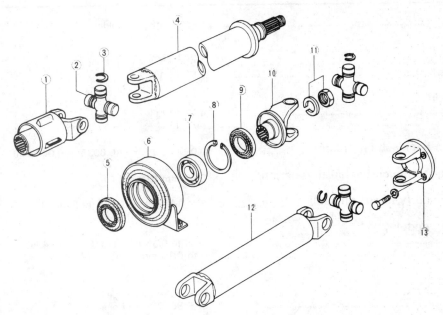

Fig. 7.6 Exploded view of the propeller shaft (Sec 4)

1 Front yoke	5 Oil seal	8 Circlip	11 Nut and spring washer
2 Trunnion	6 Support	9 Oil seal	12 Rear propeller shaft
3 Circlip	7 Ball bearing	10 Centre yoke	13 Rear yoke
4 Front propeller shaft			

5   Fault diagnosis – propeller shaft

Symptom	Reason(s)
Vibration	Propeller shaft out of balance Worn universal joint bearings Centre support bearing worn Wear in sliding sleeve splines
Knock or clunk when taking up drive	Worn universal joint bearings Wear in sliding sleeve splines Loose flange securing bolts
Metallic grating consistent with road speed	Worn and dry universal joint bearings

Chapter 8 Rear axle

Contents

Specifications

Type .... Semi-floating, hypoid

Ratio
1600 models .... 3.909 : 1
2000 models .... 3.636 : 1

Number of gear teeth
1600 models .... 43 : 11
2000 models .... 40 : 11

Ring gear-to-pinion backlash (standard) .... 0.09 to 0.11 mm (0.0035 to 0.0043 in)

Maximum ring gear-to-pinion backlash variation .... 0.07 mm (0.0028 in)

Pinion bearing preload (without oil seal) .... 9 to 14 kgf cm (7.8 to 12.2 lbf in)

Rear wheel bearing endplay
Pre-1980 models .... 0.25 to 0.35 mm (0.010 to 0.014 in)
1980 on models .... 0 to 0.10 mm (0 to 0.004 in)

Lubricant type
Above -18°C (0°F) .... SAE 90EP hypoid gear oil
Below -18°C (0°F) .... SAE 80EP hypoid gear oil

Oil capacity .... 1.1 Imp qt; 1.3 US qt; 1.2 litre

Torque wrench settings

	lbf ft	Nm
Companion flange to pinion	94 to 130	127 to 176

1 General description

The rear axle is of semi-floating type, comprising a banjo type axle casing, removable differential carrier, and axleshafts.

The drive pinion is of hypoid type; its centre line is lower than the centre line of the ring gear (or crownwheel).

The differential side bearings and pinion bearings are of taper roller type and require preloading during assembly. However, this work is considered to be outside the scope of the home mechanic as it entails the use of specialised instruments. Any setting up of the differential carrier assembly is best left to a suitably equipped garage or engineering works.

The axleshafts are of semi-floating type, and are supported at the outer ends by ball bearings and retainers which bolt to the axle casing.

Fore-and-aft location of the rear axle is by trailing arm and link with coil spring suspension. Side-to-side movement is controlled by a Panhard rod. Oil drain and filler plugs are provided in the axle casing.

2 Axleshaft (halfshaft) – removal and refitting

1 Jack up the rear of the car and support it on axle stands. Chock the front wheels.
2 Remove the roadwheel, brake drum, brake shoe assembly, parking brake cable, and hydraulic line to the wheel cylinder, with reference to Chapter 9.
3 Remove the nuts and bolts retaining the brake backplate and bearing retainer to the axle casing.
4 Using a slide hammer bolted to the axleshaft flange, remove the axleshaft assembly from the axle casing and differential side gear. If a slide hammer is not available, it may be possible to remove the

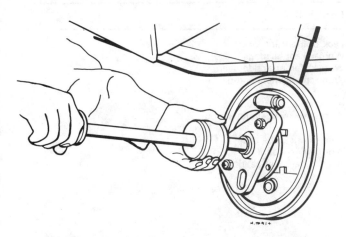

Fig. 8.1 Removing rear axleshaft with a slide hammer (Sec 2)

Fig. 8.2 Checking rear wheel bearing endplay with a dial gauge (Sec 2)

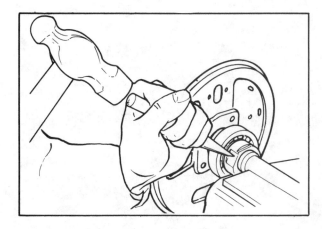

Fig. 8.3 Splitting rear wheel bearing retaining collar (Sec 3)

axleshaft by temporarily refitting the roadwheel, but take care to avoid toppling the car from the supports.

5   If necessary extract the oil seal from the casing.

6   Tap the new oil seal into the casing using a block of wood to keep it square. Make sure that the seal lip faces inward. Smear the lip with a little axle oil.

7   Insert the axleshaft assembly and make sure that it enters the differential side gear. Align the holes then insert and tighten the bolts retaining the backplate and retainer to the axle casing.

8   Using a dial gauge, check that the rear wheel bearing endplay is within the specified limits by measuring the axleshaft end movement. If not, the bearing must be renewed.

9   The remaining refitting procedure is a reversal of the removal procedure, with reference to Chapter 9 as necessary. Do not forget to bleed the brake hydraulic system.

3   Rear wheel bearing – renewal

1   Remove the axleshaft as described in Section 2.

2   Grind the bearing retaining collar close, but not into the axleshaft. Grip the axleshaft in a vice and use a cold chisel to split the collar.

3   Remove the collar, then support the bearing and either press or drive the axleshaft from it.

4   If necessary withdraw the bearing retainer and brake backplate.

5   Clean up the axleshaft collar contact area as necessary with a fine file, but do not remove more metal than necessary otherwise the collar interference fit will be incorrect.

6   Fit the bearing retainer and backplate, and tap the new bearing onto the shaft using a length of metal tube against the inner track.

7   Make sure that the collar and contact area on the axleshaft are completely dry, then press or drive the collar onto the axleshaft until it is in firm contact with the bearing inner track.

8   Refit the axleshaft as described in Section 2.

4   Differential carrier assembly – removal and refitting

1   Remove both rear axleshafts as described in Section 2.

2   Remove the drain plug and drain the rear axle oil into a suitable container. When completed, clean the plug then refit and tighten it.

3   Mark the rear axle and propeller shaft flanges in relation to each other.

4   Hold the propeller shaft stationary by inserting a long screwdriver through the rear universal joint, then unscrew the bolts and separate the propeller shaft from the rear axle companion flange. Tie the shaft to one side.

5   Unscrew the retaining nuts and lift the differential carrier assembly from the axle casing.

6   Clean the mating faces of the differential carrier and axle casing of all sealant.

7   Refitting is a reversal of removal, but apply a non-setting sealant to the mating faces, and tighten the retaining nuts evenly in diagonal sequence. With the rear wheels on the ground, fill the rear axle with oil to the bottom of the filler plug aperture, then refit the plug. Do not forget to bleed the brake hydraulic system.

5   Rear axle assembly – removal and refitting

1   Remove the rear coil springs with reference to Chapter 11.

2   Remove the rear brake shoes and disconnect the parking brake cable with reference to Chapter 9.

3   Disconnect and plug the rear brake hydraulic feed hose at the rear axle end. To reduce fluid loss, tighten the master cylinder reservoir filler cap onto a piece of polythene sheet.

4   Mark the rear axle and propeller shaft flanges in relation to each other.

5   Hold the propeller shaft stationary by inserting a long screwdriver through the rear universal joint, then unscrew the bolts and separate the propeller shaft from the rear axle companion flange.

6   Withdraw the rear axle assembly from under the car.

7   Refitting is a reversal of removal, with reference to Chapter 9 and 11 as necessary. Do not forget to remove the polythene sheeting from the brake master cylinder reservoir before bleeding the hydraulic system as described in Chapter 9. Check, and if necessary top up, the rear axle oil level.

6 Fault diagnosis – rear axle

Symptom	Reason(s)
Noise from rear axle	Lack of lubricant Worn wheel bearings Worn differential side bearings Worn crownwheel and pinion
'Clonk' on acceleration or deceleration	Axleshaft splines worn Worn crownwheel and pinion
Vibration	Wheels out of balance Worn wheel bearings Worn differential bearings

Chapter 9 Braking system

Refer to Chapter 13 for revisions and information related to 1982 models

Contents

Specifications

Type — Hydraulic; disc front, drum rear; servo assisted, with differential proportioning valve in rear brake circuit. Handbrake mechanical to rear wheels

Hydraulic circuit type — Dual, split front and rear

Front brakes
Disc diameter — 231 mm (9.095 in)
Minimum disc thickness — 12 mm (0.4724 in)
Maximum disc run-out — 0.10 mm (0.004 in)
Minimum disc pad thickness (including braking) — 1.0 mm (0.04 in)

Rear brakes (except 1980 US models)
Drum inner diameter (new) — 228.6 mm (9.0 in)
Maximum drum inner diameter — 229.6 mm (9.04 in)
Minimum lining thickness — 1.0 mm (0.04 in)

Rear brakes (1980 US models)
Drum inner diameter (new) — 200 mm (7.874 in)
Maximum drum inner diameter — 201 mm (7.914 in)
Minimum lining thickness — 1.0 mm (0.04 in)

Master cylinder
Type — Tandem
Maximum clearance between piston and bore — 0.15 mm (0.006 in)

Rear wheel cylinder
Maximum clearance between piston and bore — 0.15 mm (0.006 in)

Handbrake adjustment — 5 to 7 notches with pull of 10 kgf (22 lbf)

Footbrake pedal height
UK models — 193 to 198 mm (7.6 to 7.8 in)
US and Canadian models — 220 to 225 mm (8.66 to 8.86 in)

Footbrake pedal free travel — 7 to 9 mm (0.28 to 0.35 in)

Servo unit pushrod-to-master cylinder piston clearance — 0.1 to 0.5 mm (0.004 to 0.020 in)

Torque wrench settings
	lbf ft	Nm
Master cylinder union nut	47	63
Caliper slide pin	37	50

1 General description

The braking system is of dual hydraulic circuit type, with discs at the front and manually or automatically adjusted drum brakes at the rear. A vacuum servo unit is fitted as standard equipment to reduce braking effort at the footpedal.

The tandem type master cylinder feeds hydraulic fluid to the front calipers and rear wheel cylinders on independent circuits; if one circuit fails, the remaining circuit still functions normally.

The rear brake circuit incorporates a differential proportioning valve to prevent the rear wheel locking in advance of the front wheels during heavy applications of the brakes.

The handbrake is mechanically operated on the rear wheels only, and a warning light on the instrument panel is illuminated when the handbrake is applied with the ignition on. On most models the same light is used as a warning for low brake fluid level.

Caution: *When working on the braking system, note that brake fluid is poisonous and will also damage paintwork if spilt. Also take care not to inhale brake lining dust as it is injurious to health.*

2 Routine maintenance

1   Every 6000 miles (10 000 km) adjust the manually adjusted rear brakes as described in Section 7, and check the handbrake lever adjustment – if necessary adjust the handbrake as described in Section 13.
2   Every 12 000 miles (20 000 km) examine the hydraulic circuit lines, hoses and connections for damage and leakage.
3   Every 24 000 miles (40 000 km) or 24 months renew the brake fluid. If the car is operated in humid climates or under extreme conditions, renew the brake fluid earlier.

3 Hydraulic system – bleeding

1   If any of the hydraulic components in the braking system has been removed or disconnected, or if the fluid level in the reservoir has been allowed to fall appreciably, it is inevitable that air will have been introduced into the system. The removal of all this air from the hydraulic system is essential if the brakes are to function correctly, and the process of removing it is known as bleeding.
2   There are a number of one-man, do-it-yourself brake bleeding kits currently available from motor accessory shops. It is recommended that one of these kits should be used wherever possible, as they greatly simplify the bleeding operation and also reduce the risk of expelled air and fluid being drawn back into the system.
3   If one of these kits is not available, then it will be necessary to gather together a clean jar and a suitable length of clear plastic tubing which is a tight fit over the bleed screw, and also to engage the help of an assistant.
4   Before commencing the bleeding operation, check that all rigid pipes and flexible hoses are in good condition and that all hydraulic unions are tight. Take great care not to allow hydraulic fluid to come into contact with the car paintwork, otherwise the finish will be seriously damaged. Wash off any spilled fluid immediately with cold water.
5   If hydraulic fluid has been lost from the master cylinder, due to a leak in the system, ensure that the cause is traced and rectified before proceeding further, or a serious malfunction of the braking system may occur.
6   To bleed the system, clean the area around the bleed screw and remove the rubber cap (photo). If the hydraulic system has only been partially disconnected and suitable precautions were taken to prevent further loss of fluid, it should only be necessary to bleed that part of the system. However, if the entire system is to be bled, start at the right-hand rear wheel – on US and Canadian models bleed the master cylinder first, followed by the right-hand rear wheel.
7   Remove the filler cap and top up the reservoir. Periodically check the fluid level during the bleeding operation and top up as necessary.
8   Several types of one-man brake bleeding kits are available; with the type illustrated, connect the outlet tube to the bleed screw and then open the screw half a turn (photo). If possible position the unit so that it can be viewed from the car, then depress the brake pedal to the floor and slowly release it. The one-way valve in the kit will prevent expelled air from returning to the system at the end of each stroke. Repeat this operation until clean hydraulic fluid, free from air bubbles, can be seen coming through the tube. Now tighten the bleed screw, remove the outlet tube, and refit the cap.
9   If a one-man brake bleeding kit is not available, connect one end of the plastic tubing to the bleed screw and immerse the other end in the jam jar containing sufficient clean hydraulic fluid to keep the end of the tube submerged. Open the bleed screw half a turn and have your assistant depress the brake pedal to the floor and then slowly release it. Tighten the bleed screw at the end of each downstroke to prevent expelled air and fluid from being drawn back into the system. Repeat this operation until clean hydraulic fluid, free from air bubbles, can be seen coming through the tube. Now tighten the bleed screw, remove the plastic tube and refit the cap.
10 If the entire system is being bled, the procedures described above should now be repeated at the left-hand rear wheel followed by the

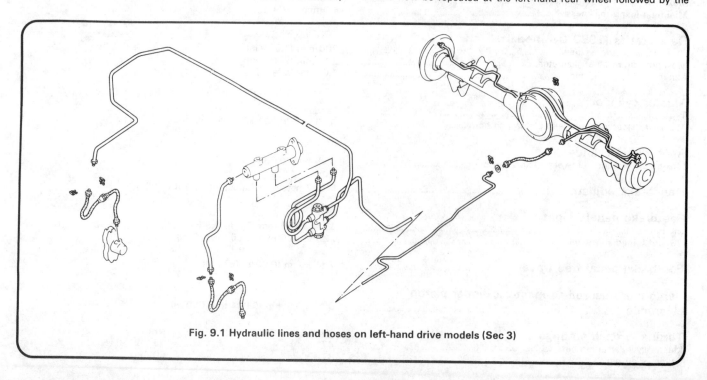

Fig. 9.1 Hydraulic lines and hoses on left-hand drive models (Sec 3)

3.6 Bleed screw and rubber cap on front caliper

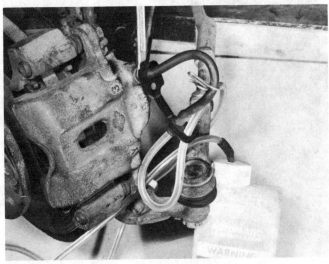

3.8A One-man brake bleeding kit connected to front caliper

3.8B Removing filler cap from brake fluid reservoir

3.8C Fitting holder ...

3.8D ... and one-man brake bleeding kit automatic dispenser to brake fluid reservoir

passenger's side front wheel, then driver's side front wheel. Do not forget to recheck the fluid level in the reservoir at regular intervals and top up as necessary.

11 When completed, recheck the fluid level in the reservoir, top up if necessary, and refit the cap. Check the 'feel' of the brake pedal, which should be firm and free from any 'sponginess'; this would indicate air still present in the system.

12 Discard any expelled hydraulic fluid, as it is likely to be contaminated with moisture, air and dirt which makes it unsuitable for further use.

4 Disc pads – inspection and renewal

1 Every 6000 miles (10 000 km) inspect the disc pad friction linings for wear. To do this, jack up the front of the car and support it on axle stands. Apply the handbrake and remove the roadwheel.

2 Unscrew and remove the caliper slide pins, withdraw the caliper and springs, and suspend the caliper on a length of wire to prevent straining the flexible hose (photos).

3 Where fitted, disconnect the disc pad wear indicator wire connection.

4 Remove the disc pads and shims from the caliper bracket (photos).

5 Check the thickness of the friction lining and backing of each disc

4.2A Removing a caliper slide pin

4.2B Removing a front brake caliper

4.4A Removing front brake shims ...

4.4B ... and disc pads

4.7 Removing plate from caliper piston

6.2 Checking brake disc for wear

pad; if it is less than the specified minimum amount, renew all four disc pads. At the same time examine the brake disc for wear as described in Section 6.

6   The caliper piston must now be pushed into the caliper to allow room for the new pads. Use a block of wood to do this.

7   Brush any dust or dirt from the caliper recesses and the bracket, taking care not to inhale the dust. Make sure that the plate is fully engaged with the piston (photo).

8   Smear the pad contact surfaces of the caliper with a little brake grease.

9   Fit the new disc pads with their friction surfaces towards the disc, then fit the shims. Reconnect the wear indicator wire when fitted.

10   Locate the caliper over the pads, fit the springs, and insert the slide pins, tightening them to the specified torque.

11   Refit the roadwheel and lower the car to the ground. Before driving the car, pump the footbrake pedal several times to set the disc pad-to-disc operating clearance.

5   Disc caliper – removal, servicing and refitting

Removal

1   Jack up the front of the car and support it on axle stands. Apply the handbrake and remove the roadwheel.

2   Remove the brake fluid reservoir filler cap, then tighten it down onto a piece of polythene sheeting. This will reduce the loss of fluid when the caliper is disconnected. Alternatively, use a brake pipe clamp on the lower flexible hose.

3   Loosen, but do not remove, the flexible hose union at the caliper.

4   Unscrew and remove the slide pins and withdraw the caliper and springs.

5   Unscrew the caliper from the hose, and plug the hose to prevent entry of dust and dirt.

Servicing

6   Clean the disc caliper with methylated spirit and wipe dry.

7   Prise off the rubber dust boot.

8   Using *low* air pressure (eg tyre footpump) in the hose aperture, withdraw the piston from the caliper.

9   Extract the seal from the caliper bore. Unscrew and remove the bleed screw.

10   Clean all the components with methylated spirit and dry them with a lint-free cloth. Examine the surfaces of the piston and bore; if these are scratched or show any bright wear areas, renew the complete caliper. If the components are in good order, discard the seal and dust boot and obtain new ones in the form of a repair kit. Note that the kit contains two types of grease which must be applied as described in the following paragraphs.

11   Smear the red grease on the piston seal and locate the seal in the bore groove using the fingers only to manipulate it.

12   Insert the piston then smear the rubber dust boot with orange grease and refit it.

Refitting

13   Screw the caliper onto the hydraulic hose, then fit the caliper and springs to the bracket and insert the slide pins. Tighten the slide pins and the flexible hose union.

14   Provided there has not been excessive loss of brake fluid, it will only be necessary to bleed the front brake disc caliper removed; otherwise, bleed both front brakes with reference to Section 3. Do not forget to remove the polythene sheeting or clamp.

15   Refit the roadwheel and lower the car to the ground.

6   Brake disc – examination, removal and refitting

1   Jack up the front of the car and support it on axle stands. Apply the handbrake and remove the roadwheel.

2   Examine the disc for deeper scoring or grooving. Light scoring is normal, but if it is severe the disc must be removed and either renewed or ground within limits by an engineering specialist (photo).

3   Check the disc for run-out to determine whether it is distorted. To do this accurately, a dial gauge will be necessary, but if this is not available feeler blades can be used against a fixed block as the disc is rotated slowly. Do not confuse wear in the hub bearings with disc run-out.

4   The brake disc is an integral part of the front hub, and the removal and refitting procedure is fully described in Chapter 11. Make sure that the hub bearings are adjusted correctly as described in Chapter 11.

7   Rear brake shoes – inspection and renewal

1   Every 12 000 miles (20 000 km) inspect the rear brake shoe friction linings for wear. To do this, jack up the rear of the car and support it on axle stands placed in front of the lower arms. Chock the front wheels, and remove the rear roadwheels.

2   Remove the two cross-head screws and withdraw the brake drum after making sure that the handbrake lever is fully released (photo). If difficulty is experienced, back off the adjustment with reference to paragraphs 14 to 26.

3   Brush any accumulated dust from the linings and brake drum taking care not to inhale it. Inspect the linings; if they are worn below the specified minimum thickness, renew them as a set. If the linings are in good condition, refit the drum and adjust the brakes as described in paragraphs 14 to 26.

4   To remove the shoes, first note how they are fitted, with particular reference to the return springs. Unhook and remove the upper return spring (photos).

5   Using a pair of pliers, depress the hold-down springs, turn them through 90°, and remove them (photo).

6   Pull the leading brake shoe outward and withdraw the handbrake operating strut (adjustable on some models).

7   Disengage both shoes from the lower anchor pins and withdraw

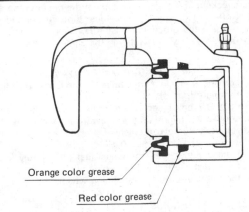

Fig. 9.2 Cross-section of the disc caliper, showing grease location (Sec 5)

Orange color grease

Red color grease

Fig. 9.3 Rear brake shoes fitted with adjustable handbrake operating strut (Sec 7)

1	Upper return spring	4	Trailing shoe
2	Lower return spring	5	Leading shoe
3	Hold-down springs	6	Operating strut

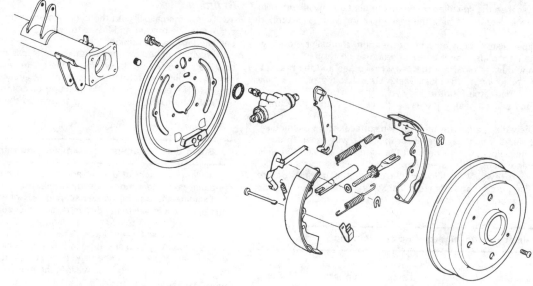

Fig. 9.4 Self-adjusting rear brakes (type 'A') fitted to later models (Sec 7)

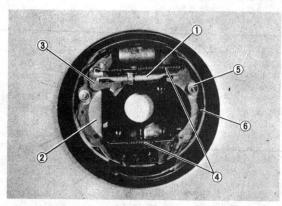

Fig. 9.5 Type 'B' self-adjusting rear brakes (Sec 7)

1	Operating strut	4	Return springs
2	Lever	5	Hold-down springs
3	Pawl lever	6	Brake shoe

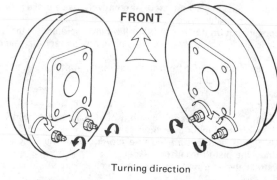

FRONT

Turning direction

— Anchor pin (to expand brake shoe)

— Lock nut (to tighten)

Fig. 9.6 Method of rear brake adjustment – adjustable anchor pin type (Sec 79

them from the backplate, at the same time disconnecting the handbrake cable from the arm on the trailing shoe. Remove the lower return spring.

8　Clean the brake backplate and check for leakage of brake fluid from the wheel cylinder, and leakage of oil from the axleshaft oil seal. If evident, rectify the fault before proceeding. Examine the brake drum for deep scoring; if evident either renew the drum or have it machined within limits by an engineering specialist.

9　To fit the new shoes, first connect the handbrake cable to the arm on the trailing shoe.

10　Hook the lower return spring to both shoes and locate the shoes on the lower anchor pins with the spring below the support.

11　Fit the handbrake operating strut in the shoe slots and attach the upper return spring. Where the strut is adjustable, turn the adjuster to shorten the strut as far as possible before fitting it.

12　Refit the hold-down springs. Where applicable, fully back off the brake adjustment by referring to paragraph 16.

13　Refit the brake drum and roadwheel and adjust the shoes as follows.

14　There are two types of manual rear brake adjustment; adjustable acnhor pins and adjustable handbrake operating strut. There are also two types of self-adjusting rear brakes which will be referred to as type 'A' and type 'B' since they are similar. The adjustment procedure for the self-adjusting brakes is for initial setting only.

15　First make sure that the handbrake lever is fully released and the rear wheels clear of the ground.

Adjustable anchor pin type

16　Working on one wheel at a time, loosen the locknuts and turn the adjustment pins as far as possible in the opposite direction to that shown in Fig. 9.6.

17　Hold one locknut stationary, then tighten the pin until the drum is locked. Back off the pin until the wheel just turns freely, and tighten the locknut. Repeat the procedure on the remaining adjustment pin, then adjust the remaining rear wheel in the same manner.

Adjustable handbrake operating strut type

18　Working on one wheel at a time, prise out the rubber plug from the rear of the backplate (photo).

19　Refer to Fig. 9.7 and insert a screwdriver so that it engages the adjuster, then push the handle of the screwdriver downward to rotate the adjuster (photo). Remove the screwdriver then repeat the action until the drum is locked.

20　Back off the adjuster until the wheel just turns freely (normally three or four notches). Refit the rubber plug.

21　Repeat the procedure on the remaining wheel.

Self-adjusting rear brakes

22　Prise out the rubber plugs from the rear of the backplate. On type 'B' brakes (see accompanying illustrations) check that the handbrake arm is fully released by inserting a screwdriver through the elongated hole in the backplate.

7.2 Removing brake drum screws

7.4A Correct installation of rear brake shoes (manual adjustment)

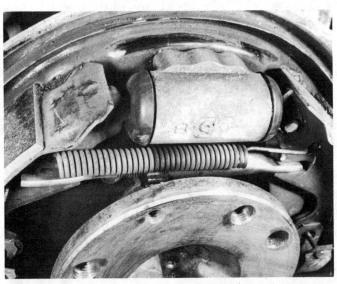

7.4B Rear brake shoe upper return spring location (manual adjustment)

7.5 Rear brake shoe hold-down spring location

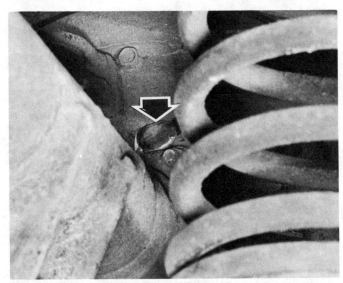

7.18 Rear brake shoe adjustment aperture plug location

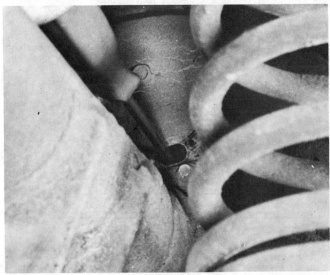

7.19 Adjusting rear brakes with a screwdriver

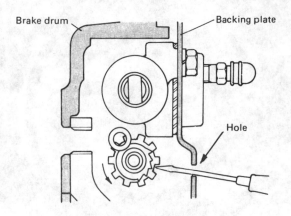

Fig. 9.7 Method of expanding rear brake shoes – adjustable handbrake operating strut type (Sec 7)

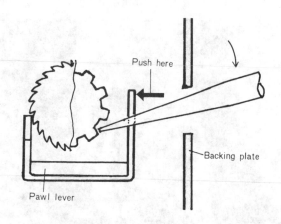

Fig. 9.9 Adjusting type 'B' self-adjusting rear brakes (Sec 7)

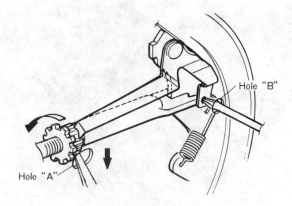

Fig. 9.8 Adjusting type 'A' self-adjusting rear brakes (Sec 7)

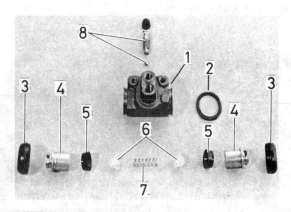

Fig. 9.10 Rear wheel cylinder components (Sec 8)

1	Body	5	Seals
2	Gasket	6	Plastic cups
3	Dust boots	7	Spring
4	Pistons	8	Bleed screw

23 On both type 'A' and 'B' brakes insert a screwdriver through the central hole in the backplate and engage it with the adjuster, then turn the adjuster in the direction of the arrow marked on the backplate until the drum is locked.

24 On type 'A' brakes insert a screwdriver through the outer hole in the backplate and depress the pawl lever, then back off the adjuster three or four notches (see Fig. 9.8). Refit the rubber plugs.

25 On type 'B' brakes use an additional screwdriver to depress the pawl lever through the central hole, then back off the adjuster six to eight notches so that the wheel rotates freely (see Fig. 9.9). Refit the rubber plugs.

26 On both types repeat the procedure on the remaining wheel, taking care to release the adjusters the identical amount of notches, then depress the footbrake pedal several times to set the self-adjusting mechanism.

All types
27 Lower the car to the ground.

8   Rear wheel cylinder – removal, servicing and refitting

Removal
1 Remove the rear brake shoes as described in Section 7.
2 Remove the brake fluid reservoir filler cap, then tighten it down onto a piece of polythene sheeting. This will reduce the loss of fluid when the wheel cylinder is disconnected. Alternatively, use a brake pipe clamp on the rear brake supply flexible hose.
3 Unscrew the union nut (preferably with a split ring spanner) and disconnect the hydraulic pipe from the wheel cylinder. Plug the end of the pipe.
4 Unscrew the retaining bolts and withdraw the wheel cylinder from the brake backplate together with the gasket.

Servicing
5 Clean the wheel cylinder with methylated spirit and wipe dry.
6 Prise off the rubber dust boots and withdraw the pistons.
7 Tap the wheel cylinder on the workbench to remove the seals, plastic cups, and spring. If necessary, unscrew the bleed screw and remove the ball.
8 Clean all the components with methylated spirit and dry them with a lint-free cloth. Examine the surfaces of the pistons and bores for scratches and bright wear areas. Temporarily refit each piston, and using a feeler blade, check that the clearance between it and the bore does not exceed the specified maximum amount. If the wheel cylinder is worn excessively it must be renewed, but if the components are in good order, discard the seals and rubber dust boots and obtain new ones in the form of a repair kit.
9 Refit the spring and plastic cups to the wheel cylinder.
10 Dip the seals in new brake fluid and insert them into the bores with their lips facing inward.
11 Dip the inner surfaces of the pistons in new brake fluid and insert them into the bores, then refit the rubber dust boots.
12 Refit the ball and bleed screw.

Refitting
13 Refitting is a reversal of removal, but always fit a new gasket; refer to Section 7 when refitting the brake shoes, and bleed the rear hydraulic system as described in Section 3.

Fig. 9.11 Master cylinder location on US and Canadian models
(Sec 9)

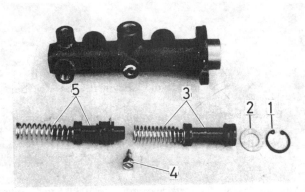

Fig. 9.12 Master cylinder components – early UK models (Sec 9)

1   Circlip   4   Stop bolt
2   Washer   5   Secondary piston assembly
3   Primary piston assembly

Fig. 9.13 Master cylinder components – later UK models (Sec 9)

1   Primary piston assembly   3   Secondary piston assembly
2   Stop bolt

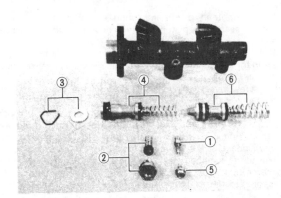

Fig. 9.14 Master cylinder components – US and Canadian models
(Sec 9)

1   Bleed screw   4   Primary piston assembly
2   Check valve and spring 5   Stop bolt
3   Spring clip and washer 6   Secondary piston assembly

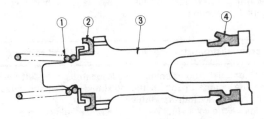

Fig. 9.15 Master cylinder primary piston components (Sec 9)

1   Return spring   3   Piston
2   Front seal   4   Rear seal

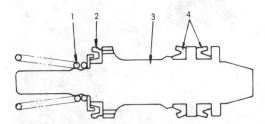

Fig. 9.16 Master cylinder secondary piston components (Sec 9)

1   Return spring   3   Piston
2   Front seal   4   Rear seals

9   Master cylinder – removal, servicing and refitting

Removal

1   Apply the handbrake and chock the wheels.
2   Unscrew the brake fluid reservoir filler cap and syphon out the fluid with a pipette.
3   Where applicable, disconnect the wiring to the brake level sensor.
4   On US and Canadian models remove the air cleaner (Chapter 3), then disconnect the brake fluid reservoir hoses from the master cylinder and plug them.
5   On all models unscrew the union nuts (preferably with a split ring spanner) and disconnect the hydraulic pipes from the master cylinder. Cover the ends of the pipes with masking tape to prevent the ingress of dust and dirt.
6   Unscrew the mounting nuts, remove the spring washers, and withdraw the master cylinder from the front of the servo unit – wrap the unit in cloth to prevent spilling brake fluid onto the paintwork.

Servicing

7   Operate the pistons slowly to expel the remaining fluid, then wash the exterior of the unit with methylated spirit and wipe dry.
8   On UK models remove the reservoir cover, unscrew the bolts, and withdraw the reservoir and seals.
9   On US and Canadian models unscrew and remove the bleed screw.
10 On all models unscrew the union and remove the check valve and spring.

10.2A Inserting a brake hose retaining clip.

10.2B Fitted position of a brake hose retaining clip

11.1 Brake differential proportioning valve

11 Depress the primary piston with a screwdriver, then extract the circlip (or spring clip) and washer (if fitted) from the mouth of the master cylinder.
12 Withdraw the primary piston and spring assembly.
13 Depress the secondary piston with a screwdriver, then unscrew the stop bolt.
14 Withdraw the secondary piston and spring assembly by tapping the cylinder on the workbench. If the rear seal lip engages the stop bolt hole, use a small screwdriver to release it.
15 Using a screwdriver, remove the seals from the pistons, taking care not to damage the pistons.
16 Clean all the components with methylated spirit and dry them with a lint-free cloth. Examine the surfaces of the pistons and bore for scratches and bright wear areas. Temporarily refit each piston, and using a feeler blade, check that the clearance between it and the bores does not exceed the specified maximum amount. If the master cylinder is worn excessively it must be renewed, but if the components are in good order, discard the seals and obtain new ones in the form of a repair kit.
17 Dip the new seals in new brake fluid and assemble them to the pistons using the fingers only to manipulate them. Make sure that they are fitted correctly by referring to Figs. 9.15 and 9.16. Fit the plates and springs to the pistons.
18 Dip the secondary piston and seals in new brake fluid and insert the assembly into the cylinder, spring end first. Make sure that the seal lips do not engage the stop bolt hole and use a small screwdriver to release them if necessary.
19 Depress the secondary piston with a screwdriver, then insert and tighten the stop bolt.
20 Dip the primary piston and seals in new brake fluid and insert the assembly into the cylinder, spring end first.
21 Depress the primary piston with a screwdriver and refit the washer and circlip (or spring clip).
22 Refit the check valve and spring and tighten the union.

23 Refit the reservoir and seals on UK models, and the bleed screw on US and Canadian models.

Refitting
24 Refitting is a reversal of removal, but bleed the entire hydraulic system as described in Section 3.

10 Hydraulic hoses and brake lines – maintenance

1 At the intervals given in the Routine Maintenance Section, inspect the condition of the flexible hoses and rigid brake lines.
2 If the hoses are chafed, perished, or swollen, they must be renewed. When fitting a hose, make sure that it is not twisted or touching any other components which may chafe or damage it (photos).
3 The rigid brake lines should be wiped clean regularly and examined for signs of corrosion or denting by flying stones. Make sure that the support clips are in place and that the lines are not touching any moving component. If a brake line is damaged or corroded it must be renewed immediately.
4 After fitting a new hose or brake hose, bleed the hydraulic system as described in Section 3.

11 Differential proportioning valve – removal and refitting

1 The differential proportioning valve is located on the left-hand side of the engine compartment on the bulkhead (right-hand drive cars) (photo) or side panel (left-hand drive cars).
2 To remove the valve, first remove the brake fluid reservoir cap and tighten it down onto a piece of polythene sheeting. This will reduce the loss of fluid when the valve is removed. Place rags or newspaper

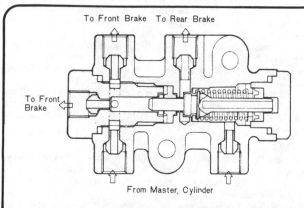

Fig. 9.17 Cross-section of differential proportioning valves (Sec 11)

To Front Brake   To Rear Brake

To Front Brake

From Master, Cylinder

Fig. 9.18 Testing the brake fluid level sensor on right-hand drive models (Sec 12)

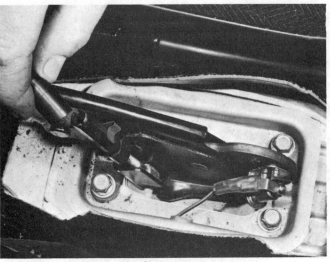

13.2A Removing handbrake cable adjusting screw cover

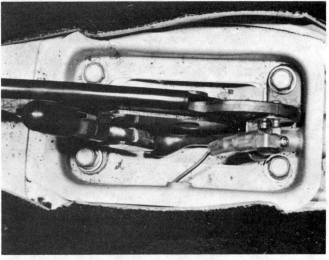

13.2B Handbrake lever and cable adjusting screw

beneath the valve to catch spilled fluid.

3   Unscrew the union nuts (preferably with a split ring spanner) and disconnect the hydraulic pipes from the valve.

4   Unscrew the retaining bolt and withdraw the valve.

5   Refitting is a reversal of removal, but note that front and rear circuits are identified by 'F' and 'R', and the arrows indicate the flow of fluid when operating the brakes.

12   Brake fluid level sensor – testing

1   The brake fluid level sensor is located in the reservoir. On right-hand drive models it is integral with the filler cap, but on left-hand drive models it is part of the reservoir.

2   To test the sensor fitted to right-hand drive models, separate the supply wire connector and use an ohmmeter to check for continuity as the filler cap is moved up and down. With the float down there should be zero resistance, but with the float up maximum resistance.

3   The testing method is identical for left-hand drive models, but use a clean screwdriver to move the float up and down. Note that the switch contacts will operate at the 'MIN' level mark.

13   Handbrake – adjustment

1   Jack up the rear of the car and support it on axle stands placed in front of the lower arms. Chock the front wheels.

2   Fully release the handbrake lever, then apply it 5 to 7 notches and check that the rear wheels are locked. If not, turn the adjusting nut at the base of the lever until correct (photos).

3   Apply the handbrake several times and recheck the adjustment. When fully released check that the rear wheels rotate freely.

4   Lower the car to the ground.

14   Handbrake cable – renewal

1   Remove the brake shoes from the appropriate side as described in Section 7.

2   Release the front of the cable from the equaliser by turning the cable and sliding out the end fitting (photo).

3   Unhook the support spring from the outer cable, then unscrew the locknuts and remove the outer cable from the bracket (photo).

4   Withdraw the handbrake cable from under the car, after releasing the inner cable ferrule (photo).

5   Fit the new cable using a reversal of the removal procedure. Adjust the handbrake as described in Section 13.

Fig. 9.19 Testing the brake fluid level sensor on left-hand drive models (Sec 12)

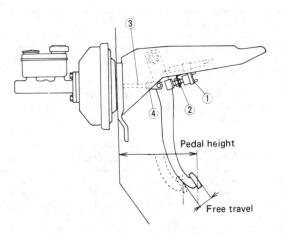

Fig. 9.20 Footbrake pedal adjustment diagram (Sec 15)

1	Stoplamp switch	3	Pushrod
2	Locknut	4	Locknut

14.2 Handbrake cable equaliser

14.3 Handbrake outer cable locknuts and bracket

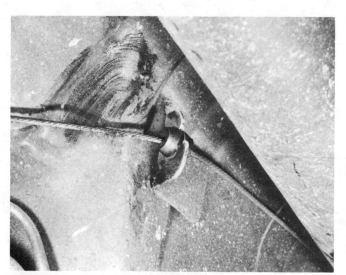

14.4 Handbrake inner cable ferrule location

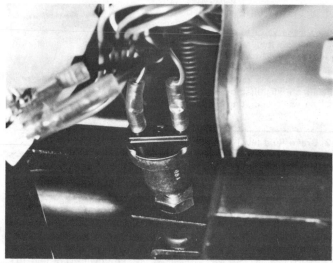

15.1 Stoplamp switch

15 Footbrake pedal/stoplamp switch – adjustment

1   Refer to Fig. 9.20 and the Specifications and check the pedal height dimension. If adjustment is necessary, loosen the locknut and turn the stoplamp switch until the dimension is correct, then tighten the locknut (photo).

2   Now check that the footbrake pedal free travel is as specified. If not, loosen the locknut and turn the servo unit pushrod as necessary. Tighten the locknut.

16 Servo unit – testing, removal and refitting

1   The servo unit is located between the footbrake pedal and the master cylinder and its purpose is to reduce the braking effort at the pedal. It does this by utilising vacuum from the inlet manifold when the engine is running.

2   To test the servo unit, depress the footbrake pedal several times with the engine switched off, in order to dissipate the vacuum.

3   Depress the pedal, then start the engine – the pedal will move toward the floor if the unit is serviceable.

4   To remove the servo unit, first remove the master cylinder as described in Section 9.

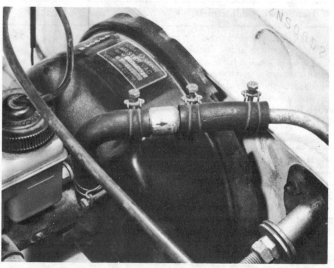

16.5 Servo unit vacuum hose and non-return valve

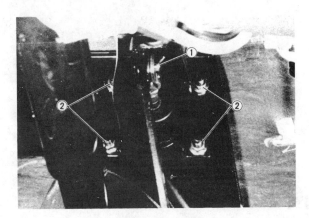

Fig. 9.21 Servo unit pushrod clevis pin (1) and mounting nuts (2) (Sec 16)

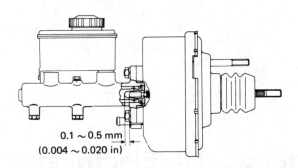

0.1 ~ 0.5 mm
(0.004 ~ 0.020 in)

Fig. 9.22 Master cylinder primary piston-to-servo unit pushrod clearance (Sec 16)

5   Disconnect the vacuum hose (photo).
6   Working inside the car, extract the split pin and remove the washer and clevis pin securing the pushrod to the pedal.
7   Unscrew the mounting nuts, remove the washers, and withdraw the servo unit from the engine compartment.
8   Refitting is a reversal of removal with reference to Section 9 as

necessary; however, before refitting the master cylinder check the servo unit pushrod-to-master cylinder primary piston clearance, and if not as specified, adjust the length of the pushrod. Use vernier calipers to determine the distances of the primary piston hole and pushrod extremity from the mating faces, then subtract the latter from the former.

17 Fault diagnosis – braking system

Symptom	Reason(s)
Brake pedal 'spongy'	Air in hydraulic system
Excessive effort required to stop car	Servo unit faulty Excessively worn brake linings or pads Incorrect linings or pads fitted Linings or pads contaminated with oil, grease or brake fluid Failure of one braking circuit
Excessive pedal travel	Rear brakes out of adjustment Free travel adjustment incorrect Air in hydraulic system
Brakes pull to one side	Linings or pads contaminated with oil, grease or brake fluid Caliper or wheel cylinder pistons seized Brake disc worn or distorted
Brakes overheat	Caliper or wheel cylinder pistons seized Rear brakes overadjusted (where applicable) Handbrake cable seized Master cylinder faulty
Brakes judder	Brake disc worn or distorted Brake drum worn or distorted Caliper or bracket bolts loose

Chapter 10 Electrical system

Refer to Chapter 13 for revisions and information related to 1982 models

Contents

Specifications

System type .... 12 volt, negative earth

Battery capacity (at 20 hour discharge rate) .... 35 amp hr, 45 amp hr, or 60 amp hr

Alternator
Brush length:
  New .... 18 mm (0.71 in)
  Minimum .... 8 mm (0.31 in)
Minimum slip ring diameter .... 32.2 mm (1.268 in)
Field resistance .... 3 to 6 ohm

Starter motor
Type .... Pre-engaged
Free running test current at 11.5 volts:
  Except 1979 US models .... 53 amp maximum
  1979 US models .... 60 amp maximum
Brush length:
  New .... 17 mm (0.67 in)
  Minimum .... 11.5 mm (0.45 in)
Armature shaft bush running clearance .... 0.2 mm (0.008 in)
Armature shaft endplay .... 0.2 to 0.5 mm (0.008 to 0.020 in)
Pinion-to-stop collar clearance .... 0.5 to 2.0 mm (0.02 to 0.08 in)

Wiper motor
Wiper motor no-load current .... 4 amp maximum

Fusible links 3

Fuses
Right-hand drive models .... 3 x 15 amp, 6 x 10 amp, 1 x 20 amp
Left-hand drive models .... 4 x 15 amp, 6 x 10 amp, 1 x 20 amp.

Bulbs

	Wattage	Wattage
	UK models	US and Canadian models
Headlight	60/55	65/55
Front parking	5	8
Direction indicators	21	27
Tail/stop	5/21	8/27
Reverse	21	27
Number plate	4	6
Boot light	5	5
Interior light	5	5
Spot light	6	6
Glovebox	3.4	3.4
Warning lights:		
Direction indicator	3.4	3.4
Main beam	3.4	3.4
Oil pressure	3.4	3.4
Brake fluid	3.4	3.4
Hazard	3.4	–
Heat hazard (without tachometer)	–	3.4
Heat hazard (with tachometer)	–	1.4
Seat belt	–	3.4
Automatic selector lever	3.4	3.4
Alternator	3.4	3.4
Heated rear window	1.4	–
Disc pad wear	1.4	–
Stop light	1.4	1.4
Tail light	1.4	1.4
Washer level	1.4	1.4
Fuel	3.4	3.4
Illumination lights:		
Instrument panel, cigarette lighter, radio, and clock	3.4	3.4
Heater and stereo	1.4	1.4

Torque wrench settings

	lbf ft	Nm
Wiper arm locknut	8	10

1 General description

The electrical system is of 12 volt negative earth type. The battery is charged by a belt-driven alternator incorporating an integral regulator. The starter is of pre-engaged type whereby the drive pinion is engaged with the flywheel ring gear before the starter motor is energised.

Although repair procedures are given in this Chapter, it may be more economical over a long period to renew complete components when they develop a fault, especially if they are well worn.

2 Battery – removal and refitting

1 The battery is located in the engine compartment, on the front left-hand side.

2 Switch off the ignition switch and all electrical components, then disconnect the lead from the negative (–) terminal followed by the lead from the positive (+) terminal.

3 Where fitted, disconnect the lead to the battery electrolyte level sensor.

4 Unscrew the clamp nut and remove the clamp.

5 Lift the battery from its mounting platform, taking care not to spill any electrolyte on the bodywork.

6 Refitting is a reversal of removal, but make sure that the polarity is correct before connecting the leads, and do not overtighten the clamps.

3 Battery – maintenance

1 Normal weekly battery maintenance consists of checking the electrolyte level of each cell to ensure that the separators are covered by 10 to 20 mm (0.4 to 0.8 in) of electrolyte. The electrolyte, viewed through the translucent battery casing, should be at or near the upper level mark. If necessary top up the cells with distilled or de-ionized water. If electrolyte is spilt, immediately wipe away the excess, as electrolyte attacks and corrodes any metal it comes into contact with very rapidly. In an *emergency*, where the electrolyte level is too low, it

is permissible to use boiled drinking water which has been allowed to cool, but this is *not* recommended as a regular practice.

2 If the battery terminals are showing signs of corrosion, brush or scrape off the worst, taking care not to get the deposits on the vehicle paintwork or your hands. Prepare a solution of household ammonia, washing soda or bicarbonate of soda and water. Brush this onto all the corroded parts, taking care that none enters the battery. This will neutralize the corrosion. When all the fizzing and bubbling has stopped the parts can be wiped clean with a dry, lint-free cloth. Smear the terminals and clamps with petroleum jelly afterwards to prevent further corrosion.

3 Inspect the battery clamp and mounting tray and treat these in the same way. Where the paintwork has been damaged, after neutralizing, the area can be painted with a zinc based primer and the appropriate finishing colour, or an underbody paint can be used.

4 At the same time inspect the battery case for cracks. If a crack is found, clean and plug it with one of the proprietary compounds marketed for this purpose. If leakage through the crack has been excessive, then it will be necessary to refill the appropriate cell with fresh electrolyte as described later. Cracks are frequently caused at the top of the battery case by pouring in distilled water in the middle of winter *after* instead of *before* a run. This gives the water no chance to mix with the electrolyte so the former freezes and splits the battery case.

5 If topping up becomes excessive and the case has been inspected for cracks that could cause leakage, but none are found, the battery is being overcharged and the voltage regulator will have to be checked.

6 With the battery on the bench, measure the specific gravity with a hydrometer to determine the state of charge and condition of the electrolyte. There should be very little variation between the different cells and, if a variation in excess of 0.025 is present, it will be due to either:

   (a) *Loss of electrolyte from the battery at some time caused by spillage or a leak, resulting in a drop in the specific gravity of the electrolyte when the deficiency was replaced with distilled water instead of fresh electrolyte, or*

   (b) *An internal short circuit caused by buckling of the plates or similar malady, pointing to the likelihood of total battery failure in the near future*

7   The specific gravity of the electrolyte at different states of charge is given in the following table:

	Ambient temperature over 32°C (90°F)	Ambient temperature under 32°C (90°F)
Fully charged	1.210 to 1.230	1.270 to 1.290
Half discharged	1.130 to 1.150	1.190 to 1.210
Fully discharged	1.050 to 1.070	1.110 to 1.130

4   Battery – electrolyte replenishment

1   If the battery is in a fully charged state and one of the cells maintains a specific gravity reading which is 0.025 or lower than the others, and a check of the cells has been made with a high discharge battery tester, then it is likely that electrolyte has been lost from the cell with the low reading at some time.
2   Top up the cell with a solution of 1 part sulphuric acid to 2.5 parts of distilled or de-ionized water. If the cell is already fully topped up draw some electrolyte out of it with a pipette.
3   When mixing the sulphuric acid and water **never add water to sulphuric acid** – always pour the acid slowly onto the water in a glass container. **If water is added to sulphuric acid it will explode.**
4   Continue to top up the cell with the freshly made electrolyte, and to recharge the battery and check the hydrometer readings.

5   Battery – charging

1   In winter time when a heavy demand is placed on the battery, such as when starting from cold, and much electrical equipment is continually in use, it is a good idea to occasionally have the battery fully charged from an external source at a rate of approximately 5 amps.
2   Continue to charge the battery at this rate until no further rise in specific gravity is noted over a four hour period.
3   Alternatively, a trickle charger, charging at the rate of 1.5 amps can be safely used overnight.
4   Special rapid 'boost' charges, which are claimed to restore the power of the battery in 1 to 2 hours, are most dangerous unless they are thermostatically controlled, as they can cause serious damage to the battery plates through overheating.
5   While charging the battery note that the temperature of the electrolyte should never exceed 131°F (55°C).
Caution: *If the battery is to remain in the car when being charged, disconnect both leads to prevent possible damage to the electrical circuits.*

6   Alternator – maintenance and special precautions

1   Periodically wipe away any dirt or grease which has accumulated on the outside of the unit, and check the security of the leads. At the same time check the tension of the fanbelt, and adjust it if necessary

as described in Chapter 2.
2   Take extreme care when making electrical circuit connections on the car, otherwise damage may occur to the alternator. Always make sure that the battery leads are connected to the correct terminals. Before using electric-arc welding equipment to repair any part of the car, disconnect the battery and alternator leads. Disconnect the battery leads before using a mains charger. Never run the alternator with the output wire disconnected.
3   The alternator warning light relay is located on the right-hand side of the engine compartment (photo).

7   Alternator – testing in situ

1   The following test procedure is made with the engine stationary, and will indicate whether the alternator or regulator circuits are defective.
2   With the ignition switched off, disconnect the warning lamp wiring plug from the back of the alternator and connect a voltmeter to each of the exposed terminals in turn. In Fig. 10.1 the terminals are 'L' and 'R'. The reading should be zero, but if voltage is registered, the alternator is faulty.
3   Reconnect the plug with the voltmeter still connected to the 'L' terminal, and switch on the ignition – if the reading is zero, the alternator and regulator are faulty. If the reading is near battery voltage, insert a small screwdriver in the hole near the 'B' terminal on the back of the alternator (see Fig. 10.2) and short circuit the 'F' terminal (located at a depth of 20 mm/0.79 in) to the alternator housing (photo). If the voltmeter reading is now lower than battery voltage, the regulator is faulty and should be renewed.
4   Switch off the ignition and remove the voltmeter.

8   Alternator – removal, servicing and refitting

Removal
1   Disconnect the battery negative lead.
2   Disconnect the main cable and warning lamp plug from the back of the alternator (photo).
3   Loosen the adjustment and pivot bolts, swivel the alternator toward the engine, and disconnect the fanbelt. Note the location of the cable clip on the pivot bolt.
4   Remove the adjustment and pivot bolts and withdraw the alternator from the engine (photo).

Servicing
5   Mark the drive end bracket, stator, and slip ring end bracket in relation to each other.
6   Unscrew the through-bolts, then use a screwdriver in the slots provided to prise the drive end bracket and rotor assembly from the stator.
7   Clamp the rotor segments in a soft-jawed vice, unscrew the pulley nut, and withdraw the pulley, fan, spacer, and rotor from the drive end bracket.

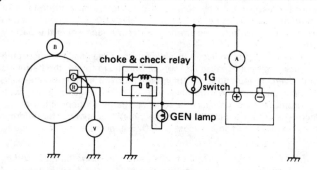

Fig. 10.1 Alternator and charging circuit showing voltmeter test (Sec 7)

Fig. 10.2 Hole location (arrowed) for shorting alternator 'F' terminal (Sec 7)

6.3 Alternator warning light relay location

7.3 Short-circuiting the alternator 'F' terminal with a screwdriver

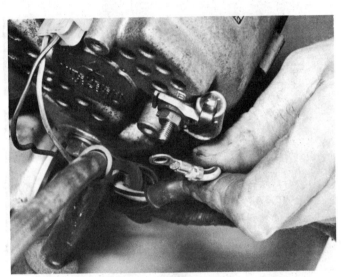

8.2 Disconnecting wiring from alternator

8.4 Removing the alternator

8.17 Inserting wire to hold brushes during alternator reassembly

8   Note the location of the stator leads on the rectifier, then unsolder them in less than 20 seconds, otherwise the excessive heat may damage the diodes.

9   Remove the stator followed by the condenser.

10   Unsolder the 'L' and 'B' plates from the rectifier, then remove the regulator and brush assembly, and the rectifier.

11   Check the front and rear bearings for smooth running, and if necessary renew them.

12   Check the stator for insulation by connecting a circuit tester between the core and each of the wires in turn. If current flows, the stator winding insulation is faulty. Check the windings for continuity by connecting the tester between each of the wires. If no current flows, there is an open circuit in the windings.

13   Check the rotor windings using the method described in paragraph 12, but connecting to the slip rings instead of the stator wires. In addition check that the rotor field resistance is as specified by connecting an ohmmeter between the two slip rings.

14   Check the rectifier diodes using an ohmmeter as shown in Fig. 10.7 – a good diode will give a low reading with the probes connected one way round, but a high reading with them reversed.

15   Check the length of the brushes and if less than the specified minimum, renew them.

16   Clean the rotor slip ring with fine glasspaper. If they are excessively worn, it may be possible to have them skimmed by an engineering

Fig. 10.3 Alternator drive end bracket and rotor assembly (Sec 8)

1	Pulley and nut	3	Rotor
2	Fan	4	Drive end bracket

Fig. 10.4 Alternator slip ring end bracket and stator components

1	Stator	3	Rectifier
2	Regulator and brush holder		

Fig. 10.5 Alternator brush holder assembly (Sec 8)

Fig. 10.6 Alternator front and rear bearings (1) (Sec 8)

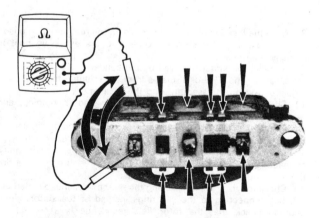

Fig. 10.7 Checking rectifier diodes with an ohmmeter (Sec 8)

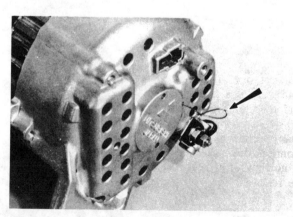

Fig. 10.8 Temporary wire location to hold brushes during reassembly (Sec 8)

works provided the diameter is not reduced to less that the specified minimum amount.

17 Reassembly of the alternator is a reversal of dismantling, but it will be necessary to insert a length of stiff wire through the hole in the slip ring end bracket to hold the brushes while the rotor is being inserted. Do not forget to remove the wire (photo).

Refitting

18 Refitting is a reversal of removal, but adjust the fanbelt tension as described in Chapter 2.

9 Starter motor – testing in situ

1 If the starter motor fails to operate, first check the condition of the battery by switching on the headlamps. If they glow brightly, then gradually dim after a few seconds, the battery is in an uncharged condition.

Fig. 10.9 Starter motor components (Sec 10)

1 *Drive end bracket*	5 *Pinion and overrun clutch*
2 *Solenoid*	6 *Yoke*
3 *Pinion lever*	7 *Armature*
4 *Stop collar*	8 *Brush holder assembly*

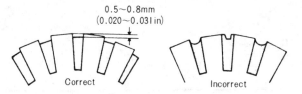

Fig. 10.10 Starter motor commutator mica undercut dimension (Sec 10)

2 If the battery is in good condition, check the terminal connections for security, and also check that the engine earth lead is making good contact with the body.

3 If the starter motor still fails to turn, check that the solenoid is being energised. To do this, connect a 12 volt test lamp and leads between the starter side solenoid terminal and earth. When the ignition key is turned to the starting position, the lamp should flow. If not, either the supply circuit is open due to a broken wire or faulty ignition switch, or the solenoid is defective. If the solenoid is supplying current to the starter motor, the fault must be in the starter motor.

10 Starter motor – removal, servicing and refitting

Removal

1 Disconnect the battery negative lead.
2 Remove the air cleaner as described in Chapter 3.
3 Unscrew the terminal nut and disconnect the supply cable from the solenoid.
4 Disconnect the ignition switch wire from the solenoid.
5 Unbolt the starter motor and withdraw it from the engine (photo).

Servicing

6 Unscrew the nut and disconnect the starter cable from the solenoid.
7 Unbolt the solenoid from the drive end bracket.
8 Unhook the plunger from the pinion lever.
9 Mark the drive end bracket, yoke and rear cover in relation to each other.
10 Unscrew the through-bolts and remove the rear cover.
11 Remove the brush holder assembly followed by the yoke.
12 Extract the pinion lever and armature assembly from the drive end bracket.
13 Using a suitable size socket, drive the top collar toward the pinion, then remove the stop ring and collar and slide off the pinion and overrun clutch assembly.
14 Clean the components with paraffin and wipe dry, then examine them for wear and damage.
15 Check the armature windings insulation by connecting an ohmmeter between the core and each commutator segment in turn – if an infinite reading is not given, the insulation is faulty. Similarly check the windings for continuity by connecting the ohmmeter to connected segments – a low reading should be obtained.
16 Clean the commutator with fine glasspaper, then wash with fuel. Using an old hacksaw blade, undercut the mica between the segments to a depth of 0.5 to 0.8 mm (0.020 to 0.031 in) as shown in Fig. 10.10.
17 Check the field windings in the yoke for insulation and continuity using the method described in paragraph 15.
18 Check the length of the brushes, and if less than the specified minimum, renew them as follows. Pull the brush from the holder and squeeze it with pliers to cause it to disintegrate, leaving the lead exposed. Clean the lead, then fit the new brush to it, small chamfer side first. Heat the lead with a soldering iron and fill the large chamfer with solder.

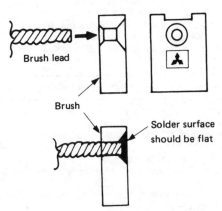

Fig. 10.11 Starter motor brush installation (Sec 10)

Fig. 10.12 Starter motor pinion-to-stop collar clearance (Sec 10)

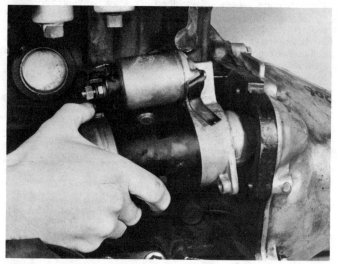

10.5 Removing starter motor

11.1A Fusebox location (UK models)

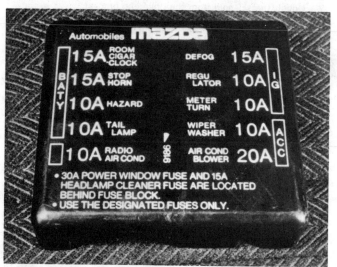

11.1B Fusebox cover (UK models)

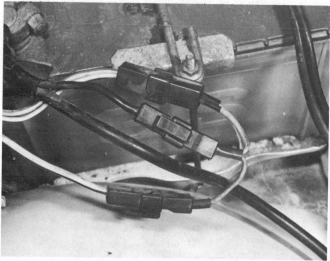

11.1C Fusible links

19 Check the armature bushes for wear and renew them if necessary.

20 Reassembly is a reversal of dismantling. When completed check that the armature endplay is within the specified limits. If not, change the rear thrust washer as necessary. Also check the pinion-to-stop collar clearance as shown in Fig. 10.12. If it is not within the specified limits, insert a washer between the solenoid and drive end bracket as necessary.

Refitting

21 Refitting is a reversal of the removal procedure.

11 Fuses and fusible links – general

1 The fusebox is located inside the car, beneath the driver's side of the facia. Three fusible links are located on the left-hand side of the engine compartment by the battery (photos).

2 The circuits protected by the fuses and fusible links are shown on the wiring diagrams at the end of this Chpater.

3 Before renewing a fuse or fusible link, always try to trace the source of trouble and rectify the fault. Always renew the fuse or fusible link with one of identical rating.

12 Direction indicator flasher system – general

1 The flasher unit is located inside the car on the driver's side below the facia.

2 If the flashers become faulty in operation, first check the bulbs for security and good contact, and also check that the bulbs have not blown. Check the relevant fuse in the fusebox. If all is in order but the flashers are still inoperative, renew the flasher unit.

3 The hazard warning system also uses the same flasher unit.

13 Combination switch – removal and refitting

1 Remove the steering wheel as described in Chapter 11.

2 Remove the screws and withdraw the steering column shrouds – prise the cover from the right-hand shroud and remove the ring from the ignition lock. Where applicable disconnect the ignition switch illumination light wiring (photos).

3 Remove the switch panel next to the steering lock (where applicable).

4 Extract the stop ring from the inner column and remove the cancel cam and spring (photo).

5 Disconnect the combination switch multi-plug.

13.2A Removing screws ...

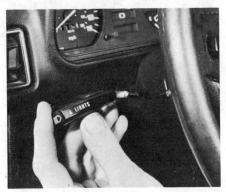

13.2B ... light switch and ...

13.2C ... ignition lock ring ...

13.2D ... cover ...

13.2E ... and steering column shrouds

13.4 Combination switch location

6 Remove the retaining screws and withdraw the combination switch assembly.
7 Refitting is a reversal of removal.

14 Ignition switch – removal and refitting

The procedure is as given for the steering lock, and full details are to be found in Chapter 11.

15 Courtesy light switches – removal and refitting

1 Courtesy light switches are located on both the front and rear doors.
2 To remove a switch, unscrew the two screws, withdraw the switch, and disconnect the wire (photo).
3 Removal of the boot compartment light switch is similar, but the switch is retained by a nut (photo).
4 Refitting is a reversal of removal.

16 Switch panel – removal and refitting

1 Remove the steering wheel as described in Chapter 11.
2 Remove the screws and withdraw the steering column shrouds – prise the cover from the right-hand shroud and remove the ring from the ignition lock, Where applicable disconnect the ignition switch illumination light wiring.
3 Remove the retaining screws, disconnect the multi-plugs, and withdraw the switch panel (photos).
4 If necessary, remove the remote control mirror switch, heated rear window switch, boot lid opener switch, and headlight cleaner switch as applicable.
5 Refitting is a reversal of removal.

17 Instrument panel – removal and refitting

1 Remove the steering wheel as described in Chapter 11. Although not essential, this provides better access.
2 Remove the screws and withdraw the steering column shroud (where applicable).
3 Reach under the facia and disconnect the speedometer cable by pressing the plastic extension.
4 Unscrew the screws (if fitted) and remove the panel hood. To do this press the inner faces outward and downward to release the clips (photo).

Fig. 10.13 Switch panel retaining screw locations (Sec 16)

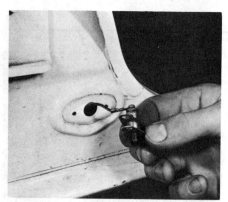
15.2 Removing a courtesy light switch

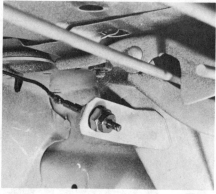
15.3 Boot compartment light switch location

16.3A Removing switch panel screws

16.3B Removing the switch panel

17.4 Removing instrument panel hood

17.5A Removing retaining screws ...

17.5B ... and instrument panel

17.5C Instrument panel multi-plugs and speedometer cable

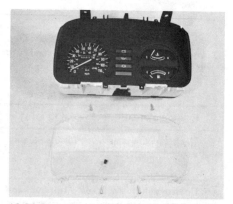
18.2A Removing instrument panel outer cover

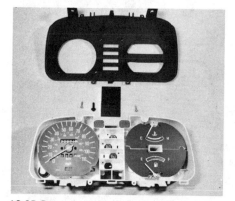
18.2B Removing instrument panel inner cover

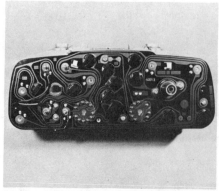
18.3 Instrument panel circuit board and warning lamp bulb holders

19.2 Removing radio control knobs

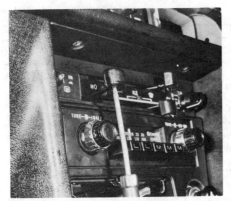
19.3A Removing heater knob

19.3B Removing fan switch knob

19.4A Removing upper screw ...

19.4B ... centre screw ...

19.4C ... tray ...

19.4D ... and facia centre panel

19.6A Withdrawing the air vents ...

19.6B ... and clock

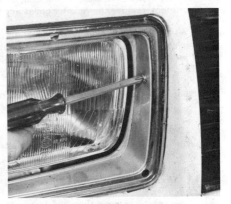
20.2A Removing retaining screw ...

20.2B ... and headlamp bezel

20.3 Headlamp unit retaining post

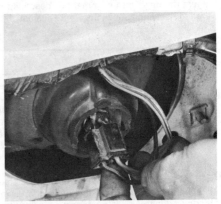
20.6 Removing headlamp plug connector

5   Remove the screws and withdraw the instrument panel sufficiently to disconnect the multi-plugs, then withdraw the panel (photos).
6   Refitting is a reversal of removal.

18 Instruments and gauges – removal and refitting

1   Remove the instrument panel as described in Section 17.
2   Remove the screws and withdraw the covers (photos).
3   The temperature and fuel gauges, speedometer, or tachometer (as applicable) can now be removed by unscrewing the relevant nuts or screws (photo).
4   Refitting is a reversal of removal, but make sure that the warning light panel and odometer knob are refitted correctly.

19 Facia centre panel and clock – removal and refitting

1   Disconnect the battery negative lead.
2   Remove the ashtray and pull off the radio control knobs. Remove the large washers (photo).
3   Pull off the heater and fan switch (one screw) knobs (photos).
4   Remove the securing screws and withdraw the centre panel sufficiently to disconnect all of the electrical connections, noting carefully where they are located (photos).
5   Remove the centre panel from the car.
6   To move the clock, prise out the two air vents, remove the two screws and disconnect the wiring (photos).
7   Refitting is a reversal of removal.

20 Headlamps – bulb removal

Sealed beam type

1   On late models release the headlamp bezel retainer in the engine compartment, remove the radiator grilles and withdraw the headlamp bezel.
2   On early models unscrew the direction indicator lens and bezel screws and remove the headlamp bezel (photos).
3   Push the sealed beam unit inward and slide it sideways (photo).
4   Disconnect the plug from the unit.
5   Fit the new sealed beam unit using a reversal of the removal procedure, then adjust the headlamp alignment as described in Section 21.

Semi-sealed beam type

6   Working in the engine compartment, pull the plug connector from the rear of the headlamp (photo).
7   Remove the sealing rubber. Push the retainer toward the bulb and turn it anti-clockwise, or release the clip, then remove the retainer and bulb (photos).
8   If necessary, remove the headlamp unit with reference to paragraphs 1 to 5 (photo).
9   Fit the new bulb using a reversal of the removal procedure, then adjust the headlamp alignment as described in Section 21. Make sure that the sealing rubber fits firmly against the rear of the headlamp.

21 Headlamp – alignment

1   Accurate headlamp alignment should be carried out by a garage equipped with an optical beam setter. However, in an emergency the following procedure will provide an acceptable light pattern.
2   Position the car on a level surface, with tyres correctly inflated, approximately 10 metres (33 feet) in front of and facing a garage door or wall.
3   Mark the headlamp bulb centres on the wall in line with the direction of the car.
4   Switch on the main beam and check that the areas of maximum illumination coincide with the marks on the wall. If not, turn the spring-loaded adjustment screws (using a screwdriver inserted through the holes provided in or near the headlamp bezel) until the correct alignment is obtained (photo).

22 Lamp bulbs – removal

1   The bulbs should always be renewed with ones of identical type and rating as listed in the Specifications.

Front parking and direction indicator lamp

2   Unscrew the retaining screws and withdraw the lens (photo).
3   Push and twist the bulb to remove it (photos).
4   Refitting is a reversal of removal.

Rear lamp cluster

5   Open the boot lid and release the four tabs to enable the lamp cluster to be withdrawn from the housing (photos).
6   Push and twist the relevant bulb to remove it.
7   Refitting is a reversal of removal.

Interior light and map light

8   To remove the interior light bulb, unclip the lens, then extract the festoon type bulb from between the spring contacts (photo).
9   If a map light is fitted, remove the cross head screws and withdraw the cover.
10   Push and twist the relevant bulb to remove it.
11   Refitting is a reversal of removal.

Side marker lamp and foglamp

12   Unscrew the retaining screws and withdraw the lens (photos).
13   Push and twist the bulb to remove it.

Glovebox lamp

14   Open the glovebox and pull the wedge type bulb from its holder (photo).

Luggage compartment bulb

15   Open the boot lid, remove the bulb holder and push and twist the bulb to remove it (photo).

Rear number plate lamp bulb

16   Unscrew the nut and remove the bulb cover.
17   Remove the bulb holder, then push and twist the bulb to remove it (photo).

Instrument panel warning lamp

18   Remove the instrument panel as described in Section 17.
19   Twist the appropriate bulb holder from the back of the panel and pull out the wedge type bulb (photo).

23 Wiper blade – renewal

1   Pull the wiper arm away from the windscreen.
2   Lift the clip and extract the wiper blade from the arm (photo).
3   Fit the new blade using a reversal of the removal procedure.

24 Wiper arm – removal, refitting and adjustment

1   Make sure that the wiper motor is stopped in the parked position. Lift the cover from the securing nut.
2   Unscrew the securing nut and prise the arm from the spindle with a wide-bladed screwdriver. Take care not to damage the paintwork (photo).
3   Refitting is a reversal of removal, but check that the blade wiping area is as shown in Fig. 10.14. If not, adjust the position of the arm on the spindle as necessary.

25 Wiper motor – removal, testing and refitting

1   Operate the wipers until they are positioned as shown in Fig. 10.15, then switch off the ignition.
2   Disconnect the battery negative lead.
3   Remove the wiper arms and blades with reference to Section 24.
4   Remove the retaining screws, withdraw the heater intake panel,

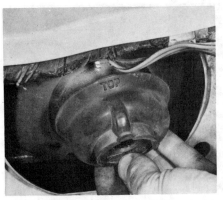

20.7A Removing sealing rubber ...

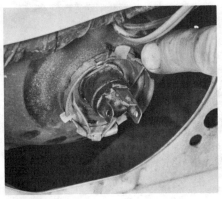

20.7B ... clip ...

20.7C ... and headlamp bulb

20.8 Removing semi-sealed beam headlamp

21.4 Adjusting the headlamp alignment unit

22.2 Removing front parking and direction indicator lamp lens

22.3A Removing front direction indicator bulb

22.3B Removing front parking bulb

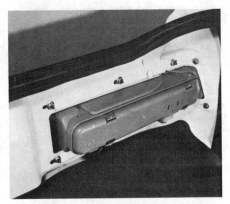

22.5A Rear lamp cluster assembly

22.5B Rear lamp cluster bulb location

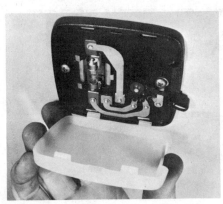

22.8 Interior light bulb location

22.12A Side marker lamp bulb location

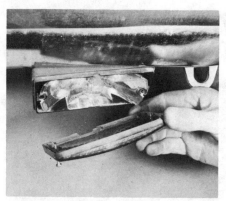
22.12B Foglamp bulb location

22.14 Removing glovebox lamp bulb

22.15 Luggage compartment bulb location

22.17 Removing rear number plate lamp bulb

22.19 Removing instrument panel warning lamp bulb

23.2 Disconnecting wiper blade from arm

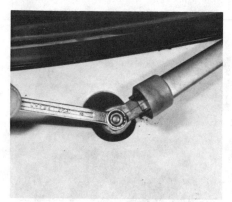
24.2A Unscrewing wiper arm nut ...

24.2B ... and withdrawing wiper arm

25.4A Washer tube location and heater intake panel

25.4B Wiper motor and linkage location

25.5 Wiper motor showing wiring connector

26.2 Speedometer cable (head end)

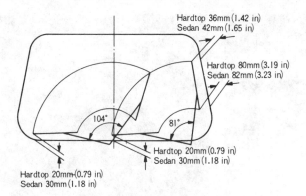

Fig. 10.14 Wiper blade wiping area on left-hand drive models (Sec 24)

Fig. 10.15 Wiper position for removing motor (Sec 25)

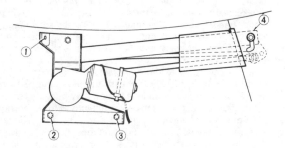

Fig. 10.16 Wiper linkage mounting bolt tightening sequence (Sec 25)

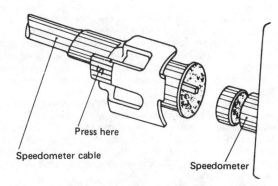

Fig. 10.17 Speedometer cable-to-head connection (Sec 26)

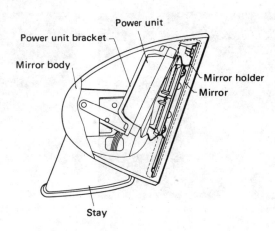

Fig. 10.18 Cutaway view of the remote control mirror (Sec 27)

and disconnect the washer tube. Remove the wiper motor cover bag and band (photos).

5   Disconnect the wiring connector and unbolt the wiper motor and linkage assembly from the bulkhead (photo).

6   Remove the wiper motor from the linkage.

7   To test the wiper motor, connect the supply wires in series with an ammeter to a 12 volt battery. The no-load current should not exceed that given in the Specifications. If it does, the motor is faulty.

8   Refitting is a reversal of removal, but tighten the linkage mounting bolts in the order shown in Fig. 10.16. Adjust the wiper arm rest position if necessary with reference to Section 24.

26 Speedometer cable – removal and refitting

1   Disconnect the battery negative lead.

2   Working inside the car, reach up behind the instrument panel and disconnect the speedometer cable from the head by pressing the plastic extension (photo).

3   Jack up the front of the car and support it on axle stands. Apply the handbrake.

4   Unscrew the collar and disconnect the speedometer cable from the left-hand side of the gearbox or automatic transmission (photo).

5   Release the cable from the body clips and withdraw it.

6   Refitting is a reversal of removal.

27 Remote control mirror – removal and refitting

1   Disconnect the battery negative lead.

2   Remove the two screws and detach the mirror body from the stay. Disconnect the wiring plug.

3   Remove the screws and extract the power unit and mirror from the body.

4   To separate the power unit from the holder, break the glass and remove the exposed screws.

5   Refitting is a reversal of removal, but attach the mirror to the holder with suitable cement.

28 Horn – removal and refitting

1   Disconnect the battery negative lead.

2   Reach under the front bumper and unscrew the horn mounting nut (photo).

3   Disconnect the wiring and withdraw the horn.

4   Refitting is a reversal of removal.

26.4 Speedometer cable attachment to gearbox

28.2 Horn location

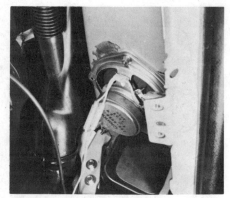

29.1 Standard radio speaker location with glovebox removed

29 Radios and tape players – fitting (general)

A radio or tape player is an expensive item to buy, and will only give its best performance if fitted properly. It is useless to expect concert hall performance from a unit that is suspended from the dashpanel by string with its speaker resting on the back seat or parcel shelf! If you do not wish to do the fitting yourself, there are many in-car entertainment specialists who will do the fitting for you.

Make sure the unit purchased is of the same polarity as the vehicle. Ensure that units with adjustable polarity are correctly set before commencing installation.

It is difficult to give specific information with regard to fitting, as final positioning of the radio/tape player, speakers and aerial is entirely a matter of personal preference. However, the following paragraphs give guidelines to follow which are relevant to all installations.

Radios

Most radios are a standardised size of 7 in wide by 2 in deep. This ensures that they will fit into the radio aperture provided in most cars. If your car does not have such an aperture, then the radio must be fitted in a suitable position either in or beneath the dashboard. Alternatively, a special console can be purchased which will fit between the dashpanel and the floor or on the transmission tunnel. These consoles can also be used for additional switches and instrumentation if required. Where no radio aperture is provided, the following points should be borne in mind before deciding exactly where to fit the unit.

(a) The unit must be within easy reach of the driver wearing a seat belt

(b) The unit must not be mounted in close proximity to an electronic tachometer, the ignition switch and its wiring, or the flasher unit and associated wiring

(c) The unit must be mounted within easy reach of the aerial lead, and in such a place that the aerial lead will not have to be routed near the components detailed in the preceding paragraph 'b'

(d) The unit should not be positioned in a place where it might cause injury to the car occupants in an accident; for instance under the dashpanel above the driver's or passenger's legs

(e) The unit must be fitted really securely

Some radios will have mounting brackets provided, together with instructions; others will need to be fitted using drilled and slotted metal strips, bent to form mounting brackets. These strips are available from most accessory shops. The unit must be properly earthed by fitting a separate earthing lead between the casing of the radio and the vehicle frame.

Use the radio manufacturers' instructions when wiring the radio into the vehicle's electrical system. If no instructions are available, refer to the relevant wiring diagram to find the location of the radio feed connection in the vehicle's wiring circuit. A 1 to 2 amp 'in-line' fuse must be fitted in the radio's 'feed' wire – a choke may also be necessary (see next Section).

The type of aerial used and its fitted position, is a matter of personal preference. In general, the taller the aerial the better the reception. It is best to fit a fully retractable aerial; especially if a mechanical car-wash is used or if you live in an area where cars tend

to be vandalised. In this respect, electric aerials which are raised and lowered automatically when switching the radio on or off are convenient, but are more likely to give trouble than the manual type.

When choosing a position for the aerial, the following points should be considered:

(a) The aerial lead should be as short as possible; this means that the aerial should be mounted at the front of the vehicle

(b) The aerial must be mounted as far away from the distributor and HT leads as possible

(c) The part of the aerial which protrudes beneath the mounting point must not foul the roadwheels, or anything else

(d) If possible, the aerial should be positioned so that the coaxial lead does not have to be routed through the engine compartment

(e) The plane of the panel on which the aerial is mounted should not be so steeply angled that the aerial cannot be mounted vertically (in relation to the end-on aspect of the car). Most aerials have a small amount of adjustment available

Having decided on a mounting position, a relatively large hole will have to be made in the panel. The exact size of the hole will depend upon the specific aerial being fitted, although generally the hole required is of $\frac{3}{4}$ in (19 mm) diameter. On metal bodied cars, a tank-cutter of the relevant diameter is the best tool to use for making the hole. This tool needs a small diameter pilot hole drilled through the panel, through which the tool clamping bolt is inserted. When the hole has been made the raw edges should be de-burred with a file and then painted to prevent corrosion.

Fit the aerial according to the manufacturer's instructions. If the aerial is very tall, or if it protrudes beneath the mounting panel for a considerable distance, it is a good idea to fit a stay beneath the aerial and the vehicle frame. This stay can be manufactured from the slotted and drilled metal strips previously mentioned. The stay should be securely screwed or bolted in place. For best reception, it is advisable to fit an earth lead between the aerial and the vehicle frame.

It will probably be necessary to drill one or two holes through bodywork panels in order to feed the aerial lead into the interior of the car. Where this is the case, ensure that the holes are fitted with rubber grommets to protect the cable and to stop possible entry of water.

Positioning and fitting of the speaker depends mainly on its type. Generally, the speaker is designed to fit directly into the aperture already provided in the car. Where this is the case, fitting the speaker is just a matter of removing the protective grille from the aperture and screwing or bolting the speaker in place. Take great care not to damage the speaker diaphragm whilst doing this. It is a good idea to fit a gasket beneath the speaker frame and the mounting panel. In order to prevent vibration, some speakers will already have such a gasket fitted.

If a 'pod' type speaker was supplied with the radio, this can be secured to the mounting panel with self-tapping screws.

When connecting a rear mounted speaker to the radio, the wires should be routed through the vehicle beneath the carpets or floor mats, preferably along the side of the floorpan where they will not be trodden on by passengers. Make the relevant connections as directed by the radio manufacturer.

By now you will have several yards of additional wiring in the car; use PVC tape to secure this wiring out of harm's way. Do not leave electrical leads dangling. Ensure that all new electrical connections are properly made (wires twisted together will not do) and completely secure.

The radio should now be working, but before you pack away your tools it will be necessary to trim the radio to the aerial. Follow the radio manufacturer's instructions regarding this adjustment.

Tape players

Fitting instructions for both cartridge and cassette stereo tape players are the same, and in general the same rules apply as when fitting a radio. Tape players are not usually prone to electrical interference like radios, although it can occur, so positioning is not so critical. If possible, the player should be mounted on an even keel. Also it must be possible for a driver wearing a seat belt to reach the unit in order to change or turn over tapes.

For the best results from speakers designed to be recessed into a panel, mount them so that the back of the speaker protrudes into an enclosed chamber within the car (eg door interiors or the boot cavity).

To fit recessed type speakers in the front doors, first check that there is sufficient room to mount a speaker in each door without it fouling the latch or window winding mechanism. Hold the speaker against the skin of the door and draw a line around the periphery of the speaker. With the speaker removed, draw a second cutting line within the first to allow enough room for the entry of the speaker back, but at the same time providing a broad seat for the speaker flange. When you are sure that the cutting-line is correct, drill a series of holes around its periphery. Pass a hacksaw blade through one of the holes and then cut through the metal between the holes until the centre section of the panel falls out.

De-burr the edges of the hole and then paint the raw metal to prevent corrosion. Cut a corresponding hole in the door trim panel, ensuring that it will be completely covered by the speaker grille. Now drill a hole in the door edge and a corresponding hole in the door surround. These holes are to feed the speaker leads through, so fit grommets. Pass the speaker leads through the door trim, door skin and out through the holes in the side of the door and door surround. Refit the door trim panel and then secure the speaker to the door using self-tapping screws. **Note**: *If the speaker is fitted with a shield to prevent water dripping on it, ensure that this shield is at the top.*

'Pod' type speakers can be fastened to the shelf behind the rear seat, or anywhere offering a corresponding mounting point on each side of the car. If the 'pod' speakers are mounted on each side of the shelf behind the rear seat, it is a good idea to drill several large diameter holes through to the boot cavity, beneath each speaker – this will improve the sound reproduction. 'Pod' speakers sometimes offer a better reproduction quality if they face the rear window (which then acts as a reflector) so it is worthwhile experimenting before finally fixing the speakers.

30 Radios and tape players – suppression of interference (general)

To eliminate buzzes and other unwanted noises costs very little and is not as difficult as sometimes thought. With a modicum of common sense and patience, and following the instructions in the following paragraphs, interference can be virtually eliminated.

The first cause for concern is the generator. The noise this makes over the radio is like an electric mixer and the noise speeds up when you rev up the engine (if you wish to prove the point, you can remove the fan and try it). The remedy for this is simple; connect a 1.0 to 3.0 mfd capacitor between earth (probably the bolt that holds down the generator base) and the *output* terminal on the alternator. This is most important for if it is connected to the small terminal, the generator will probably be damaged permanently (see Fig. 10.19).

A second common cause of electrical interference is the ignition system. Here a 1.0 mfd capacitor must be connected between earth and the SW or – terminal on the coil (see Fig. 10.20). This may stop the tick-tick sound that comes over the speaker. Next comes the spark itself.

There are several ways of curing interference from the ignition HT system. One is the use of carbon-cored HT leads as original equipment. Where copper cable is substituted then you must use the resistive spark plug caps (see Fig. 10.21). These should be of about 10 000 to 15 000 ohm resistance. If due to lack of room these cannot be used, an alternative is to use 'in-line' suppressors. If the interference is not too bad, it may be possible to get away with only one suppressor in the coil-to-distributor line. If the interference does continue (a 'clacking' noise), then modify all HT leads.

At this stage it is advisable to check that the radio and aerial are well earthed, and to see that the aerial plug is pushed well into the set and that the radio is properly trimmed (see preceding Section). In addition, check that the wire which supplies the power to the set is as short as possible. At this stage it is a good idea to check that the fuse is of the correct rating. For most sets this will be about 1 to 2 amps.

At this point, the more usual causes of interference have been suppressed. If the problem still exists, a look at the cause of interference may help to pinpoint the component generating the stray electrical discharges.

The radio picks up electromagnetic waves in the air; now some are made by regular broadcasters and some, which we do not want, are made by the car itself. The home made signals are produced by stray electrical discharges floating around in the car. Common producers of these signals are electrical motors, ie the windscreen wipers, electric screen washers, electric window winders, heater fan or an electric aerial if fitted. Other sources of interference are flashing turn signals and instruments. The remedy for these cases is shown in Fig. 10.22 for an electric motor whose interference is not too bad and Fig. 10.23 for instrument suppression. Turn signals are not normally suppressed. In recent years, radio manufacturers have included in the live line of the radio, in addition to the fuse, an in-line choke. If your circuit lacks one of these, put one in as shown in Fig. 10.24.

All the foregoing components are available from radio stores or accessory stores. If you have an electric clock fitted, this should be suppressed by connecting a 0.5 mfd capacitor directly across it as shown for a motor in Fig. 10.22.

If after all this you are still experiencing radio interference, first assess how bad it is, for the human ear can filter out unobtrusive unwanted noises quite easily. But if you are still adamant about eradicating the noise, then continue.

As a first step, a few experts seem to favour a screen between the radio and the engine. This is OK as far as it goes, literally! The whole

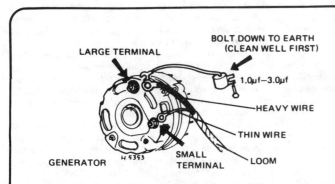

Fig. 10.19 The correct way to connect a capacitor to the generator (Sec 30)

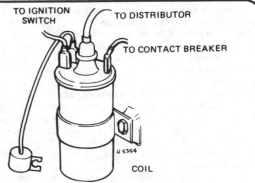

Fig. 10.20 The capacitor must be connected to the ignition switch side of the coil – conventional system only (Sec 30)

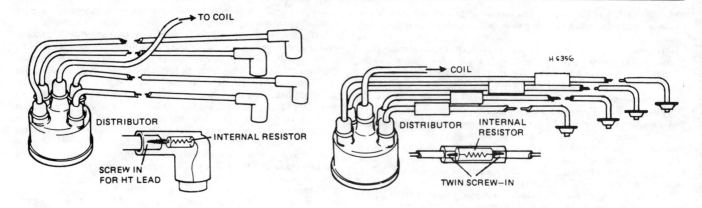

Resistive spark plug caps   'In-line' suppressors

Fig. 10.21 Ignition HT lead suppressors (Sec 30)

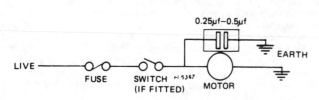

Fig. 10.22 Correct method of suppressing electric motors (Sec 30)

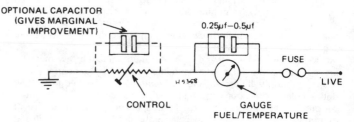

Fig. 10.23 Method of suppressing gauges and their control units (Sec 30)

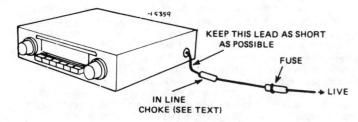

Fig. 10.24 An 'in-line' choke should be fitted into the live supply lead as close to the unit as possible (Sec 30)

set is screened anyway and if interference can get past that then a small piece of aluminium is not going to stop it.

A more sensible way of screening is to discover if interference is coming down the wires. First, take the live lead; interference can get between the set and the choke (hence the reason for keeping the wires short). One remedy here is to screen the wire and this is done by buying screened wire and fitting that. The loudspeaker lead could be screened also to prevent pick-up getting back to the radio although this is unlikely.

Without doubt, the worst source of radio interference comes from the ignition HT leads, even if they have been suppressed. The ideal way of suppressing these is to slide screening tubes over the leads themselves. As this is impractical, we can place an aluminium shield over the majority of the lead areas. In a vee or twin-cam engine this is relatively easy but for a straight engine, the results are not particularly good.

Now for the really difficult cases, here are a few tips to try out. Where metal comes into contact with metal, an electrical disturbance is caused which is why good clean connections are essential. To remove interference due to overlapping or butting panels, you must

bridge the join with a wide braided earth strap (like that from the frame to the engine/transmission). The most common moving parts that could create noise and should be strapped are, in order of importance:

(a) Silencer to frame
(b) Exhaust pipe to engine block and frame
(c) Air cleaner to frame
(d) Front and rear bumpers to frame
(e) Steering column to frame
(f) Bonnet and boot lids to frame

These faults are most pronounced when the engine is idling or labouring under load. Although the moving parts are already connected with nuts, bolts, etc, these do tend to rust and corrode, thus creating a high resistance interference source.

If you have a 'ragged' sounding pulse when mobile, this could be wheel or tyre static. This can be cured by buying some anti-static powder and sprinkling inside the tyres.

If the interference takes the shape of a high pitched screeching noise that changes its note when the car is in motion and only comes now and then, this could be related to the aerial, especially if it is of the telescopic or whip type. This source can be cured quite simply by pushing a small rubber ball on top of the aerial as this breaks the electric field before it can form; but it would be much better to buy yourself a new aerial of a reputable brand. If, on the other hand, you are getting a loud rushing sound every time you brake, then this is brake static. This effect is most prominent on hot dry days and is cured only by fitting a special kit, which is quite expensive.

In conclusion, it is pointed out that it is relatively easy and therefore cheap, to eliminate 95 per cent of all noise, but to eliminate the final 5 per cent is time and money consuming. It is up to the individual to decide if it is worth it. Please remember also, that you cannot get a concert hall performance out of a cheap radio.

Finally, cassette players and eight track players are not usually affected by car noise, but in a very bad case, the best remedies are the first three suggestions plus using a 3 to 5 amp choke in the live line and in difficult cases, screening the live and speaker wires.

Note: *If your car is fitted with electronic ignition, then it is not recommended that either the spark plug resistors or the ignition coil capacitor be fitted as these may damage the system. Most electronic ignition units have built-in suppression and should, therefore, not cause interference.*

31 Central door locking system – general

1   As from late 1980 a central door locking system may be fitted. The wiring diagram is given in Fig. 10.47 and the system comprises a control switch switch and separate solenoids to operate the door locks.

2   To remove a door lock switch first remove the door trim panel as described in Chapter 12. Disconnect the remote control rod and the wiring plug, then remove the screws and withdraw the door lock. Remove the screws and withdraw the switch from the door lock. Refitting is a reversal of removal.

3   To remove a door lock solenoid, remove the trim panel as described in Chapter 12, and disconnect the remote control rod. Disconnect the solenoid wiring plug, unscrew the mounting nuts, and withdraw the solenoid through the aperture in the door. Refitting is a reversal of removal.

Wiring diagrams commence overleaf

Fig. 10.25 Key to wiring diagram for pre-1980 right-hand drive models

1 Side turn signal light (UK models only)
2 Horn
3 Front combination light
 -1 Turn signal light
 -2 Parking light
4 Headlight
 -1 (Low beam)
 -2 (High beam)
5 Earth
6 Headlight
 -1 (Low beam)
 -2 (High beam)
7 Front combination light
 -1 Turn signal light
 -2 Parking light
8 Horn
9 Side turn signal light (UK models only)
10 Headlight cleaner motor (If equipped)
11 Oil pressure switch
12 Alternator
13 Starter
14 Battery electrolyte low level sensor (If equipped)
15 Fusible link
16 Brake fluid low level switch (If equipped)
17 Alternator warning light relay
18 Ignition coil
19 Frost switch (If equipped)
20 Thermo switch (If equipped)
21 Thermo control relay (If equipped)
22 'Register (for air conditioner)
23 Short switch (for air conditioner)
24 Air conditioner switch (If equipped)
25 Air conditioner indicator light (If equipped)
26 Slow fuel cut valve
27 Magnet clutch (If equipped)
28 Air conditioner solenoid valve (If equipped)
29 Water temperature gauge unit
30 Connector
31 Interior light
32 Light checker relay
33 Kickdown switch (For automatic transmission)
34 Fan switch (If equipped)
35 Fan motor (If equipped)
36 Connector
37 Kickdown solenoid valve (For automatic transmission)
38 Reversing light switch
39 Earth
40 Connector
41 Oscillator
42 Flasher unit

43 Intermittent wiper relay
44 Horn relay
45 Stop light switch
46 Fuse holder (For headlight cleaner)
47 Fuse holder (For power window)
48 Windscreen washer motor
49 Washer fluid low level switch (If equipped)
50 Windscreen wiper motor
51 Remote control mirror (UK models only)
52 Headlight cleaner switch (If equipped)
53 Remote control mirror (UK models only)
54 Remote boot lid release switch (If equipped)
55 Fusebox
56 Parking brake switch
57 Inhibitor switch (For automatic transmission)
58 Select lever illumination light (For automatic transmission)
59 Stereo (If equipped)
60 Radio (If equipped)
61 Speaker (If equipped)
62 Speaker (If equipped)
63 Rear window heater switch (If equipped)
64 Connector
65 Glovebox light (If equipped)
66 Glovebox light switch (If equipped)
67 Cigarette lighter
68 Earth
69 Clock (If equipped)
70 Clock light)If equipped)
71 Heater control illumination light (If equipped)
72 Chime (If equipped)
73 Ignition switch
74 Instrument panel illumination light control
75 Combination meter
 -1 Instrument panel illumination light
 -2 High beam indicator light
 -3 Turn signal indicator light
 -4 Fuel gauge
 -5 Voltage regulator
 -6 Water temperature gauge
 -7 Tachometer (If equipped)
 -8 Oil pressure warning light
76 Combination meter
 -1 Turn signal light
 -2 Alternator warning light
 -3 Parking brake and brake fluid low level warning light (If equipped)
 -4 Battery electrolyte low level warning light (If equipped)
 -5 Low fuel level warning light (If equipped)

 -6 Tail light malfunction warning light (If equipped)
 -7 Stop light malfunction warning light (If equipped)
 -8 Washer fluid low level warning light (If equipped)
77 Combination switch
 -1 Windscreen washer switch
 -2 Windscreen wiper switch
 -3 Light switch
 -4 Dimmer switch
 -5 Passing switch
 -6 Turn signal switch
 -7 Hazard switch
 -8 Horn switch
78 Connector
79 Connector
80 Earth
81 Power window motor (for UK models, if equipped)
82 Power window motor (for UK models, if equipped)
83 Power window switch (for UK models, if equipped)
84 Power window switch (for UK models, if equipped)
85 Power window motor (for UK models, if equipped)
86 Power window motor (for UK models, if equipped)
87 Power window motor (for UK models, if equipped)
88 Earth
89 Door switch
90 Door switch
91 Fuel pump
92 Luggage compartment light
93 Luggage compartment light switch
94 Rear window heater earth (If equipped)
95 Rear window heater (If equipped)
96 Door switch
97 Earth
98 Fuel tank unit
99 Door switch
100 Rear combination light
 -1 Turn signal light
 -2 Reversing light
 -3 Stop light
 -4 Tail light
101 Remote boot lid release motor (If equipped)
102 Number plate light
103 Rear combination light
 -1 Turn signal light
 -2 Reversing light
 -3 Stop light
 -4 Tail light

Note: The wiring is traced through the harness using the small numbers in circles in each wire where it enters the harness – these indicate the other components to which the particular item is connected

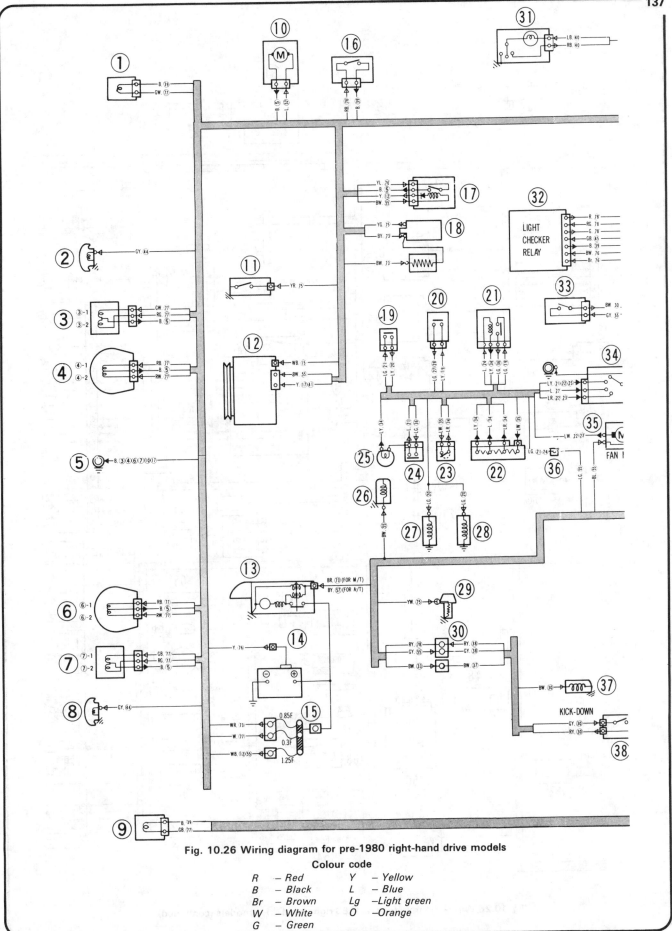

Fig. 10.26 Wiring diagram for pre-1980 right-hand drive models

Colour code

R	– Red	Y	– Yellow
B	– Black	L	– Blue
Br	– Brown	Lg	– Light green
W	– White	O	– Orange
G	– Green		

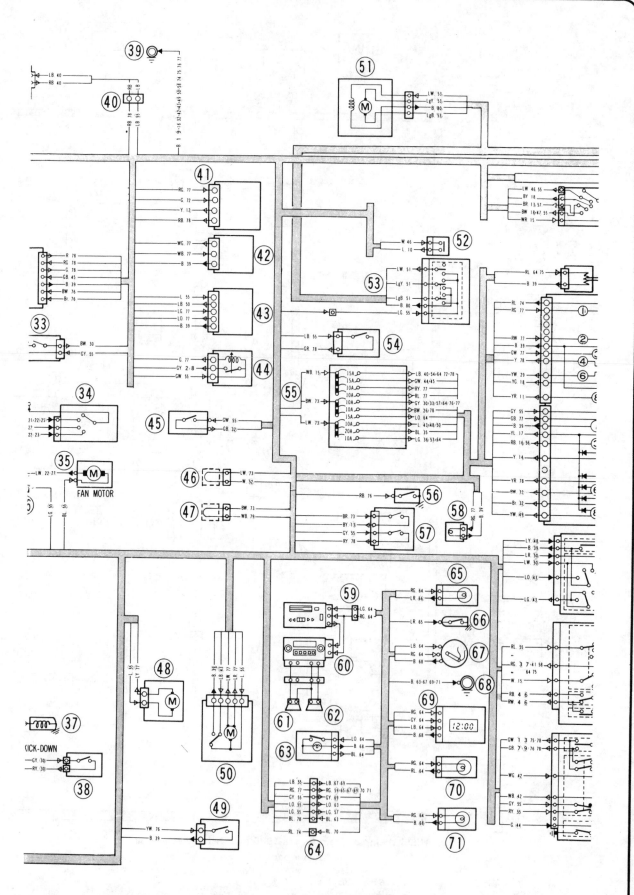

Fig. 10.26 Wiring diagram for pre-1980 right-hand drive models (continued)

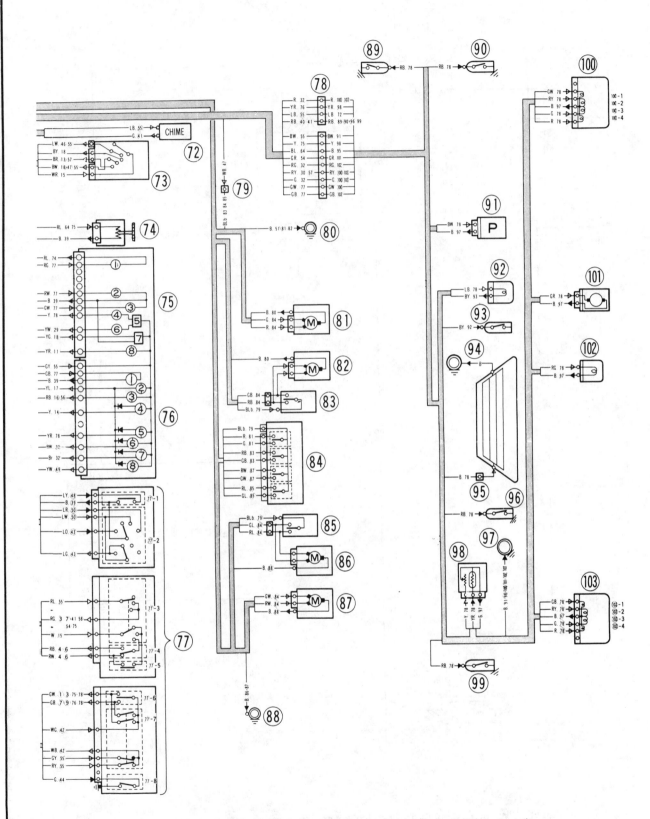

Fig. 10.26 Wiring diagram for pre-1980 right-hand drive models (continued)

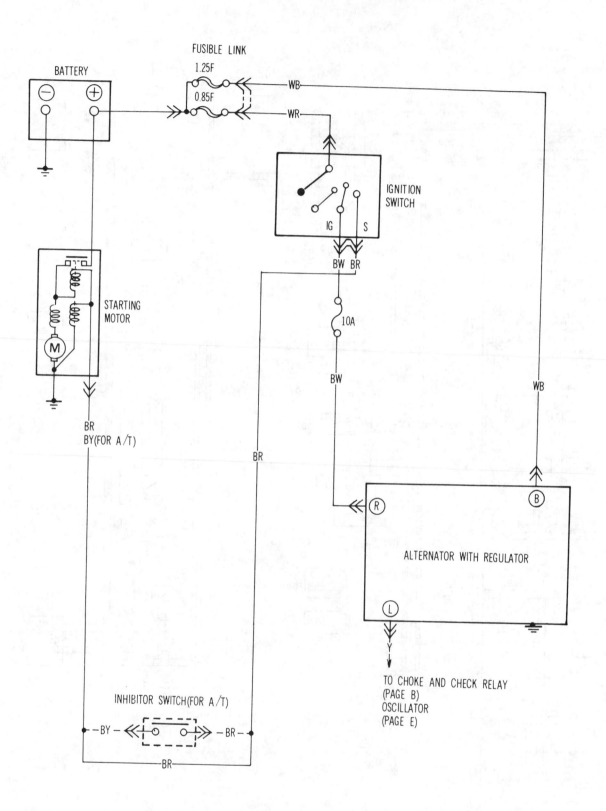

Fig. 10.27 Wiring diagram (A) for charging and starting systems on North American models

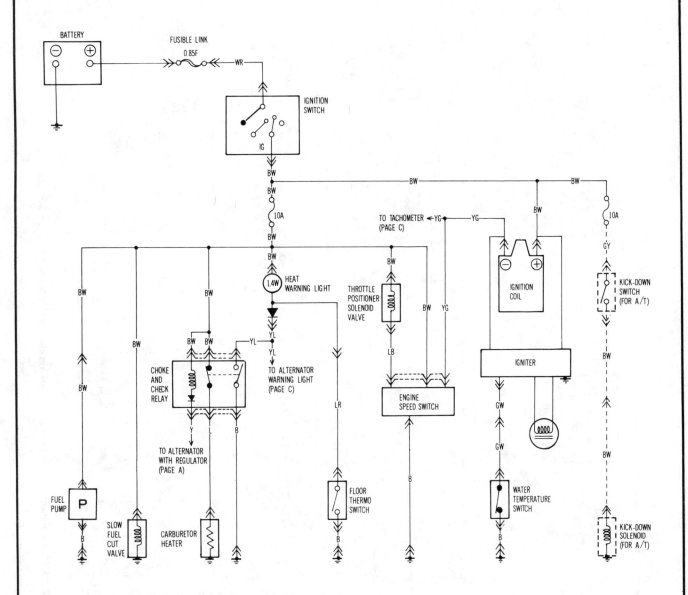

Fig. 10.28 Wiring diagram (B) for ignition, emission control and fuel systems on North American models

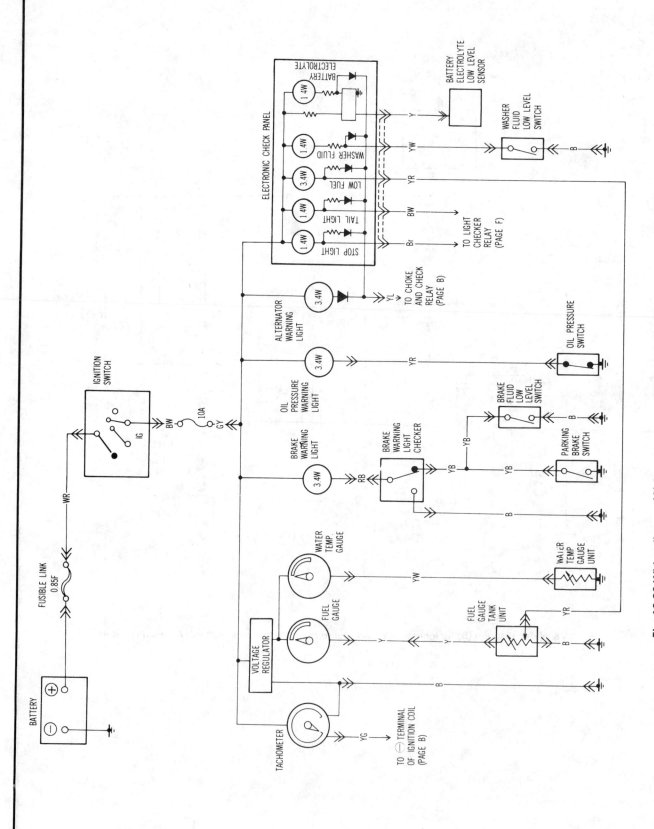

Fig. 10.29 Wiring diagram (C) for meter and warning systems on North American models

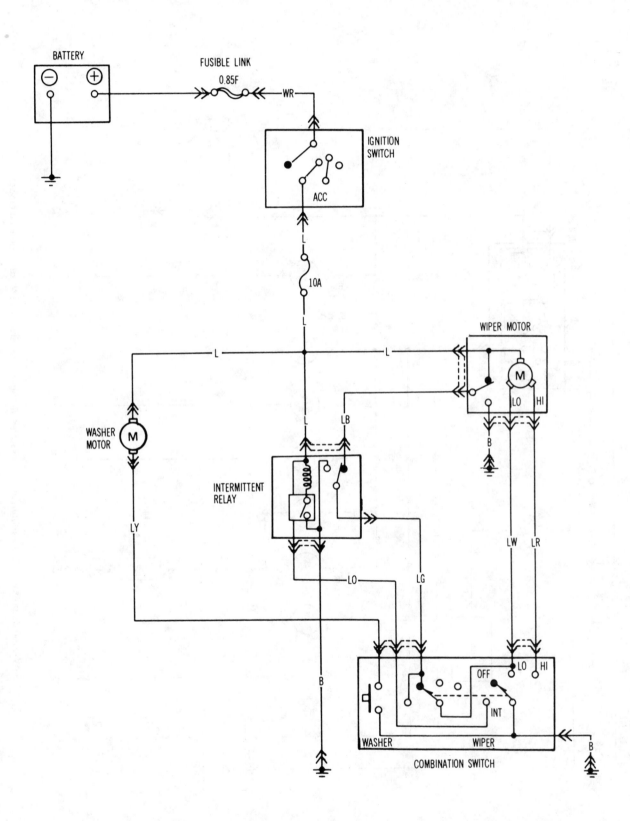

Fig. 10.30 Wiring diagram (D) for wiper and washer systems on North American models

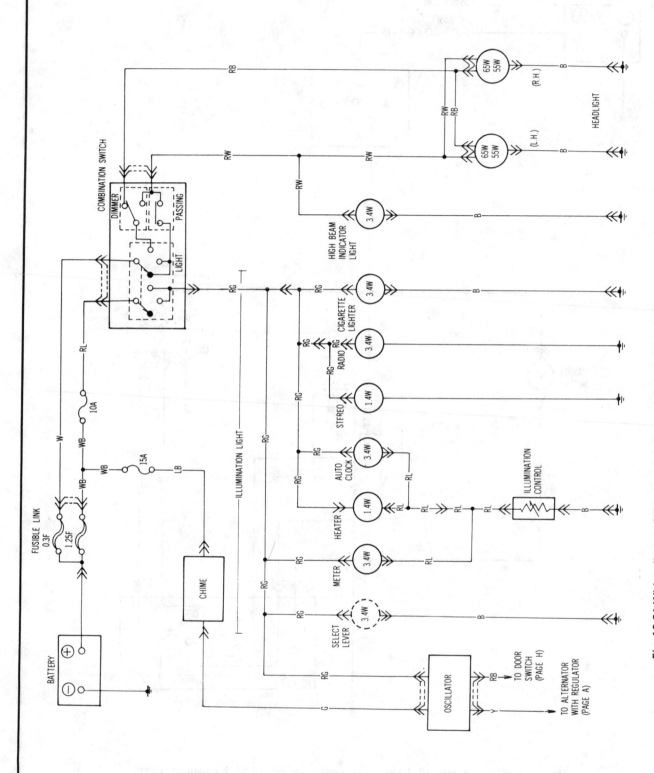

Fig. 10.31 Wiring diagram (E) for headlight and accessories illumination systems on North American models

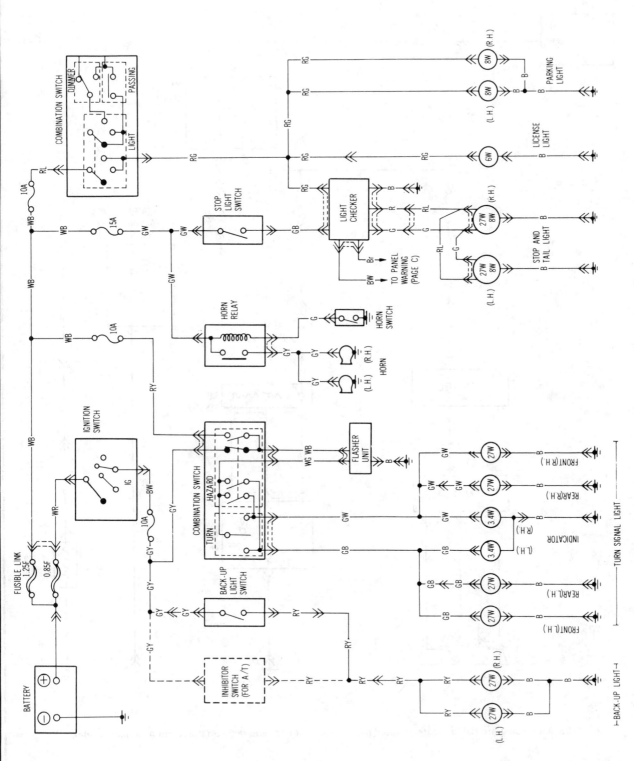

Fig. 10.32 Wiring diagram (F) for main lighting and horn systems on North American models

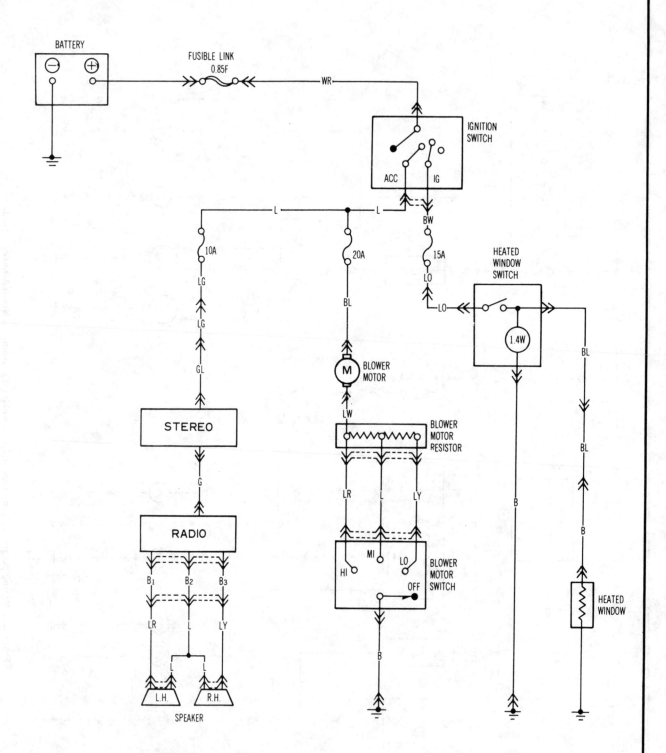

Fig. 10.33 Wiring diagram (G) for heater, heated rear window, stereo, and radio on the North American models

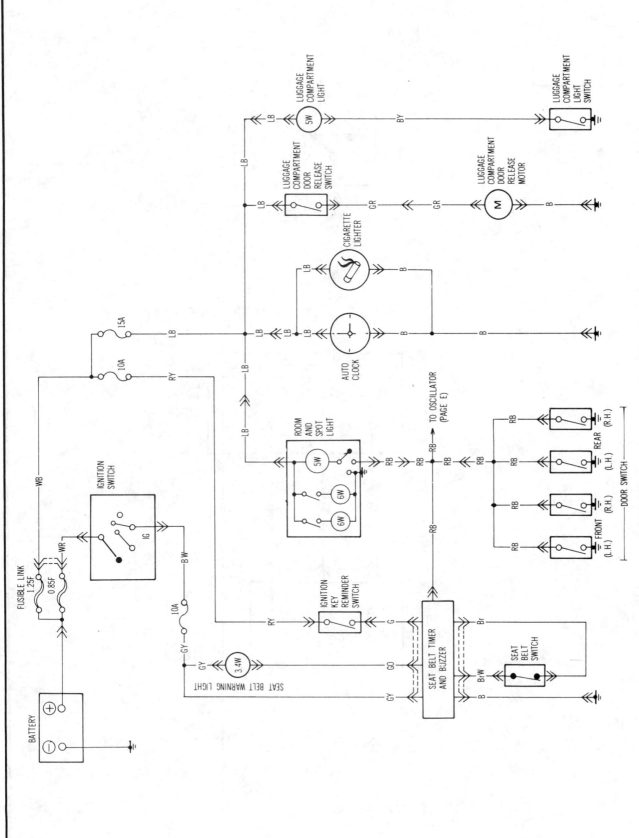

Fig. 10.34 Wiring diagram (H) for general accessories on North American models

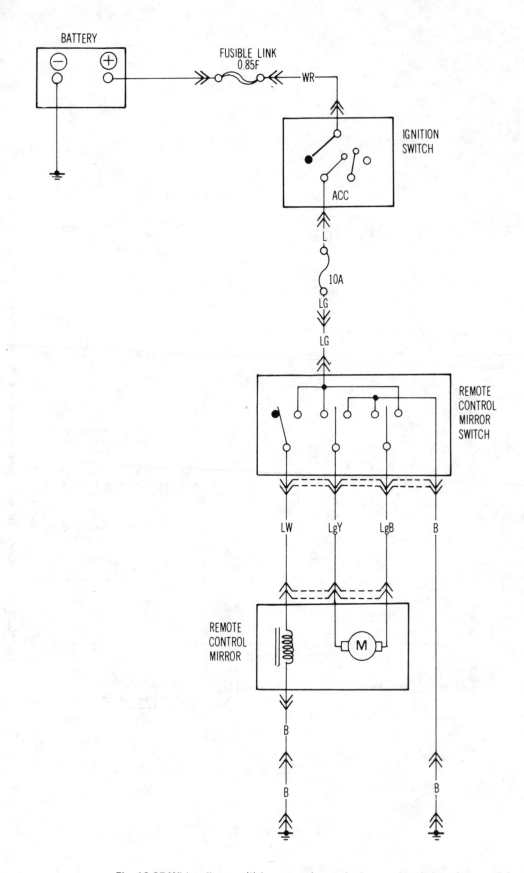

Fig. 10.35 Wiring diagram (I) for remote control mirror on North American models

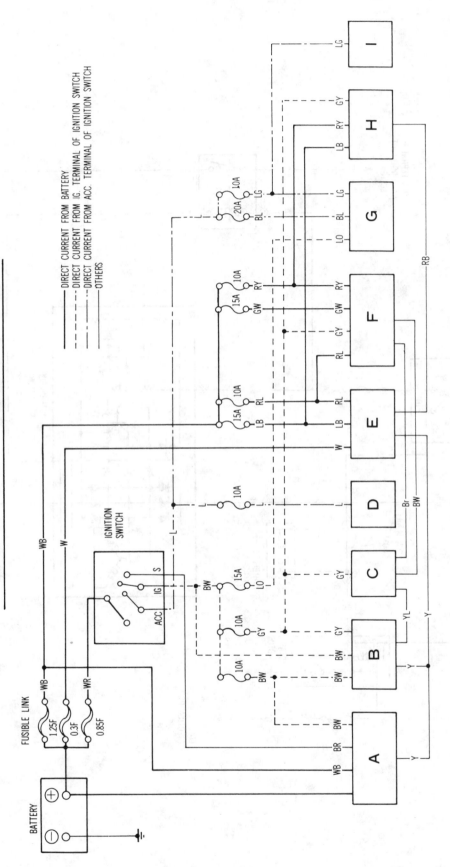

SUB SYSTEM CONNECTIONS

Fig. 10.36 Wiring diagram showing sub-system connections on North American models

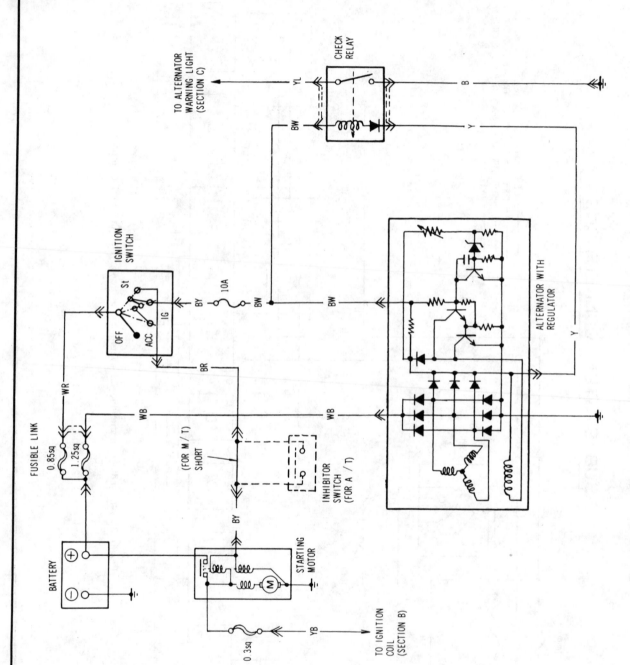

Fig. 10.37 Wiring diagram (A) for charging and starting systems on UK models (1980 on)

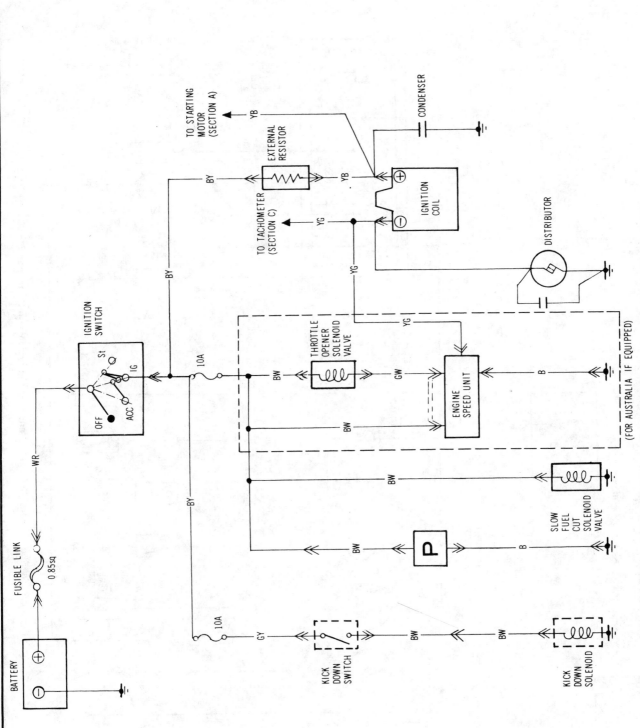

Fig. 10.38 Wiring diagram (B) for ignition and fuel systems on UK models (1980 on)

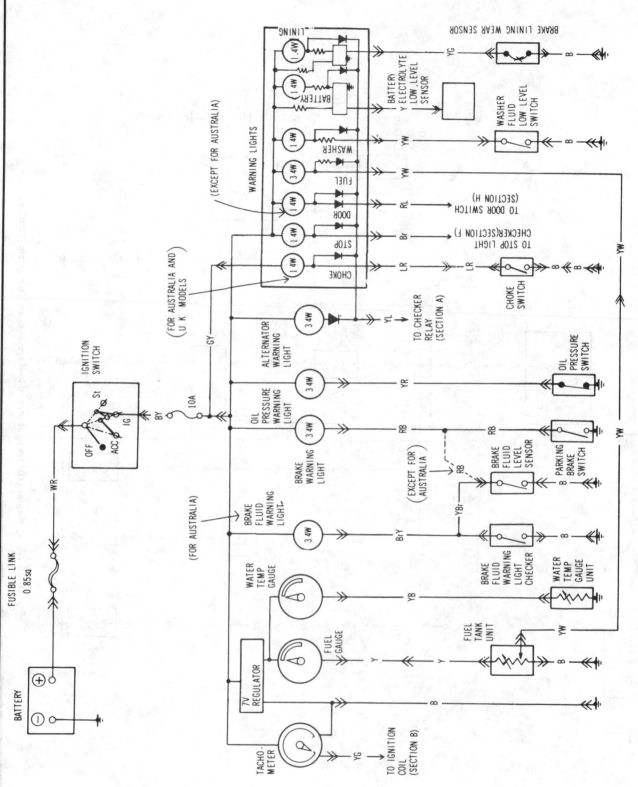

Fig. 10.39 Wiring diagram (C) for meter and warning systems on UK models (1980 on)

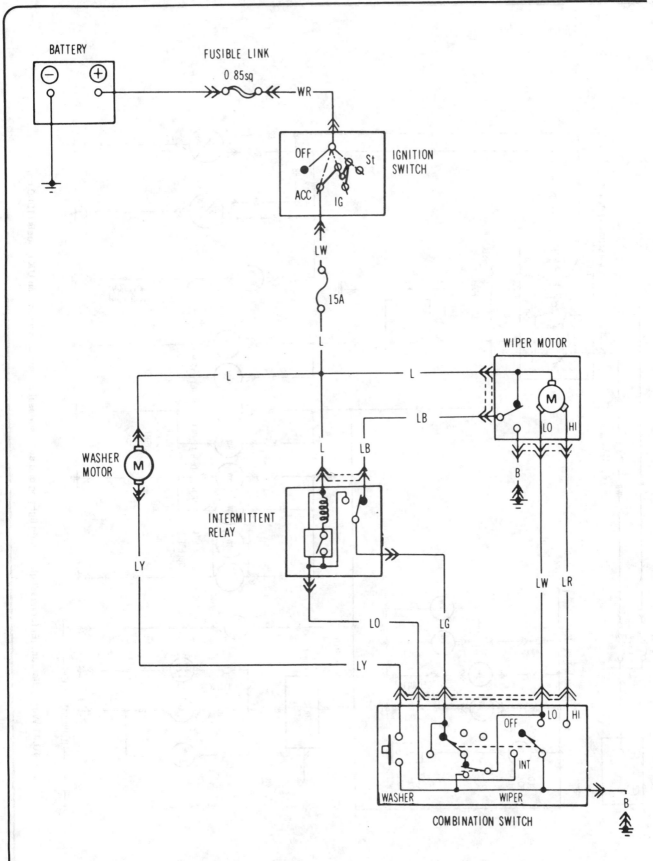

Fig. 10.40 Wiring diagram (D) for wiper and washer systems on UK models (1980 on)

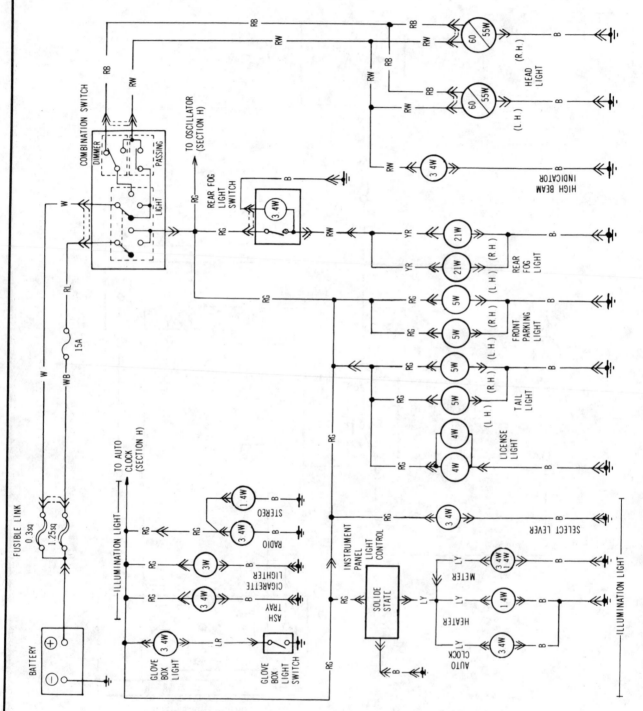

Fig. 10.41 Wiring diagram (E) for headlights, main lighting and accessories illumination systems on UK models (1980 on)

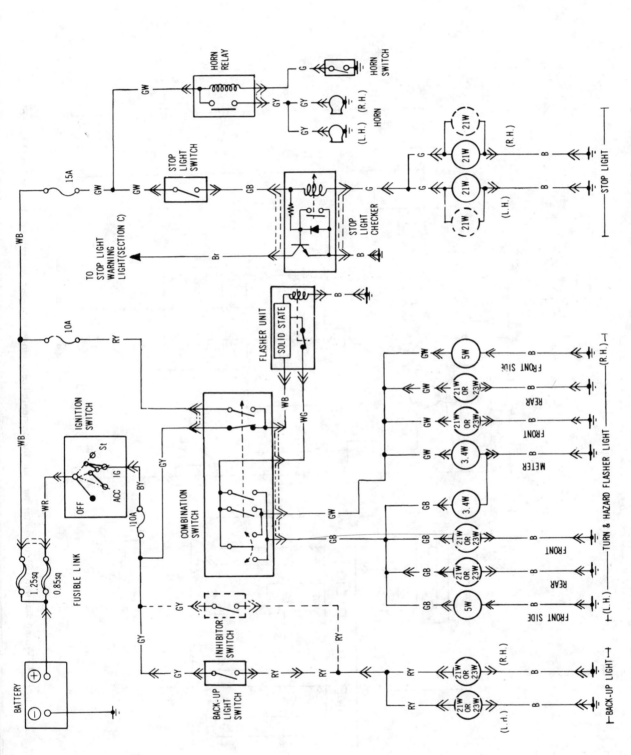

Fig. 10.42 Wiring diagram (F) for hazard flasher, additional main lighting and horn systems on UK models (1980 on)

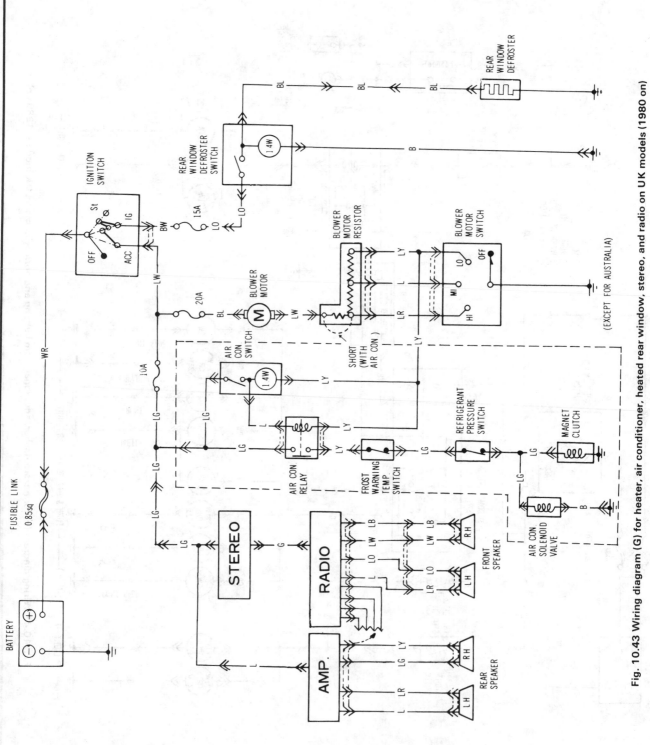

Fig. 10.43 Wiring diagram (G) for heater, air conditioner, heated rear window, stereo, and radio on UK models (1980 on)

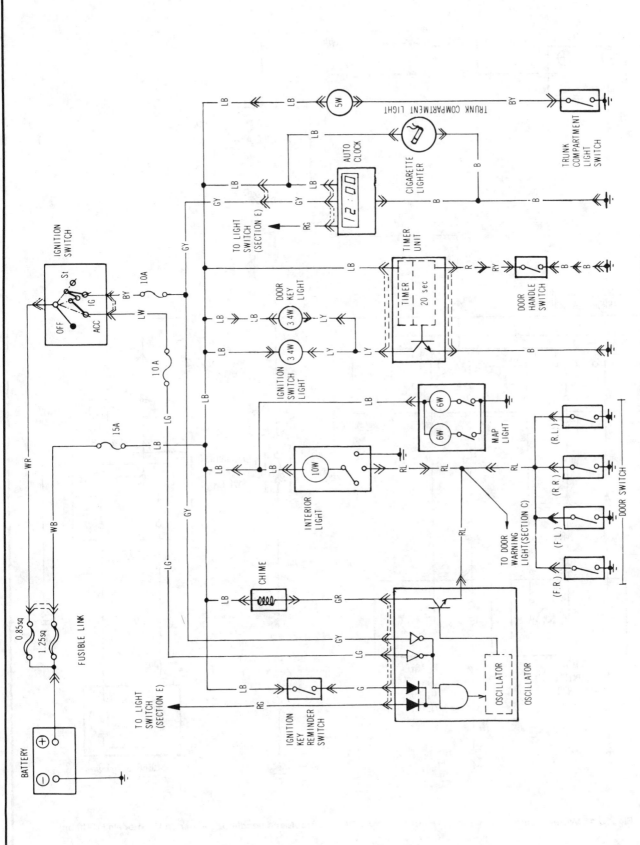

Fig. 10.44 Wiring diagram (H) for general accessories on UK models (1980 on)

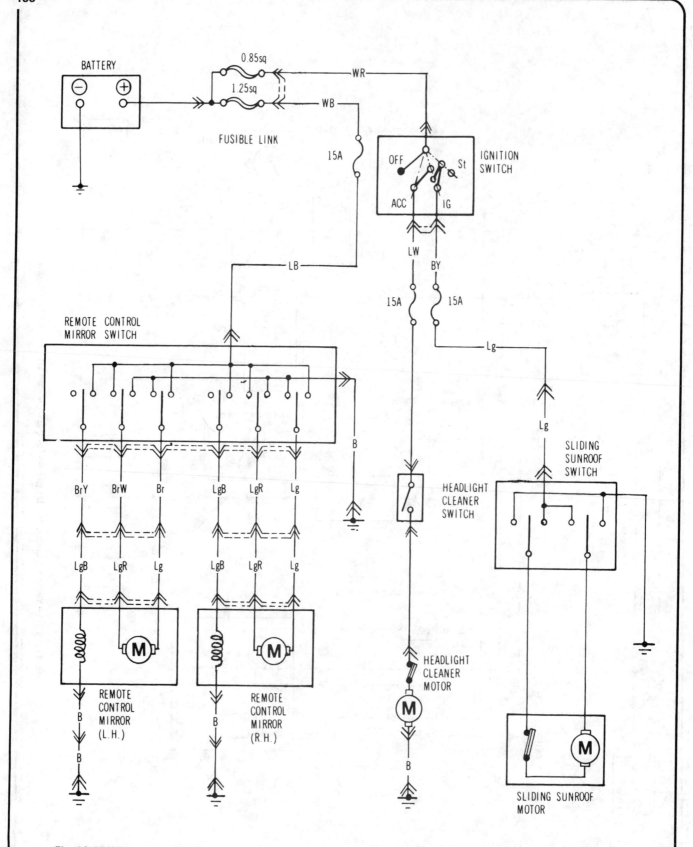

Fig. 10.45 Wiring diagram (I) for remote control mirror, sliding sunroof, and headlight cleaner on UK models (1980 on)

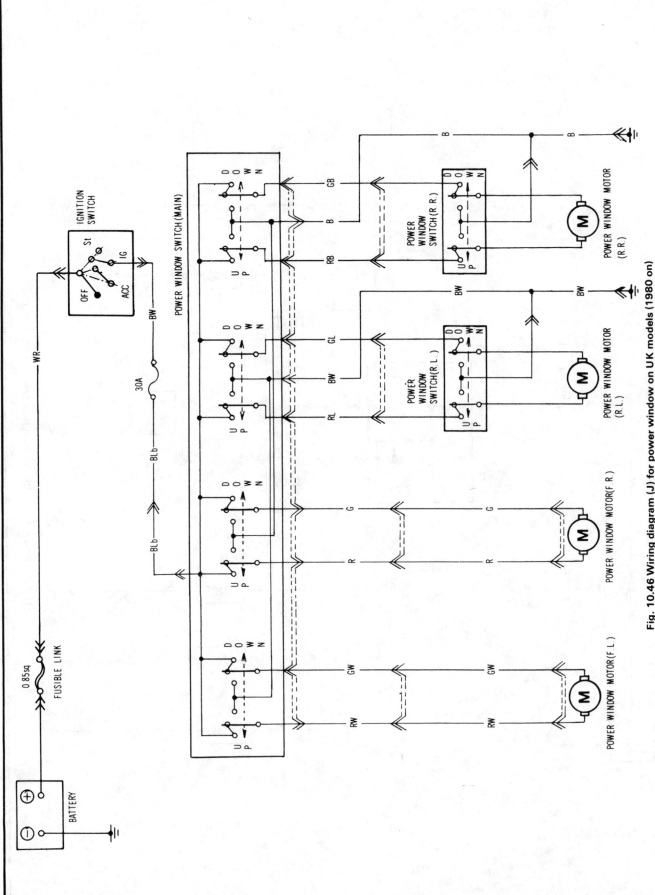

Fig. 10.46 Wiring diagram (J) for power window on UK models (1980 on)

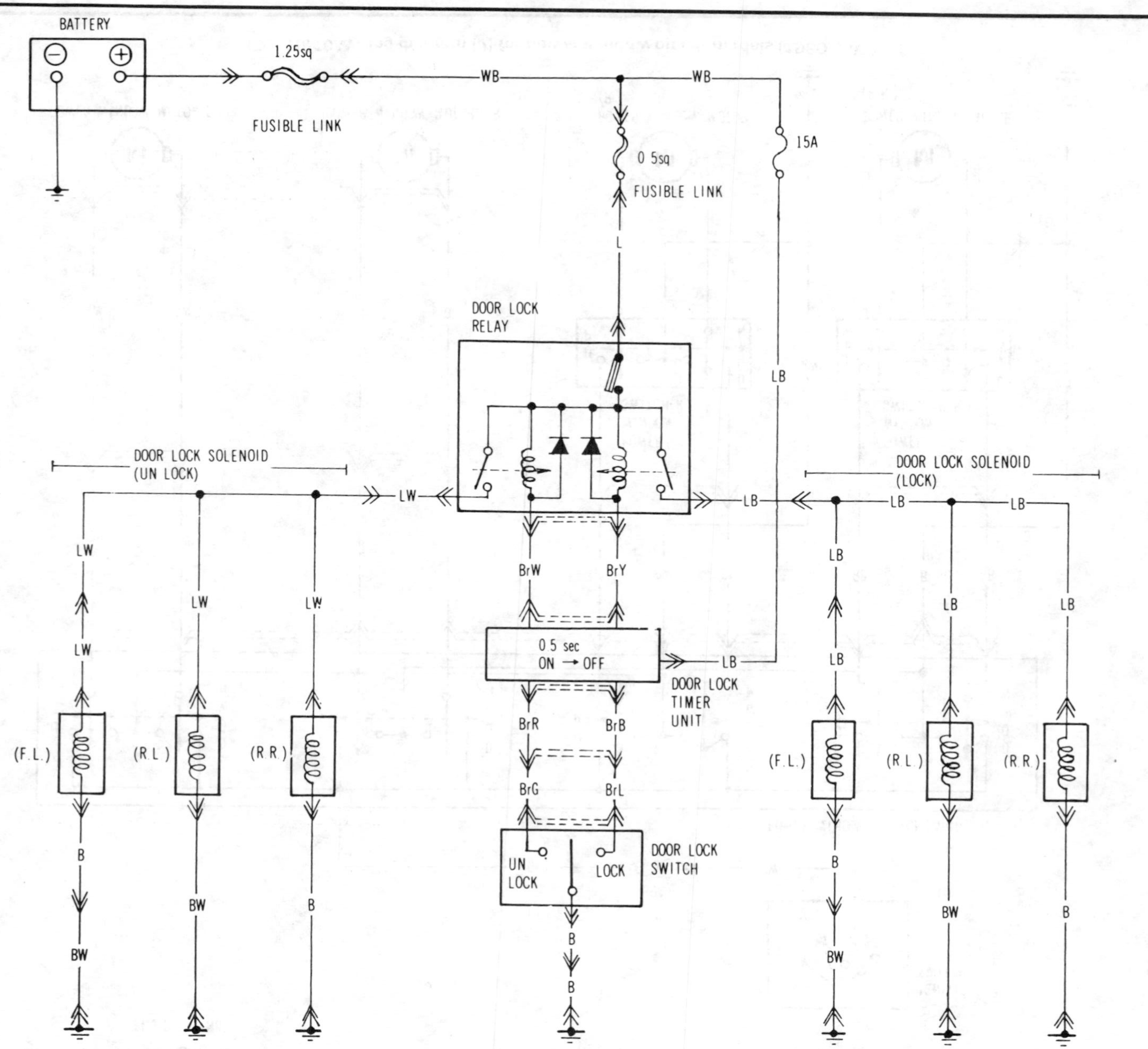

Fig. 10.47 Wiring diagram (K) for door lock system on UK models (1980 on)

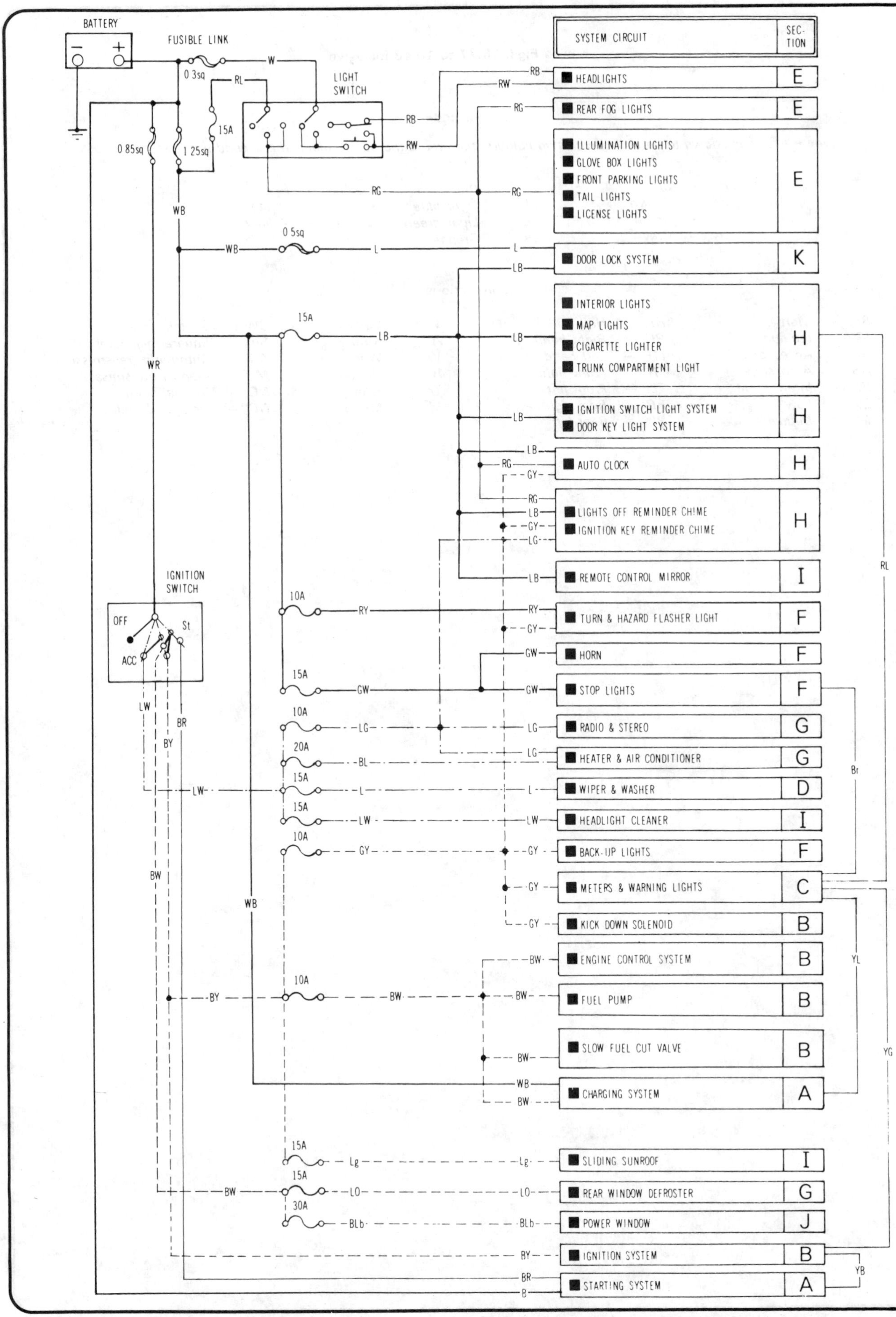

BATTERY

FUSIBLE LINK

0 3sq

RL

W

15A

0 85sq   1 25sq

WB

LIGHT SWITCH

RB

RW

WR

0 5sq

WB   L

15A

LB

IGNITION SWITCH

OFF   St

ACC

LW   BR

BY

10A   RY

15A   GW

10A   LG

20A   BL

15A   L

15A   LW

10A   GY

BW

10A   BY   BW

WB
BW

15A   Lg

15A   BW   LO

30A   BLb

BY

BR
B

SYSTEM CIRCUIT	SEC-TION
■ HEADLIGHTS	E
■ REAR FOG LIGHTS	E
■ ILLUMINATION LIGHTS ■ GLOVE BOX LIGHTS ■ FRONT PARKING LIGHTS ■ TAIL LIGHTS ■ LICENSE LIGHTS	E
■ DOOR LOCK SYSTEM	K
■ INTERIOR LIGHTS ■ MAP LIGHTS ■ CIGARETTE LIGHTER ■ TRUNK COMPARTMENT LIGHT	H
■ IGNITION SWITCH LIGHT SYSTEM ■ DOOR KEY LIGHT SYSTEM	H
■ AUTO CLOCK	H
■ LIGHTS OFF REMINDER CHIME ■ IGNITION KEY REMINDER CHIME	H
■ REMOTE CONTROL MIRROR	I
■ TURN & HAZARD FLASHER LIGHT	F
■ HORN	F
■ STOP LIGHTS	F
■ RADIO & STEREO	G
■ HEATER & AIR CONDITIONER	G
■ WIPER & WASHER	D
■ HEADLIGHT CLEANER	I
■ BACK-UP LIGHTS	F
■ METERS & WARNING LIGHTS	C
■ KICK DOWN SOLENOID	B
■ ENGINE CONTROL SYSTEM	B
■ FUEL PUMP	B
■ SLOW FUEL CUT VALVE	B
■ CHARGING SYSTEM	A
■ SLIDING SUNROOF	I
■ REAR WINDOW DEFROSTER	G
■ POWER WINDOW	J
■ IGNITION SYSTEM	B
■ STARTING SYSTEM	A

RB   RW
RG
RB
RW

RG   RG

L

LB   LB

LB

LB
RG   GY

RG
LB
GY
LG

LB

RY
GY

GW

GW

LG
LG

L

LW

GY   GY

GY

GY

BW

BW

BW

WB
BW

Lg

LO

BLb

RL

Br

YL

YG

YB

Fig. 10.48 Wiring diagram showing sub-system connections on UK models (1980 on)

Key to Figs. 10.27 to 10.48 inclusive

Colour code

Where a wire is shown to be coded with two colours, the first is the basic colour, the second is the stripe colour

B	–	Black	L	–	Blue	R	– Red
Br	–	Brown	Lb	–	Light blue	W	– White
G	–	Green	Lg	–	Light green	Y	– Yellow
Gy	–	Grey	O	–	Orange		

Abbreviations

St	–	Start	Hi	–	High	V	–	Volt	SW	– Switch
IG	–	Ignition	RH	–	Right-hand	A	–	Amp	Sq	– Square millimeter
ACC	–	Accessory	LH	–	Left-hand	W	–	Watt	A/T	– Automatic transmission
AS	–	Auto stop	FR	–	Front right	R	–	Resistance	M/T	– Manual transmission
INT	–	Intermittent	FL	–	Front left	Tr	–	Transistor	NO	– Normal open
Lo	–	Low	RR	–	Rear right	M	–	Motor	NC	– Normal closed
Mi	–	Middle	RL	–	Rear left					

32 Fault diagnosis – electrical system

Symptom	Reason(s)
Starter motor fails to turn engine	Battery discharged Battery defective internally Battery terminal leads loose or earth lead not securely attached to body Loose or broken connections in starter motor circuit Starter motor solenoid switch faulty Starter brushes badly worn, sticking or brush wires loose Commutator dirty, worn or burnt Starter motor armature faulty Field coils earthed
Starter motor turns engine very slowly	Battery in discharged condition Starter brushes badly worn, sticking or brush wires loose Loose wires in starter motor circuit
Starter motor operates without turning engine	Pinion or flywheel gear teeth broken or worn
Starter motor noisy or engagement excessively rough	Pinion or flywheel teeth broken or worn Starter motor retaining bolts loose
Battery will not hold charge for more than a few days	Battery defective internally Electrolyte level too weak or too low Battery plates heavily sulphated Fanbelt slipping Alternator faulty
Horn will not operate or operates intermittently	Loose connections Defective switch Defective relay Defective horn
Horns blow continually	Faulty relay Relay wiring earthed Horn button stuck (earthed)
Lights do not come on, or come on but fade out	If engine not running, battery discharged Light bulb filament burnt out, or bulbs or sealed beam units broken Wire connections loose, disconnected or broken Light switch shorting or otherwise faulty
Lights give very poor illumination	Lamp glasses dirty Lamps badly out of adjustment
Lights work erratically – flashing on and off, especially over bumps	Battery terminals or earth connection loose Lights not earthing properly Contacts in light switch faulty
Wiper motor fails to work	Blown fuse Wire connections loose, disconnected, or broken Brushes badly worn Armature worn or faulty Field coils faulty
Wiper motor works very slowly and takes excessive current	Commutator dirty, greasy or burnt Armature bearings dirty or unaligned Armature badly worn or faulty
Wiper motor works slowly and takes little current	Brushes badly worn Commutator dirty, greasy or burnt Armature badly worn or faulty
Fuel and temperature gauge gives no reading	Wiring to gauges disconnected Voltage stabiliser faulty Fuel gauge tank unit faulty Temperature gauge transmitter faulty Gauges faulty
Fuel or temperature gauge gives maximum reading all the time	Wire from gauge to tank unit or transmitter earthed Fuel gauge tank unit faulty Temperature gauge transmitter faulty

Chapter 11 Suspension and steering

Refer to Chapter 13 for revisions and information related to 1982 models

Contents

Specifications

Front suspension

Type	Independent; MacPherson struts and coil springs, with anti-roll bar

Coil spring free length:
UK models	368 mm (14.49 in)
North America, Australia and Sweden models	370.5 mm (14.59 in)

Rear suspension

Type	Trailing lower arms, upper links, coil springs, Panhard rod, telescopic gas filled shock absorbers, anti-roll bar (on some models)

Coil spring free length:
Pre-1980 models	335 mm (13.19 in)
1980 on models	352 mm (13.86 in)

Steering

Type	Recirculating ball nut
Reduction ratio – standard	19.5 : 1 to 23.5 : 1 (variable)
– power steering	17.8 : 1
Sector-to-rack clearance	0 to 0.1 mm (0 to 0.004 in)

Worm bearing preload torque:
Without sector and column bush	2 to 5 kgf cm (1.7 to 4.3 lbf in)
With sector and column bush	6 to 12 kgf cm (5.2 to 10.4 lbf in)
Tilt steering	6 to 9 kgf cm (5.2 to 7.8 lbf in)
Maximum sector shaft-to-bush clearance	0.10 mm (0.004 in)
Sector shaft-to-adjusting screw clearance	0 to 0.10 mm (0 to 0.004 in)
Lubricant – standard	SAE 90EP hypoid gear oil
– power steering	M2 C33 F (Type F)
Maximum balljoint endplay	1.0 mm (0.04 in)

Front wheel alignment

King pin inclination:
UK models	10° 50′
North American models	10° 40′

Camber:
UK models	1° 00'
North American models	1° 15' ± 30'
Maximum camber variation side to side:	30'

Castor:
UK models	3° 10'
1979 North American models	3° 00'

1980 North American models:
RH	3° 40' ± 45'
LH	3° 10' ± 45'
Maximum castor variation side to side	40'
Toe-in	0 to 6 mm (0 to 0.24 in)

Wheels and tyres

Roadwheels:
1600 models	Pressed steel 5J x 13
2000 models	Pressed steel 5½J x 13
Coupe models	Alloy 5½J x 13
TWR models	Alloy 6J x 13

Tyres:
1600 models	6.45-13-4PR, 165 SR 13
2000 models	185/70 SR 13, 185/70 HR 13

Tyre pressures:

UK models
Front	26 lbf in² (1.8 kgf/cm²)
Rear	28 lbf/in² (2.0 kgf/cm²)
North American and Australian models — front and rear	26 lbf/in² (1.8 kgf/cm²)

Torque wrench settings

Front suspension

	lbf ft	Nm
Suspension arm to crossmember	35	47
Lower balljoint	57	77
Steering arm to strut	57	77
Anti-roll bar front mounting	42	57
Shock absorber piston rod to mounting	53	71
Shock absorber seal cap nut	83	112
Shock absorber piston rod nut	8	10
Suspension arm to steering arm	53	71
Radius arm to suspension arm	53	71

Rear suspension

	lbf ft	Nm
Shock absorber lower mounting	53	71
Shock absorber bracket:		
Bolt	29	39
Nut	33	44
Lower arm to axle casing	66	89
Lower arm to underbody	66	89
Upper link to axle casing	66	89
Upper link to flange	66	89
Panhard rod to axle casing	66	89
Panhard rod to underbody	66	89
Anti-roll bar rear mounting	29	39

Steering

	lbf ft	Nm
Steering wheel nut	36	48
Steering gear to body	36	48
Pitman arm to sector shaft	73	98
Idler to body	36	48
Idler arm to centre link	22	29
Pitman arm to centre link	28	37
Tie-rod to centre link	28	37
Tie-rod to steering arm	28	37
Tie-rod locknut	55	74
Wheel bolts	65 to 80	88 to 108

1 General description

The front suspension is of the independent MacPherson strut type incorporating coil springs and an anti-roll bar. The hydraulic telescopic shock absorbers are an integral part of the struts.

The rear suspension is of trailing arm type with coil springs bearing on the lower arms. Upper links control the up-and-down attitude of the rear axle, and a Panhard rod controls the side-to-side movement. Gas filled telescopic shock absorbers are fitted and an anti-roll bar is fitted to some models.

The steering is of recirculating ball nut type. The centre link, which is mounted behind the front suspension crossmember, connects the Pitman arm to the idler arm, and two side tie-rods are also fitted. Later models may be fitted with a tilt steering column and power steering. The power steering system comprises a hydraulic pump driven by the engine and a steering gear which assists the steering movement by hydraulic pressure.

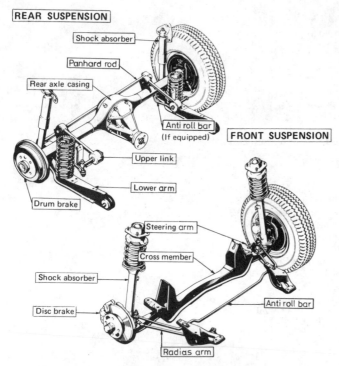

Fig. 11.1 Front and rear suspension components (Sec 1)

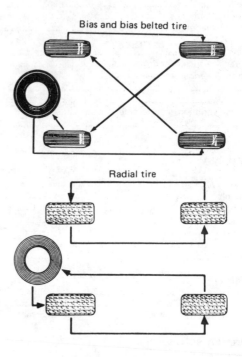

Fig. 11.2 Tyre rotation chart (Sec 2)

2 Maintenance and inspection

1   At the intervals specified in the Routine Maintenance Section, check the suspension and steering for wear and damage, and renew any components as necessary.
2   At the same time, check the tightness of all steering and suspension nuts and bolts in accordance with the torque figures listed in the Specifications.
3   Check the front tyres every 3000 miles (5000 km) for irregular wear, and if evident, check and adjust the front wheel alignment.
4   Check and, if necessary, adjust the tyre pressures every week.
5   Every 6000 miles (10 000 km) rotate the wheels in accordance with Fig. 11.2. To ensure good handling do not mix steel and textile braced tyres on the same car.

3 Front suspension strut – removal and refitting

1   Jack up the front of the car and support it on axle stands. Remove the roadwheel.
2   Support the strut with a trolley jack.
3   Working in the engine compartment, mark the top strut mounting in relation to the body, then unscrew the mounting nuts (photo).
4   Remove the front hub and disc assembly as described in Section 9 (photo).
5   Unbolt the backplate from the strut (photos).
6   Unscrew the two bolts and separate the strut from the steering arm after lowering the trolley jack (photo).
7   Withdraw the front suspension strut assembly from the car.
8   Refitting is a reversal of removal, but adjust the front wheel bearings as described in Section 9. Tighten all nuts and bolts to the specified torque, and check the front wheel alignment as described in Section 29. Make sure that the top mounting and body marks are aligned correctly.

4 Front coil spring – removal and refitting

1   Remove the front suspension strut as described in Section 3.
2   Grip the top mounting in a vice, and loosen only the piston rod nut.

Remove the mounting from the vice (photo).
3   Using coil spring compressors, compress the coil spring until it is released from the top mounting (photo).
4   Remove the piston rod nut and washer, and withdraw the mounting, spring seat, coil spring, dust cover, and rubber stop.
5   Examine the top mounting for deterioration, and the coil spring for free length. Check that the mounting bearing rotates smoothly. Examine the spring seat, dust cover, and rubber stop for deterioration. Renew any components which are unserviceable, but if the coil spring requires renewal, fit a new spring to both sides. The springs are identified by painted dots and new springs should always have identical markings.
6   Refitting is a reversal of removal, but tighten all nuts and bolts to the specified torque, and refer to Section 3 as necessary. When completed, position the car on level ground and check the ground-to-body height on each side of the car (note that tyre pressures and tread depth must be identical on each side). If the dimensions are not identical, adjusting plates (maximum of two) may be fitted to the coil springs as necessary.

5 Front shock absorber – removal, inspection and refitting

1   Remove the front coil spring as described in Section 4.
2   Grip the strut vertically in a soft-jawed vice.
3   A spanner as shown in Fig. 11.3 must now be obtained in order to unscrew the shock absorber seal cap nut. Withdraw the nut and prise out the piston rod guide O-ring.
4   Remove the piston rod and pressure tube assembly from the strut, but do not attempt to dismantle the assembly further.
5   Examine the strut and piston rod assemblies for damage and wear, and check the base of the pressure tube for cracks which would cause malfunction of the shock absorber. Renew the piston rod and pressure tube assembly or alternatively obtain a new cartridge if the shock absorber is faulty. Clean all components with methylated spirit and make sure that all old fluid is removed.
6   Insert the piston rod and pressure tube assembly into the strut, then pour 240 cc of new shock absorber fluid into the strut. Insert the guide O-ring.
7   Lubricate the cap nut seal with a little grease, then ease it onto the piston rod shoulder.
8   With the piston rod fully extended, tighten the cap nut to the

3.3 Front suspension strut upper mounting

3.4 Removing front brake caliper complete with disc pads

3.5A Removing front brake disc backplate bolt

3.5B Removing front brake disc backplate

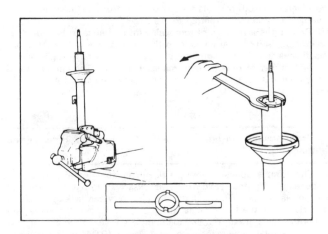

Fig. 11.3 Unscrewing the front shock absorber seal cap nut (Sec 5)

Inset shows tool for 1979 models

3.6 Unscrewing steering arm-to-strut bolts

4.2 Front suspension strut upper mounting and piston rod nut

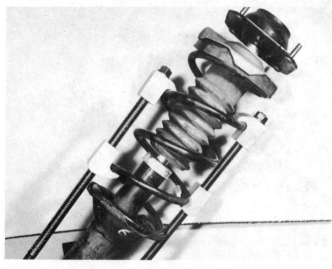

4.3 Using compressors to compress the front coil spring

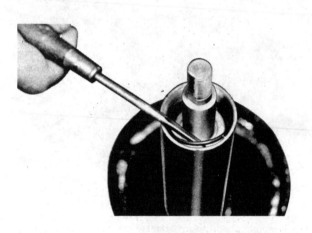

Fig. 11.4 Removing the front shock absorber piston rod guide O-ring (Sec 5)

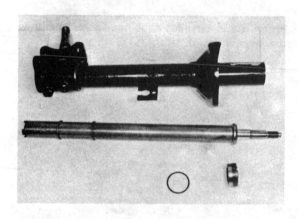

Fig. 11.5 Front suspension strut and shock absorber components (Sec 5)

specified torque using a crowsfoot adaptor or a spring balance as shown in Fig. 11.6.

9　With the strut still held in the soft-jawed vice, operate the piston rod several times through its full stroke. The strut must now be kept in a vertical position until refitted to the car.

10　Refitting is a reversal of removal, with reference to Section 4 as necessary. With the car lowered to the ground, check that the shock absorber is functioning correctly by placing one's full weight on the relevant corner of the car, then releasing the car. The corner should move upwards then settle half way down the next stroke if the shock absorber is good.

6　Front suspension arm and balljoint – checking, removal and refitting

1　The front suspension lower balljoint is an integral part of the suspension arm, and if worn it is necessary to renew the arm and balljoint as one unit. To check the balljoint for wear, jack up the front of the car until the wheels clear the ground, then grip the wheel top and bottom and attempt to pull the complete wheel alternately in and out. If the total movement exceeds 1.0 mm (0.04 in) the balljoint should be renewed, but take care not to confuse wheel bearing play with balljoint movement.

2　To remove the suspension arm, first remove the roadwheel, and support the car on axle stands.

Fig. 11.6 Tightening the front shock absorber seal cap nut (Sec 5)

6.9A Front suspension arm balljoint

6.9B Front suspension components with suspension strut removed, showing balljoint

7.3 Front suspension radius arm front mounting

8.4 Anti-roll bar front mounting plate

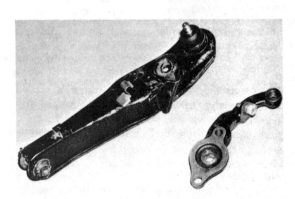

Fig. 11.7 Front suspension arm and steering arm (Sec 6)

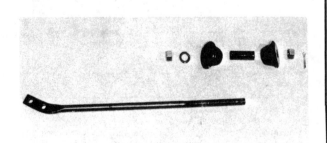

Fig. 11.8 Front radius arm components (Sec 7)

12 ± 1.0 mm
(0.472 ± 0.039 in)

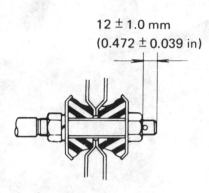

Fig. 11.9 Front radius arm fitting dimension (Sec 7)

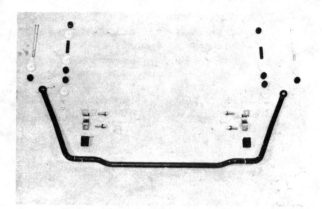

Fig. 11.10 Front anti-roll bar components (Sec 8)

3 Extract the split pin and unscrew the tie-rod end nut, then using a balljoint separator tool, disconnect the tie-rod from the steering arm.
4 Unscrew the two bolts retaining the steering arm to the bottom of the suspension strut.
5 Disconnect the anti-roll bar from the suspension arm with reference to Section 8.
6 Unbolt the radius arm from the suspension arm.
7 Unscrew the pivot nut, then drive out the pivot bolt, noting which way round it is fitted.
8 Withdraw the suspension arm and balljoint.
9 Extract the split pin and unscrew the balljoint nut, then use a balljoint separator tool to remove the steering arm (photos).
10 Examine the steering arm, suspension arm, and balljoint for wear and damage, and also check the condition of the balljoint dust seal and pivot bushes. Renew the components as necessary.
11 Refitting is a reversal of removal, but tighten all nuts and bolts to the specified torque wrench settings; delay tightening the pivot bolt until the weight of the car is on the front suspension. Refer to Section 8 when refitting the anti-roll bar to the suspension arm. Fit new split pins to the balljoints.

7 Front radius arm – removal and refitting

1 Jack up the front of the car and support it on axle stands.
2 Unbolt the radius arm from the suspension arm.
3 Extract the split pin, then unscrew the front nut and withdraw the radius arm together with the bushes, spacer, and spring washer (photo).
4 Examine the components for wear, damage or deterioration and renew them as necessary.
5 Refitting is a reversal of removal, but tighten the nuts and bolts in the following sequence. First tighten the bolts on the suspension arm to the specified torque. Tighten the front mounting nut until it is between 11 and 13 mm (0.433 and 0.512 in) from the end of the radius arm (Fig. 11.9), then fit the split pin. Tighten the rear mounting nut to 94 lbf ft (127 Nm).

8 Front anti-roll bar – removal and refitting

1 Jack up the front of the car and support it on axle stands.
2 Remove the engine splash guard.
3 Unscrew the two nuts on each side and disconnect the anti-roll bar from the link bolts. Remove the link bolts, bushes and spacers.
4 Unbolt the front mounting plates and withdraw the anti-roll bar (photo).
5 Examine the anti-roll bar, mounting plates, link bolts and spacers for wear and damage. Check the rubber bushes for deterioration. Renew the components as necessary.
6 Refitting is a reversal of removal, but note the following additional points:

13 mm (0.512 in)

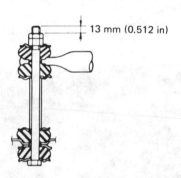

Fig. 11.11 Front anti-roll bar fitting dimension (Sec 8)

(a) The split end of the front support mounting rubbers must face the front of the car
(b) Delay tightening the front mounting plate bolts to the specified torque until the weight of the car is on the front suspension
(c) Tighten the link bolt nuts until the dimension of the exposed bolt is 13 mm (0.512 in) as shown in Fig. 11.11

9 Front hub bearings – lubrication and adjustment

Lubrication
1 The front hub bearings should be packed with new grease every 24 000 miles (40 000 km). To do this jack up the front of the car and support it on axle stands. Remove the roadwheel.
2 Remove the brake caliper with reference to Chapter 9 and tie it to the coil spring – do not disconnect the hydraulic hose.
3 Remove the disc pads and unbolt the caliper mounting bracket.
4 Tap off the hub grease cap using a suitable drift (photo).
5 Extract the split pin and remove the locking cap. Unscrew the adjusting nut (photos).
6 Shake the hub and remove the washer and outer bearing (photos).
7 Withdraw the hub and brake disc assembly (photo).
8 Remove all old grease from the bearings and hub recesses. Wash clean with paraffin and allow to dry.
9 Pack the bearings with new lithium based grease; also pack the hub recesses and grease cap approximately half full. Smear the oil seal lip with a little grease.
10 Refit the hub to the stub axle together with the outer bearing and washer.
11 Refit the adjusting nut then refer to paragraphs 17 to 21 and adjust the bearings.
12 Refit the caliper mounting bracket, disc pads, and caliper with reference to Chapter 9.
13 Refit the roadwheel and lower the car to the ground.

9.4 Removing front hub grease cap

9.5A Removing front hub split pin and locking cap

9.5B Removing front hub adjusting nut

9.6A Removing front hub washer ...

9.6B ... and outer bearing

9.7 Withdrawing the front hub and brake disc assembly

Fig. 11.12 Checking front hub bearing turning torque (Sec 9)

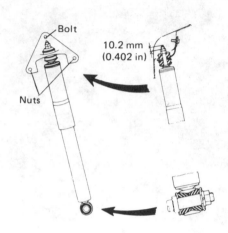

Fig. 11.13 Rear shock absorber and fitting dimension (Sec 11)

Adjustment

14 Jack up the front of the car until the roadwheel clears the ground. Grip the wheel top and bottom and attempt to rock it; with correctly adjusted hub bearings it should just be possible to feel a small amount of play in the bearings, but do not confuse movement with wear in the suspension balljoint. If considerable play is evident, adjust the bearings as follows.

15 Tap off the hub grease cap using a suitable drift.

16 Extract the split pin and remove the locking cap.

17 Tighten the adjusting nut until the hub binds when being rotated, then back off the nut one flat (60°).

18 Fit the locking cap so that the split pin holes are aligned and temporarily insert the split pin.

19 If available use a spring scale to check the timing torque of the hub after removing the wheel and refitting a wheel bolt (see Fig. 11.12). The reading should be between 0.77 and 1.92 lbf (0.35 and 0.87 kgf). If necessary adjust the adjustment nut.

20 Bend over the ends of the split pin and refit the grease cap.

21 Lower the car to the ground.

10 Front hub bearings and seal – renewal

1 Remove the front hub as described in Section 9, paragraphs 1 to 8.

2 Prise out the oil seal with a screwdriver then remove the inner bearing (photo).

3 Using a soft metal drift, remove the inner and outer bearing outer tracks from the hub (photo).

4 Wash the bearings and hub with paraffin and allow to dry. Examine the bearings and tracks for wear, pitting, and damage, and

renew the bearings as necessary.

5 Drive the outer tracks fully into the hub using a length of metal tubing.

6 Insert the inner bearing, then fit the oil seal with its lip facing into the hub. Use a block of wood and a mallet, making sure that the seal is kept square.

7 The remaining procedure is described in Section 9 paragraphs 9 to 13.

11 Rear shock absorber – removal, testing and refitting

1 Jack up the rear of the car and support it on axle stands placed in front of the lower arms. Chock the front wheels and remove the relevant rear roadwheel.

2 Unscrew the bolt and nuts securing the shock absorber upper mounting bracket to the underbody (photo).

3 Unscrew the nut and remove the washer and shock absorber from the mounting on the rear axle.

4 Unscrew the nut and remove the upper bracket, mounting rubbers and washers from the shock absorber.

5 To test the gas filled shock absorber, grip the lower mounting eye in a vice with the shock absorber vertical, then fully retract and extend the unit several times. If there is not a smooth resistance in both directions, the shock absorber should be renewed.

6 Check the mounting bushes for wear and deterioration, and if necessary renew them.

7 Refitting is a reversal of removal, but tighten all nuts and bolts to the specified torque, and tighten the upper mounting nuts until the dimension of the exposed bolt is 10.2 mm (0.402 in) as shown in Fig. 11.13.

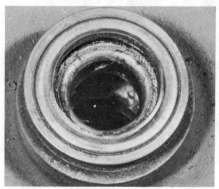

10.2 Front hub inner oil seal and bearing

10.3 Front hub outer bearing outer track

11.2 Rear shock absorber upper mounting

13.3 Rear suspension upper link-to-rear axle mounting bolt

13.4 Rear suspension upper link-to-underbody mounting bolt

12 Rear coil spring – removal and refitting

1   Jack up the rear of the car and support it on axle stands placed in front of the lower arm. Chock the front wheels and remove the relevant rear roadwheel.
2   Support the rear axle with a trolley jack.
3   Unscrew the nut and disconnect the shock absorber from the rear axle.
4   If removing the right-hand coil spring, unscrew the mat and disconnect the Panhard rod from the rear axle.
5   Unscrew the nut and remove the bolt securing the upper link to the rear axle.
6   Loosen, but do not remove, the nut and bolt securing the lower suspension arm to the rear axle.
7   Where fitted, disconnect the anti-roll bar from the underbody bracket link by unscrewing the nuts and removing the washer and rubber bush.
8   Lower the jack until the coil spring and rubber seat can be withdrawn from the rear axle. Take care not to strain the rear brake hydraulic hose.
9   Check the rubber seat for wear and deterioration, and the coil spring for free length, and renew them as necessary.
10 Refitting is a reversal of removal, but make sure that the open end of the coil spring is located in the rubber seat. Initially tighten all nuts and bolts finger tight, then with the weight of the car on the suspension tighten them to the specified torque. Refer to Section 16 when reconnecting the anti-roll bar if fitted.

13 Rear suspension upper link – removal and refitting

1   Jack up the rear of the car and support it on axle stands placed in front of the lower arms. Chock the front wheels and remove the relevant rear roadwheel.
2   Support the rear axle with a trolley jack.
3   Unscrew the nut and remove the spring washer and bolt securing the link to the rear axle (photo).
4   Unscrew the nut, remove the spring washer and plain washer and withdraw the upper link from the car (photo).
5   Examine the link and rubber bushes for wear, damage and deterioration and renew the complete link if necessary.
6   Refitting is a reversal of removal, but initially tighten the nuts finger tight, then with the weight of the car on the suspension, tighten them to the specified torque.

14 Rear suspension lower arm – removal and refitting

1   Remove the relevant rear coil spring as described in Section 12.
2   Unscrew the nuts and remove the spring washers from the mounting bolts (photos).
3   Drive out the mounting bolts, noting which way round they are fitted, then withdraw the lower arm from the car.
4   Examine the arm and bushes for wear, damage and deterioration and renew the complete arm if necessary.
5   Refitting is a reversal of removal, with reference to Section 12 as necessary. As with the other nuts and bolts, delay tightening the mounting nuts to the specified torque until the weight of the car is on the suspension.

15 Panhard rod – removal and refitting

1   Jack up the rear of the car and support it on axle stands placed in front of the lower arms. Chock the front wheels.
2   Unscrew the nut securing the Panhard rod to the rear axle, remove the spring washer and plain washer and disconnect the rod.
3   Unscrew the nut and drive out the bolt from the underbody mounting bracket, then withdraw the Panhard rod (photo). Note the location of the washers.
4   Examine the rod and bushes for wear, damage and deterioration and renew the complete rod if necessary.
5   Refitting is a reversal of removal, but initially tighten the nuts finger tight, then with the weight of the car on the suspension tighten them to the specified torque. The bolt head must face the fuel tank.

16 Rear anti-roll bar – removal and refitting

1   Jack up the rear of the car and support it on axle stands placed in front of the lower arms. Chock the front wheels.
2   Unscrew the two nuts on each side and disconnect the anti-roll bar from the link bolts. Remove the link bolts, bushes and spacers.
3   Unbolt the rear mounting plates and withdraw the anti-roll bar.
4   Examine the anti-roll bar, mounting plates, link bolts, and spacers for wear and damage. Check the rubber bushes for deterioration. Renew the components as necessary.
5   Refitting is a reversal of removal, but note the following additional points:

14.2A Rear suspension lower arm front mounting bolt

14.2B Rear suspension lower arm rear mounting bolt and Panhard rod-to-rear axle mounting

15.3 Panhard rod-to-underbody mounting bolt

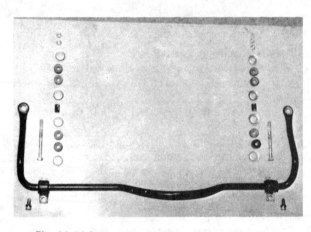

Fig. 11.14 Rear anti-roll bar components (Sec 16)

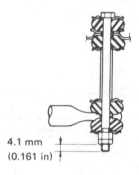

4.1 mm
(0.161 in)

Fig. 11.15 Rear anti-roll bar fitting dimension (Sec 16)

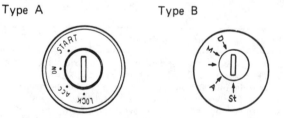

Type A   Type B

Fig. 11.16 Yuhshin (type A) and Neiman (type B) ignition switches (Sec 18)

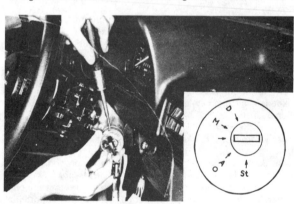

Fig. 11.17 Removing the key cylinder on a Neiman ignition switch (Sec 18)

(a)   *The split end of the rear support mounting rubbers must face the rear of the car*

(b)   *Delay tightening the rear mounting plate bolts to the specified torque until the weight of the car is on the rear suspension*

(c)   *Tighten the link bolt nuts until the dimension of the exposed bolt is 4.1 mm (0.161 in) as shown in Fig. 11.15*

17 Steering wheel – removal and refitting

1   Turn the front wheels to the straight-ahead position.
2   Disconnect the battery negative lead.
3   Remove the cap from the centre of the steering wheel (photo).
4   Mark the steering wheel hub and inner steering column in relation

to each other, then unscrew the nut and withdraw the steering wheel (photo). If it is tight, do not exert excessive force, but use a suitable puller.

5   Refitting is a reversal of removal, but align the previously made marks and the switch prongs, then tighten the nut to the specified torque (photo).

18 Steering lock/ignition switch (standard) – removal and refitting

1   Two types of steering lock/ignition switch may be fitted; Yuhshin or Neiman. To identify which type is fitted check the position of the ignition key slot – if it is central, a Yuhshin type is fitted (photo); if it is off-centre, a Neiman type is fitted.

17.3 Removing steering wheel cap

17.4 Unscrewing steering wheel nut

17.5 Switch prongs and location holes in steering wheel

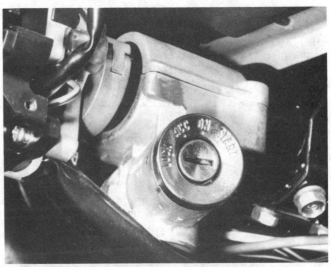

18.1 Yuhshin type steering lock/ignition switch

Yuhshin type
2   Remove the combination switch assembly as described in Chapter 10

Neiman type
3   Disconnect the battery negative lead.
4   Remove the screws and withdraw the two steering column shrouds – prise out the right-hand cover and remove the ignition lock ring. Where applicable, disconnect the ignition switch illumination light wiring.
5   On right-hand drive models remove the switch panel next to the steering lock.
6   Disconnect the ignition switch multi-plug.
7   If necessary remove the key cylinder by unscrewing the bolt, turning the ignition key to the arrow between the A and M marks, and depressing the stop key with a thin rod.

Yuhshin and Neiman types
8   Cut a groove in the shear bolts using a sharp cold chisel, then unscrew them with a screwdriver and withdraw the steering lock/ignition switch.
9   Refitting is a reversal of removal, but tighten the shear bolts finger tight initially, then tighten them further until the heads shear off.

19.7 Steering gear and mounting bolts

19 Steering gear (standard) – removal and refitting

1   Remove the steering wheel and steering lock/ignition switch as described in Section 17 and 18.
2   Unbolt the upper mounting bracket from the dash panel and steering column. Wrap masking tape around the column bolt holes to prevent loss of oil.
3   On US and Canadian models, remove the air duct.
4   Jack up the front of the car and support it on axle stands.
5   Extract the split pin and unscrew the nut securing the centre steering link to the Pitman arm. Using a balljoint separator tool, detach the centre link.
6   Unscrew the nut and use a puller to detach the Pitman arm from the sector shaft.
7   Unscrew and remove the steering gear mounting bolts (photo).
8   On UK models the steering gear and shim can be withdrawn from within the engine compartment.
9   On US and Canadian models, remove the engine splash guard, front anti-roll bar (Section 8), and left-hand engine mounting (see Chapter 1) after supporting the engine with a trolley jack and block of wood. The steering gear and shim can then be withdrawn from under the car.
10 With the steering gear removed, check the endplay of the inner column – if excessive the car has probably been involved in a collision which has caused the collapsible columns to collapse. Where this has occurred renew the complete steering gear. Note that collapsible columns are not fitted to early models.
11 Refitting is a reversal of removal with reference to Section 17 and 18 as necessary. Do not forget to fit the mounting shim in its original location, and tighten all nuts and bolts to their specified torque. Stake the end of the sector shaft in two places to lock the Pitman arm nut. Check and if necessary top up the steering gear with the specified oil.

20 Steering gear (standard) – overhaul

1   Unscrew the filler plug and drain the oil from the steering gear.
2   Mount the steering gear in a vice and remove the outer column.
3   Unscrew the locknut and side cover retaining bolts, then turn the adjusting screw clockwise to remove the side cover. Remove the gasket.
4   Slide out the adjustment screw and pad. Withdraw the sector shaft.
5   Unscrew the worm shaft bearing locknut and adjustment screw, and withdraw the worm shaft and ball nut assembly.
6   Prise out the oil seal.
7   Wash all components in paraffin and wipe dry, then examine them for wear and damage. Check the bearings and bushes for excessive play and pitting with reference to the Specifications. Obtain a new oil seal, and renew the other components as necessary. Temporarily refit the adjustment screw and pad to the sector shaft, and check the pad-to-shaft clearance with a feeler gauge. If the clearance exceeds the specified tolerance, renew the steering gear assembly.
8   Reassemble the steering gear in reverse order to dismantling, but fit a new oil seal and gasket, and make sure that the centre of the sector gear engages the centre of the ball nut. Tighten the side cover bolts to the specified torque, and before refitting the outer column make the following adjustments:

(a) Tighten the worm shaft bearing adjustment screw until the specified preload torque is obtained, then tighten the locknut
(b) With the inner column in a central position and a dial gauge on the Pitman arm (fitted temporarily) at the radius of the sector gear, adjust the end cover screw until the specified sector to rack clearance is obtained, then tighten the locknut. Check that the inner column moves freely in both directions

9   Fill the steering gear with the specified oil and refit the filler plug.

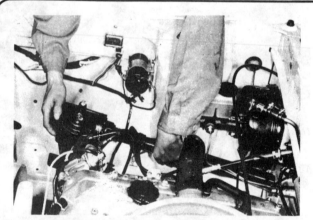

Fig. 11.18 Removing the steering gear on UK models (Sec 19)

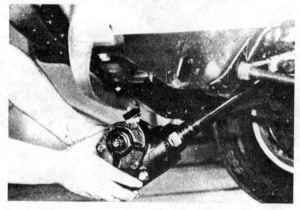

Fig. 11.19 Removing the steering gear on US and Canadian models (Sec 19)

Fig. 11.20 Removing steering gear side cover (Sec 20)

Fig. 11.21 Steering gear worm shaft and ball nut (Sec 20)

21 Steering lock/ignition switch (tilt and power steering) – removal and refitting

1　Remove the steering column as described in Section 22.
2　Cut a groove in the shear bolts using a sharp cold chisel, then unscrew them with a screwdriver and withdraw the steering lock/ignition switch.
3　Refitting is a reversal of removal, but align the lock with the groove in the column and tighten the shear bolts finger tight initially. Check the operation of the lock then tighten the bolts until the heads shear off.

22 Steering column (tilt and power steering) – removal, overhaul and refitting

1　Remove the steering wheel as described in Section 17.
2　Remove the steering column shrouds and the switch panel.
3　Remove the combination switch with reference to Chapter 10.
4　Unscrew the nuts and withdraw the cover plate from the bottom of the column.
5　Unscrew the clamp bolt from the bottom of the column.
6　Unscrew the bracket mounting bolts beneath the facia.
7　Withdraw the steering column assembly.
8　To remove the inner column and bearings, first bend straight the staking at the bottom of the outer column.

9　Grip the bottom of the inner column between two blocks of wood in a vice, then tap the mounting bracket and withdraw the outer column.
10　Extract the circlip and pull the bearing from the inner column.
11　Reassembly is a reversal of dismantling, but stake the bottom of the outer column in four new places. Before refitting the column adjust the tilt mechanism as follows.

Single lock type
12　Remove the adjusting lever and bolt, noting that the bolt has a left-hand thread.
13　Check that the adjusting nut (also left-hand thread) is tightened to 3.6 lbf ft (5.0 Nm).
14　Fit the adjusting lever and washer and insert the bolt, then turn the lever until it touches the bracket and tighten the bolt to 16 lbf ft (22 Nm).

Dual lock type
15　The upper bracket adjustment is identical to that for the single lock type. To adjust the lower bracket, first remove the adjusting lever, noting again that the bolt has a left-hand thread.
16　Check that the adjusting nut is tightened to 2.9 lbf ft (4.0 Nm).
17　Fit the adjusting lever and washer, insert the bolt, and tighten it to 16 lbf ft (22 Nm).

All types
18　Refitting the steering column is a reversal of removal.

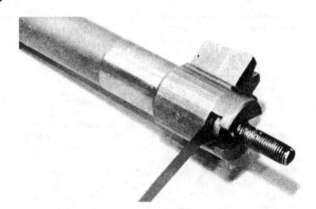

Fig. 11.22 Checking adjustment pad-to-sector shaft clearance with a feeler gauge (Sec 20)

Fig. 11.23 Correct meshing of sector gear and ball nut (Sec 20)

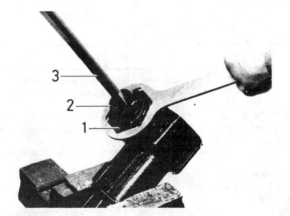

Fig. 11.24 Tightening worm shaft bearing adjustment screw locknut (Sec 20)

1　Locknut　　2　Adjustment screw　　3　Inner column

Fig. 11.25 Checking inner column turning torque (Sec 20)

Fig. 11.26 Steering column cover plate location (Sec 22)

Fig. 11.27 Inner steering column clamp bolt location (Sec 22)

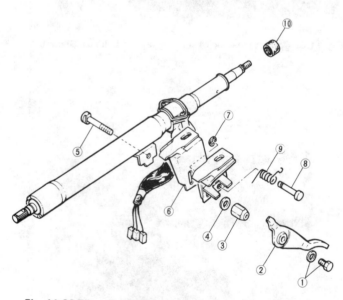

Fig. 11.28 Tilt and power steering column components (Sec 22)

1	Bolt and washer	5	Bolt	8	Bolt
2	Lever	6	Fixing bracket	9	Spring
3	Nut	7	Clip	10	Bearing
4	Washer				

23 Steering gear (tilt steering) – removal and refitting

1   Jack up the front of the car and support it on axle stands. Apply the handbrake.
2   Unscrew the nut from the end of the centre steering link and, using a balljoint separator, detach the link from the steering gear Pitman arm.
3   Unscrew the nut and use a puller to detach the Pitman arm from the sector shaft.
4   Unscrew the nuts and withdraw the cover plate from the bottom of the column.
5   Unscrew the clamp bolt from the bottom of the column.
6   Unscrew and remove the steering gear mounting bolts and nuts. Withdraw the steering gear.
7   Refitting is a reversal of removal, but stake the end of the sector shaft in two places to lock the Pitman arm nut. Check and if necessary top up the steering gear with the specified oil.

24 Steering gear (tilt steering) – overhaul

The procedure is identical to that for the non-tilt steering gear, except that the pad-to-shaft clearance of the sector shaft adjustment screw may be adjusted with shims available from a Mazda dealer. Refer to Section 20 for the procedure.

25 Power steering – air bleeding

1   Jack up the front of the car and support it on axle stands.
2   Fill the pump reservoir with fluid to the 'FULL' mark on the dipstick, then turn the steering wheel fully clockwise then anti-clockwise several times. Top up the fluid.
3   Spin the engine on the starter while turning the steering wheel fully clockwise and anti-clockwise and top up the fluid again. Do not start the engine at this stage – disconnect the distributor main HT lead.
4   Repeat the procedure in paragraph 3 until there is no need to top up the reservoir, then start the engine and turn the steering wheel fully clockwise and anti-clockwise two or three times.
5   Lower the car to the ground and check the steering wheel movement. If it is excessively noisy, or if the fluid level rises when the engine is switched off with the steering in the straight-ahead direction, repeat the bleeding operation again.
6   If complete air bleeding proves difficult, raise the temperature of the fluid to 50 to 80°C (122 to 176°F) by turning the steering repeatedly clockwise and anti-clockwise, then check the steering as in paragraph 5 after allowing it to cool for five to ten minutes.

26 Power steering gear – removal and refitting

1   Working inside the car, unscrew the nuts and withdraw the cover plate from the bottom of the steering column. Unscrew the clamp bolt from the inner column.
2   Working in the engine compartment note the location of the pressure and return lines on the steering gear, then disconnect and plug them.
3   Jack up the front of the car and support it on axle stands. Apply the handbrake.
4   Unscrew the nut from the end of the centre steering link and, using a balljoint separator, detach the link from the steering gear Pitman arm.
5   Unscrew the nut and use a puller to detach the Pitman arm from the sector shaft.
6   Unscrew and remove the steering gear mounting bolts and nuts. Withdraw the steering gear.
7   Refitting is a reversal of removal, but stake the end of the sector shaft in two places to lock the Pitman arm nut. Fill the hydraulic system with fluid and bleed it as described in Section 25.

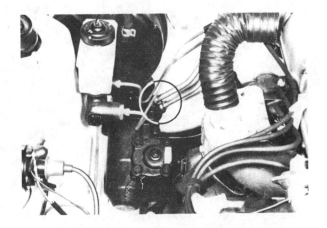

Fig. 11.29 Power steering gear pressure and return line location (Sec 26)

Fig. 11.30 Power steering pump pressure and return line location (Sec 27)

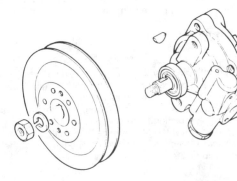

Fig. 11.31 Power steering pump and pulley components (Sec 27)

Fig. 11.32 Power steering pump drivebelt tension checking point (Sec 27)

Fig. 11.33 Steering linkage components (Sec 28)

1   Balljoints   4   Tie-rods
2   Idler arm   5   Centre link
3   Pitman arm

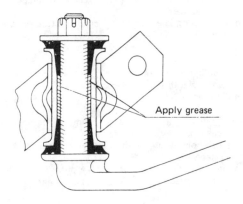

Fig. 11.34 Cross-section of steering idler (Sec 28)

Fig. 11.35 Pitman arm showing master splines (arrowed) (Sec 28)

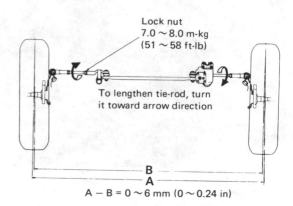

Fig. 11.36 Steering tie-rod adjustment method (Sec 29)

27 Power steering pump – removal, refitting, and drivebelt adjustment

1 Remove the guard plate from beneath the pump.
2 Note the location of the pressure and return lines on the pump, then disconnect and plug them.
3 Unscrew and remove the pulley nut and spring washer, withdraw the pulley, and disengage it from the pulley.
4 Unscrew the mounting bolts and withdraw the power steering pump.
5 Refitting is a reversal of removal, but make sure that the pulley engages with the Woodruff key correctly. Check the drivebelt tension by using firm thumb pressure between the pulleys as shown in Fig. 11.32. The deflection should be between 8 and 10 mm (0.3 and 0.4 in) for a new belt and between 11 and 13 mm (0.4 and 0.5 in) for a used belt. Fill the hydraulic system with fluid and bleed it as described in Section 25.

28 Steering linkage components – inspection, removal and refitting

1 Jack up the front of the car and support it on axle stands. Apply the handbrake.
2 To check a steering balljoint, grip the tie-rod or link and attempt to move it up and down. If the endplay exceeds that specified, the balljoint must be renewed.
3 Wear in the steering idler can be checked by attempting to move the idler arm laterally.

Steering idler

4 Extract the split pin, unscrew the nut, and detach the centre link from the idler arm using a balljoint remover tool.
5 Remove the roadwheel, then unbolt and remove the steering idler (photo).
6 If necessary, dismantle the idler by removing the split pin, nut, idler arm, and bushes.
7 Clean the components in paraffin, examine them for wear, and renew them as necessary.
8 Reassemble and refit the idler in reverse order but lubricate the bushes and reservoir space with a lithium-based grease.

Pitman arm

9 Extract the split pin, unscrew the nut, and detach the centre link from the Pitman arm using a balljoint remover tool (photo).
10 Unscrew the nut and use a puller to remove the Pitman arm from the sector shaft. Note the master spline for correct refitting.
11 Refitting is a reversal of removal, but after tightening the Pitman arm nut, lock it by staking the sector shaft in two places.

Centre link

12 Extract the split pins, unscrew the nuts, and detach the centre link from the tie-rods, idler arm, and Pitman arm using a balljoint remover tool.
13 Refitting is a reversal of removal.

Tie-rod

14 Extract the split pin, unscrew the nuts, and detach the tie-rod from the steering arm and centre link using a balljoint remover tool (photos).
15 To remove either tie-rod end, first measure the adjustable distance between the ends, then loosen the locknut (left-hand or right-hand thread according to position), and unscrew the end.
16 Refitting is a reversal of removal, but maintain the identical dimension between the ends, and when completed adjust the toe-in as described in Section 29.

29 Wheel alignment – checking and adjusting

1 Accurate wheel alignment is essential for good steering and slow tyre wear. Before checking it, make sure that the tyre pressures are correct, the wheels are not damaged, and the steering and suspension balljoints are not worn excessively.
2 Place the car on level ground with the wheels in the straight-ahead position.
3 Using a wheel alignment gauge check that the amount of toe-in is within the tolerance given in the Specifications.
4 If adjustment is necessary, loosen the tie-rod locknuts on both sides and turn the tie-rods by equal amounts until the toe-in is correct. Always recheck the adjustment after tightening the locknuts, and make sure that the distances between the tie-rod ends on both sides of the car are identical.
5 Camber and castor angles are adjustable by repositioning the front suspension strut upper mountings, but as this work entails the use of specialised equipment it is best entrusted to a garage.

30 Roadwheels and tyres – general

1 Clean the insides of the roadwheels whenever they are removed. If necessary, remove any rust and repaint them.
2 Remove any flints or stones which may have become embedded in the tyres. Examine the tyres for damage and splits. Where the depth of tread is less than the legal minimum, renew them.
3 The wheels should be rebalanced half way through the life of the tyres to compensate for loss of rubber.
4 Check and adjust the tyre pressures regularly and make sure that the dust caps are correctly fitted. Remember to check the spare tyre also.

28.5 Steering idler and mounting bolts

28.9 Steering Pitman arm

28.14A Steering tie-rod end

28.14B Steering tie-rod end nut and split pin

28.14C Using a balljoint remover to separate the tie-rod end from the steering arm

---

31 Fault diagnosis – suspension and steering

Symptom	Reason(s)
Car pulls to one side	Uneven tyre pressures Suspension or steering balljoint worn Wheel alignment incorrect
Excessive pitching or rolling	Worn shock absorbers Weak or broken spring
Heavy or stiff steering	Wheel alignment incorrect Tyre pressures incorrect Seized suspension or steering balljoint Steering gear lubricant low
Excessive play in steering	Worn steering gear Worn suspension or steering balljoint Worn idler bushes
Wheel wobble and vibration	Roadwheels out of balance Roadwheels buckles or damaged Wheel bearings worn or out of adjustment
Excessive tyre wear	Tyre pressures incorrect Wheel alignment incorrect Roadwheels out of balance

Chapter 12 Bodywork and fittings

Contents

1 General description

The bodyshell is of all-steel welded construction incorporating two box section members forming an integral chassis. The front wings are bolted in position and are detachable should renewal be necessary after a front end collision. The bodyshell is strengthened locally to provide for the suspension system, steering components, and engine and transmission supports.

2 Maintenance – bodywork and underframe

1   The general condition of a car's bodywork is the thing that significantly affects its value. Maintenance is easy but needs to be regular. Neglect, particularly after minor damage, can lead quickly to further deterioration and costly repair bills. It is important also to keep watch on those parts of the car not immediately visible, for instance the underside, inside all the wheel arches and the lower part of the engine compartment.

2   The basic maintenance routine for the bodywork is washing – preferably with a lot of water, from a hose. This will remove all the loose solids which may have stuck to the car. It is important to flush these off in such a way as to prevent grit from scratching the finish. The wheel arches and underframe need washing in the same way to remove any accumulated mud which will retain moisture and tend to encourage rust. Paradoxically enough, the best time to clean the underframe and wheel arches is in wet weather when the mud is thoroughly wet and soft. In very wet weather the underframe is usually cleaned of large accumulations automatically and this is a good time for inspection.

3   Periodically, it is a good idea to have the whole of the underframe of the car steam cleaned, engine compartment included, so that a thorough inspection can be carried out to see what minor repairs and renovations are necessary. Steam cleaning is available at many garages and is necessary for removal of the accumulation of oily grime which sometimes is allowed to become thick in certain areas. If steam cleaning facilities are not available, there are one or two excellent grease solvents available which can be brush applied. The dirt can then be simply hosed off.

4   After washing paintwork, wipe off with a chamois leather to give

an unspotted clear finish. A coat of clear protective wax polish will give added protection against chemical pollutants in the air. If the paintwork sheen has dulled or oxidised, use a cleaner/polisher combination to restore the brilliance of the shine. This requires a little effort, but such dulling is usually caused because regular washing has been neglected. Always check that the door and ventilator opening drain holes and pipes are completely clear so that water can be drained out. Bright work should be treated in the same way as paintwork. Windscreens and windows can be kept clear of the smeary film which often appears, by adding a little ammonia to the water. If they are scratched, a good rub with a proprietary metal polish will often clear them. Never use any form of wax or other body or chromium polish on glass.

3 Maintenance – upholstery and carpets

1   Mats and carpets should be brushed or vacuum cleaned regularly to keep them free of grit. If they are badly stained remove them from the car for scrubbing or sponging and make quite sure they are dry before refitting. Seats and interior trim panels can be kept clean by a wipe over with a damp cloth. If they do become stained (which can be more apparent on light coloured upholstery) use a little liquid detergent and a soft nail brush to scour the grime out of the grain of the material. Do not forget to keep the head lining clean in the same way as the upholstery. When using liquid cleaners inside the car do not over-wet the surfaces being cleaned. Excessive damp could get into the seams and padded interior causing stains, offensive odours or even rot. If the inside of the car gets wet accidentally it is worthwhile taking some trouble to dry it out properly, particularly where carpets are involved. *Do not leave oil or electric heaters inside the car for this purpose.*

4 Minor body damage – repair

The photographic sequences on pages 190 and 191 illustrate the operations detailed in the following sub-sections.

Repair of minor scratches in the car's bodywork

If the scratch is very superficial, and does not penetrate to the

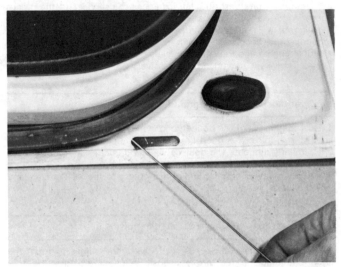

2.4A Checking door drain hole with a wire probe

2.4B Checking sill drain hole with a wire probe

metal of the bodywork, repair is very simple. Lightly rub the area of the scratch with a paintwork renovator, or a very fine cutting paste, to remove loose paint from the scratch and to clear the surrounding bodywork of wax polish. Rinse the area with clean water.

Apply touch-up paint to the scratch using a thin paint brush; continue to apply thin layers of paint until the surface of the paint in the scratch is level with the surrounding paintwork. Allow the new paint at least two weeks to harden: then blend it into the surrounding paintwork by rubbing the paintwork, in the scratch area, with a paintwork renovator or a very fine cutting paste. Finally, apply wax polish.

Where the scratch has penetrated right through to the metal of the bodywork, causing the metal to rust, a different repair technique is required. Remove any loose rust from the bottom of the scratch with a penknife, then apply rust inhibiting paint to prevent the formation of rust in the future. Using a rubber or nylon applicator fill the scratch with bodystopper paste. If required, this paste can be mixed with cellulose thinners to provide a very thin paste which is ideal for filling narrow scratches. Before the stopper-paste in the scratch hardens, wrap a piece of smooth cotton rag around the top of a finger. Dip the finger in cellulose thinners and then quickly sweep it across the surface of the stopper-paste in the scratch; this will ensure that the surface of the stopper-paste is slightly hollowed. The scratch can now be painted over as described earlier in this Section.

Repair of dents in the car's bodywork

When deep denting of the car's bodywork has taken place, the first task is to pull the dent out, until the affected bodywork almost attains its original shape. There is little point in trying to restore the original shape completely, as the metal in the damaged area will have stretched on impact and cannot be reshaped fully to its original contour. It is better to bring the level of the dent up to a point which is about $\frac{1}{8}$ in (3 mm) below the level of the surrounding bodywork. In cases where the dent is very shallow anyway, it is not worth trying to pull it out at all. If the underside of the dent is accessible, it can be hammered out gently from behind, using a mallet with a wooden or plastic head. Whilst doing this, hold a suitable block of wood firmly against the outside of the panel to absorb the impact from the hammer blows and thus prevent a large area of the bodywork from being 'belled-out'.

Should the dent be in a section of the bodywork which has double skin or some other factor making it inaccessible from behind, a different technique is called for. Drill several small holes through the metal inside the area – particularly in the deeper section. Then screw long self-tapping screws into the holes just sufficiently for them to gain a good purchase in the metal. Now the dent can be pulled out by pulling on the protruding heads of the screws with a pair of pliers.

The next stage of the repair is the removal of the paint from the damaged area, and from an inch or so of the surrounding 'sound'

bodywork. This is accomplished most easily by using a wire brush or abrasive pad on a power drill, although it can be done just as effectively by hand using sheets of abrasive paper. To complete the preparation for filling, score the surface of the bare metal with a screwdriver or the tang of a file, or alternatively, drill small holes in the affected area. This will provide a really good 'key' for the filler paste.

To complete the repair see the Section on filling and re-spraying.

Repair of rust holes or gashes in the car's bodywork

Remove all paint from the affected area and from an inch or so of the surrounding 'sound' bodywork, using an abrasive pad or a wire brush on a power drill. If these are not available a few sheets of abrasive paper will do the job just as effectively. With the paint removed you will be able to gauge the severity of the corrosion and therefore decide whether to renew the whole panel (if this is possible) or to repair the affected area. New body panels are not as expensive as most people think and it is often quicker and more satisfactory to fit a new panel than to attempt to repair large areas of corrosion.

Remove all fittings from the affected area except those which will act as a guide to the original shape of the damaged bodywork (eg headlamp shells etc). Then, using tin snips or a hacksaw blade, remove all loose metal and any other metal badly affected by corrosion. Hammer the edges of the hole inwards in order to create a slight depression for the filler paste.

Wire brush the affected area to remove the powdery rust from the surface of the remaining metal. Paint the affected area with rust inhibiting paint; if the back of the rusted area is accessible treat this also.

Before filling can take place it will be necessary to block the hole in some way. This can be achieved by the use of zinc gauze or aluminium tape.

Zinc gauze is probably the best material to use for a large hole. Cut a piece to the approximate size and shape of the hole to be filled, then position it in the hole so that its edges are below the level of the surrounding bodywork. It can be retained in position by several blobs of filler paste around its periphery.

Aluminium tape should be used for small or very narrow holes. Pull a piece off the roll and trim it to the approximate size and shape required, then pull off the backing paper (if used) and stick the tape over the hole; it can be overlapped if the thickness of one piece is insufficient. Burnish down the edges of the tape with the handle of a screwdriver or similar, to ensure that the tape is securely attached to the metal underneath.

Bodywork repairs – filling and re-spraying

Before using this Section, see the Sections on dent, deep scratch, rust holes and gash repairs.

Many types of bodyfiller are available, but generally speaking those proprietary kits which contain a tin of filler paste and a tube of resin hardener are best for this type of repair. A wide, flexible plastic or nylon applicator will be found invaluable for imparting a smooth and well contoured finish to the surface of the filler.

Mix up a little filler on a clean piece of card or board – measure the hardener carefully (follow the maker's instructions on the pack) otherwise the filler will set too rapidly or too slowly.

Using the applicator apply the filler paste to the prepared area; draw the applicator across the surface of the filler to achieve the correct contour and to level the filler surface. As soon as a contour that approximates the correct one is achieved, stop working the paste – if you carry on too long the paste will become sticky and begin to 'pick up' on the applicator. Continue to add thin layers of filler paste at twenty-minute intervals until the level of the filler is just proud of the surrounding bodywork.

Once the filler has hardened, excess can be removed using a metal plane or file. From then on, progressively finer grades of sandpaper should be used, starting with a 40 grade production paper and finishing with 400 grade wet-and-dry paper. Always wrap the abrasive paper around a flat rubber, cork, or wooden block – otherwise the surface of the filler will not be completely flat. During the smoothing of the filler surface the wet-and-dry paper should be periodically rinsed in water. This will ensure that a very smooth finish is imparted to the filler at the final stage.

At this stage the dent should be surrounded by a ring of bare metal, which in turn should be encircled by the finely 'feathered' edge of the good paintwork. Rinse the repair area with clean water, until all of the dust produced by the rubbing-down operation has gone.

Spray the whole repair area with a light coat of primer – this will show up any imperfections in the surface of the filler. Repair these imperfections with fresh filler paste or bodystopper, and once more smooth the surface with abrasive paper. If bodystopper is used, it can be mixed with cellulose thinners to form a really thin paste which is ideal for filling small holes. Repeat this spray and repair procedure until you are satisfied that the surface of the filler, and the feathered edge of the paintwork are perfect. Clean the repair area with clean water and allow to dry fully.

The repair area is now ready for final spraying. Paint spraying must be carried out in warm, dry, windless and dust free atmosphere. This condition can be created artificially if you have access to a large indoor working area, but if you are forced to work in the open, you will have to pick your day very carefully. If you are working indoors, dousing the floor in the work area with water will help to settle the dust which would otherwise be in the atmosphere. If the repair area is confined to one body panel, mask off the surrounding panels; this will help to minimise the effects of a slight mis-match in paint colours. Bodywork fittings (eg chrome strips, door handles etc) will also need to be masked off. Use genuine masking tape and several thicknesses of newspaper for the masking operations.

Before commencing to spray, agitate the aerosol can thoroughly, then spray a test area (an old tin, or similar) until the technique is mastered. Cover the repair area with a thick coat of primer; the thickness should be built up using several thin layers of paint rather than one thick one. Using 400 grade wet-and-dry paper, rub down the surface of the primer until it is really smooth. While doing this, the work area should be thoroughly doused with water, and the wet-and-dry paper periodically rinsed in water. Allow to dry before spraying on more paint.

Spray on the top coat, again building up the thickness by using several thin layers of paint. Start spraying in the centre of the repair area and then, using a circular motion, work outwards until the whole repair area and about 2 inches of the surrounding original paintwork is covered. Remove all masking material 10 to 15 minutes after spraying on the final coat of paint.

Allow the new paint at least two weeks to harden, then, using a paintwork renovator or a very fine cutting paste, blend the edges of the paint into the existing paintwork. Finally, apply wax polish.

5 Major body damage – repair

Where serious damage has occurred or large areas need renewal due to neglect, it means certainly that completely new sections or panels will need welding in, and this is best left to professionals. If the damage is due to impact it will also be necessary to completely check the alignment of the bodyshell structure. Due to the principle of construction, the strength and shape of the whole car can be affected by damage to one part. In such instances the services of the official agent with specialist checking jigs are essential. If a body is left misaligned, it is first of all dangerous as the car will not handle properly, and secondly, uneven stresses will be imposed on the steering, engine and transmission, causing abnormal wear or complete failure. Tyre wear may also be excessive.

6 Maintenance – hinges and locks

1   Oil the hinges of the bonnet, doors and boot with a drop or two of light oil periodically. A good time is after the car has been washed.
2   Similarly lubricate the door catches and bonnet and boot release mechanism.
3   Apply a smear of general purpose grease to the lock strikers and striker plates.

7 Door rattles – tracing and rectification

1   Check first that the door is not loose at the hinges and that the latch is holding the door firmly in position. Check also that the door lines up with the aperture in the body.
2   If the hinges are loose, or the door is out of alignment, it will be necessary to reset the hinge positions. This is a straightforward matter after slackening the hinge retaining screws slightly, following which the door can be repositioned in/out or up/down.
3   If the latch is holding the door properly, it should hold the door tightly when fully latched, and the door should line up with the body. If adjustment is required, slacken the striker plate screws slightly and reposition the plate in/out or up/down as necessary.
4   Other rattles from the door could be caused by wear or looseness in the window winder, or the glass channels, seal strips and interlock lock mechanism.

8 Bonnet – removal, refitting and adjustment

1   Support the bonnet in its open position, and place some cardboard or cloth between the front edge and the front crossmember.
2   Mark the location of the hinges with a pencil.
3   Unbolt the support arm from the bonnet (photo).
4   With the help of an assistant, unscrew the hinge bolts and lift the bonnet from the car (photo).
5   Refitting is a reversal of removal, but after fully closing the bonnet, check that it is central and aligned with the surrounding bodywork. If adjustment is necessary, loosen the hinge-to-bonnet bolts to position the bonnet side-to-side and front-to-rear, and loosen the hinge-to-bulkhead bolts to position the bonnet front edge height. Tighten the bolts after making the adjustment, then check that the bonnet closes correctly – if necessary adjust the bonnet lock as described in Section 9.

9 Bonnet lock – removal, refitting and adjustment

1   Open the bonnet and unbolt the lock from the bulkhead (photo).
2   Disconnect the cable and withdraw the lock from the car.
3   Refitting is a reversal of removal, but the lock must be positioned so that the striker on the bonnet aligns with the entry slot in the lock. The bonnet rear edge height is also adjusted by positioning the lock up or down. The lock position is best adjusted with the bolts only slightly loosened, then fully tightened afterward.

10 Boot lid – removal, refitting and adjustment

1   Open the boot lid and place some cardboard or cloth between the front edge and the body and rear window.
2   Mark the location of the hinges with a pencil.
3   With the help of an assistant, unscrew the hinge nuts and lift the boot lid from the car (photo).
4   Refitting is a reversal of removal, but check the boot lid is central and aligned with the surrounding bodywork when closed. If adjustment is necessary, loosen the hinge nuts and move the boot lid to the

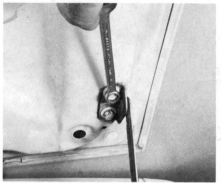

8.3 Unbolting bonnet support arm

8.4 Unscrewing bonnet hinge bolts

9.1 Bonnet lock location

10.3 Boot lid hinge location

11.2A Removing boot lid lock centre guard plate

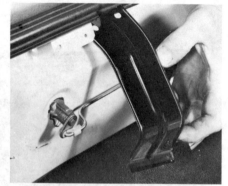

11.2B Removing boot lid private lock guard plate

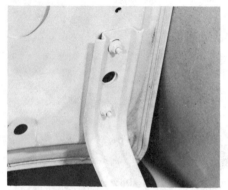

11.2C Removing boot lid lock bolts

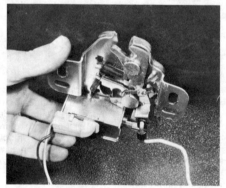

11.3 Removing boot lid lock

11.4 Boot lid lock striker location

side or front or rear. Tighten the nuts after making the adjustment, then check that the boot lid closes correctly – if necessary, adjust the boot lid lock as described in Section 11.

11 Boot lid lock – removal, refitting and adjustment

1   Disconnect the battery negative lead.
2   With the boot lid open, unbolt the lock from the rear panel. Also remove the guard plates (photos).
3   Disconnect the solenoid wiring and the rod to the private lock. Withdraw the boot lid lock (photo).
4   Refitting is a reversal of removal, but the lock must be positioned within the oversize holes so that the striker aligns with the entry slot, and the boot lid is in firm contact with the sealing rubber when shut. If necessary the striker may be adjusted within the elongated holes (photo).

12 Front and rear doors – removal, refitting and adjustment

1   Support the door with axle stands – place cloth beneath the door edge to protect the paint.
2   Unscrew the bolts securing the hinges to the body and withdraw the door (photo). Where applicable disconnect the central door locking wiring.
3   Refitting is a reversal of removal, but check that the door closes correctly and is in firm contact with the sealing rubber when shut. If necessary, loosen the striker screws on the body and reposition the striker (photo).

13 Door trim panel – removal and refitting

1   Wind down the window to its lowest position and note the

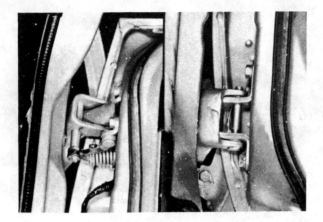

Fig. 12.1 Front door hinges (Sec 12)

Left – upper   Right – lower

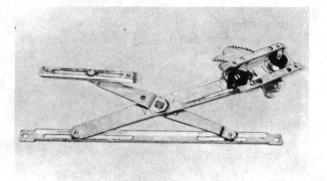

Fig. 12.2 Front door window regulator (Sec 14)

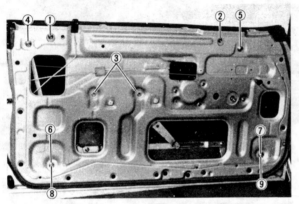

Fig. 12.3 Front door window adjustment points (Sec 14)

1 and 2   Window stops
3   Regulator guide bolts
4, 5, 6 and 7   Window channel adjustment bolts and locknuts
8 and 9   Window in/out adjustment bolts

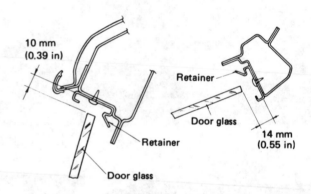

Fig. 12.4 Front door window vertical and horizontal adjustment
dimensions (Sec 14)

position of the window regulator handle.
2   Prise off the cover and unscrew the regulator handle retaining screw. Remove the handle (photos).
3   Remove the cover and screws, and withdraw the armrest (photos).
4   Remove the screw securing the inner door handle to the door (photos).
5   Using a wide-bladed screwdriver, prise the trim panel clips from the door.
6   Lift the trim panel over the locking buton, and at the same time guide the inner handle through the aperture. Remove the panel.
7   If necessary peel the polythene sheet from the door, taking care not to tear it.
8   Refitting is a reversal of removal, but fit the window regulator handle in its previously noted position.

14 Front door window regulator and glass – removal and refitting

1   Remove the trim panel as described in Section 13.
2   On Coupe models, remove the window stop.
3   Unscrew the screws or nuts (as applicable) securing the window to the regulator (photo).
4   Push the window fully upward and support it with a block of wood.
5   Unscrew the regulator mounting bolts, then, with the regulator in the middle position, withdraw it through the aperture in the door (photo).
6   Remove the inner and outer weatherstrips from the door.
7   Withdraw the glass from the top of the door.
8   Refitting is a reversal of removal, but check that the upper edge of the glass follows the contour of the frame or body aperture (as

applicable). If necessary loosen the regulator fixed guide bolts and adjust the guide up or down, but keeping it parallel to the door bottom edge. On Coupe models adjust the vertical and horizontal positions of the window with reference to Figs. 12. 3 and 12.4. To adjust the in/out position of the window top edge loosen the bottom window channel locknuts and turn the bolts until the clearance shown in Fig. 12.5 is obtained. After tightening the locknuts apply mastic to the bolts and holes.

15 Front door lock (standard) – removal and refitting

1   Remove the trim panel as described in Section 13.
2   Disconnect the control rods from the outside handle, inner handle, and private lock (photo).
3   Unclip and remove the inner handle (photo).
4   Unscrew the cross-head screws and withdraw the lock from the door aperture.
5   Refitting is a reversal of removal.

16 Front door outer handle and private lock – removal and refitting

1   Remove the trim panel as described in Section 13.
2   Disconnect the control rods from the outside handle and private lock.
3   Unscrew the nuts and remove the outer handle.
4   Prise out the spring clip and withdraw the private lock.
5   Refitting is a reversal of removal.

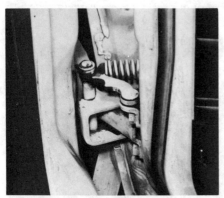

12.2 Front door lower hinge

12.3 Front door striker

13.2A Removing the cover ...

13.2B ... and window regulator handle

13.3A Removing the cover ...

13.3B ... and screws from the armrest

13.4A Removing the screw ...

13.4B ... and inner door handle

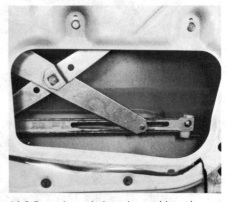

14.3 Front door window glass guide and regulator

14.5 Front door window regulator mounting bolt locations

15.2 Front door lock and control rods

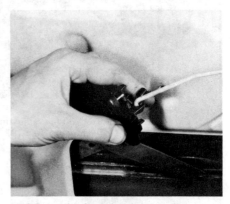

15.3 Removing front door inner handle

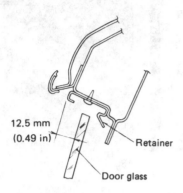

12.5 mm
(0.49 in)

Retainer

Door glass

Fig. 12.5 Front door and rear quarter window in/out adjustment
dimensions (Secs 14 and 19)

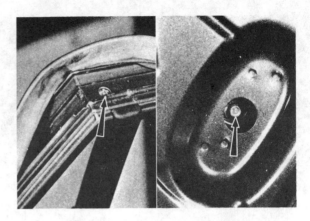

Fig. 12.6 Rear door window channel bolts (Sec 18)

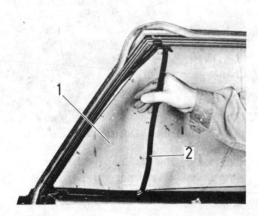

Fig. 12.7 Rear door fixed quarterlight (1) and seal (2) (Sec 18)

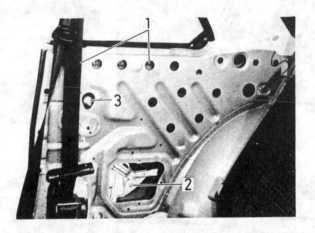

Fig. 12.8 Rear quarter window regulator location on Coupe
models (Sec 19)

1 Window stops   2 Guide bolts   3 Regulator

Fig. 12.9 Rear quarter window adjustment points on Coupe
models (Sec 19)

1 and 2   Window stops   5   In/out adjustment
3 and 4   Horizontal adjustment

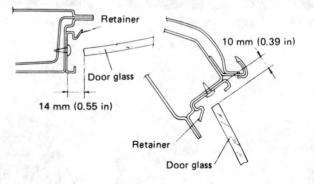

Retainer

Door glass

14 mm (0.55 in)

10 mm (0.39 in)

Retainer

Door glass

Fig. 12.10 Rear quarter window horizontal and vertical adjustment
dimensions on Coupe models (Sec 19)

17 Rear door window regulator and glass – removal and refitting

1 Remove the fixed quarterlight as described in Section 18.
2 Remove the inner and outer weatherstrips.
3 Unscrew the regulator mounting bolts, and withdraw the regulator from the door aperture, at the same time disengaging the control arm from the window guide.
4 Withdraw the glass from the top of the door.
5 Refitting is a reversal of removal.

18 Rear door fixed quarterlight – removal and refitting

1 Remove the door trim panel as described in Section 13.
2 Pull back the weatherstrip and unscrew the cross-head screws from the top of the rear window channel.
3 Unscrew the lower bolt and withdraw the rear window channel from the door.
4 Pull the fixed quarterlight from the door together with the rubber seal.
5 Refitting is a reversal of removal.

19 Rear quarter window regulator and glass (Coupe models) – removal and refitting

1 Remove the rear seat cushion, then remove the nut and bolt and lift out the seat back filler pad.
2 Prise out the cap, remove the screw, and pull off the window regulator handle.
3 Remove the seat belt reel cover then, using a wide-bladed screwdriver, prise off the trim panel. Peel off the polythene sheet.
4 Remove the outer weatherstrip and unscrew the window stops from the body panel.
5 Unscrew the bolts securing the lower guide to the regulator, and withdraw the window glass upward.
6 Unbolt the regulator and withdraw it through the body aperture.
7 Refitting is a reversal of removal, but adjust the position of the glass as follows. Fully raise the window and adjust the upper stops to provide the vertical clearance shown in Fig. 12.10. Check that the glass moves smoothly – if not, loosen the guide bolts and locknut and reposition the guide. With the window fully raised, adjust the horizontal position of the glass with reference to Fig. 12.10 by repositioning the guide. Finally adjust the in/out position with reference to Fig. 12.5 by loosening the lower locknut and turning the bolt. After tightening the locknut apply mastic to the bolt and hole.

20 Windscreen and rear window glass – removal and refitting

The windscreen and rear window glass are bonded to the body with special adhesives, and their removal and refitting are therefore best entrusted to a specialist in this work.

21 Bumpers – removal and refitting

Front bumper
1 On UK models, disconnect the headlight cleaner pipes and clips if fitted, then unscrew the bracket-to-body nuts and withdraw the bumper, noting that the side caps slide from the location slots. If necessary remove the nuts and bolts and dismantle the side caps and brackets.
2 On US and Canadian models, unscrew the nuts attaching the shock absorbers to the body, then unscrew the shock absorber inner mounting nuts from within the engine compartment. Withdraw the front bumper, and if necessary remove the shock absorbers.
3 On all models refitting is a reversal of removal, but additionally on US and Canadian models check the fitting dimensions given in Fig. 12.13 with all the tyres inflated to the correct pressure.

Rear bumper
4 On UK models, disconnect the battery negative lead, then disconnect the rear foglamp wiring. Unscrew the bracket-to-body

mounting nuts and withdraw the bumper. If necessary remove the nuts and bolts and dismantle the side caps, brackets and foglamps.
5 On US and Canadian models, unscrew the nuts attaching the shock absorbers to the body. Open the boot lid, remove the cover plate, and unscrew the shock absorber inner mounting nuts. Withdraw the rear bumper, and if necessary remove the shock absorbers.

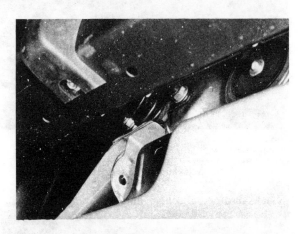

Fig. 12.11 Front bumper shock absorber outer mounting on US and Canadian models (Sec 21)

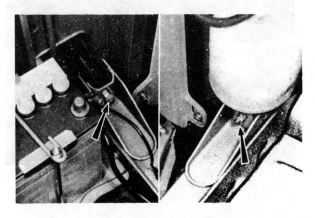

Fig. 12.12 Front bumper shock absorber inner mountings on US and Canadian models (Sec 21)

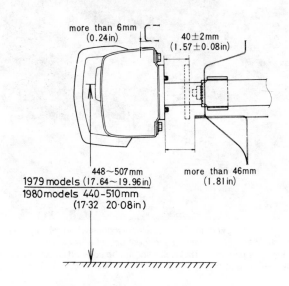

more than 6mm (0.24 in)

40 ± 2mm (1.57 ± 0.08in)

$448 \sim 507$mm
1979 models (17.64 ~ 19.96 in)
1980 models 440~510mm
(17·32 20.08 in)

more than 46mm (1.81 in)

Fig. 12.13 Front bumper shock absorber fitting dimensions on US and Canadian models (Sec 21)

This photo sequence illustrates the repair of a dent and damaged paintwork. The procedure for the repair of a hole is similar. Refer to the text for more complete instructions

After removing any adjacent body trim, hammer the dent out. The damaged area should then be made slightly concave

Use coarse sandpaper or a sanding disc on a drill motor to remove all paint from the damaged area. Feather the sanded area into the edges of the surrounding paint, using progressively finer grades of sandpaper

The damaged area should be treated with rust remover prior to application of the body filler. In the case of a rust hole, all rusted sheet metal should be cut away

Carefully follow manufacturer's instructions when mixing the body filler so as to have the longest possible working time during application. Rust holes should be covered with fiberglass screen held in place with dabs of body filler prior to repair

Apply the filler with a flexible applicator in thin layers at 20 minute intervals. Use an applicator such as a wood spatula for confined areas. The filler should protrude slightly above the surrounding area

Shape the filler with a surform-type plane. Then, use water and progressively finer grades of sandpaper and a sanding block to wet-sand the area until it is smooth. Feather the edges of the repair area into the surrounding paint.

Use spray or brush applied primer to cover the entire repair area so that slight imperfections in the surface will be filled in. Prime at least one inch into the area surrounding the repair. Be careful of over-spray when using spray-type primer

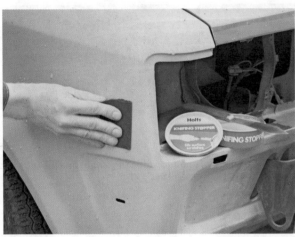

Wet-sand the primer with fine (approximately 400 grade) sandpaper until the area is smooth to the touch and blended into the surrounding paint. Use filler paste on minor imperfections

After the filler paste has dried, use rubbing compound to ensure that the surface of the primer is smooth. Prior to painting, the surface should be wiped down with a tack rag or lint-free cloth soaked in lacquer thinner

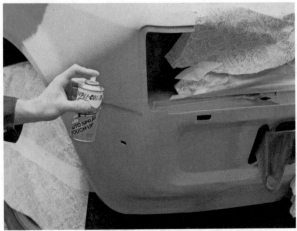

Choose a dry, warm, breeze-free area in which to paint and make sure that adjacent areas are protected from over-spray. Shake the spray paint can thoroughly and apply the top coat to the repair area, building it up by applying several coats, working from the center

After allowing at least two weeks for the paint to harden, use fine rubbing compound to blend the area into the original paint. Wax can now be applied

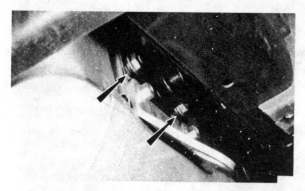

Fig. 12.14 Rear bumper shock absorber outer mounting on US and Canadian models (Sec 21)

Fig. 12.15 Rear bumper shock absorber cover plate and inner mounting on US and Canadian models (Sec 21)

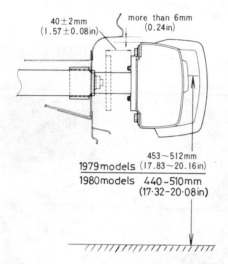

Fig. 12.16 Rear bumper shock absorber fitting dimensions on US and Canadian models (Sec 21)

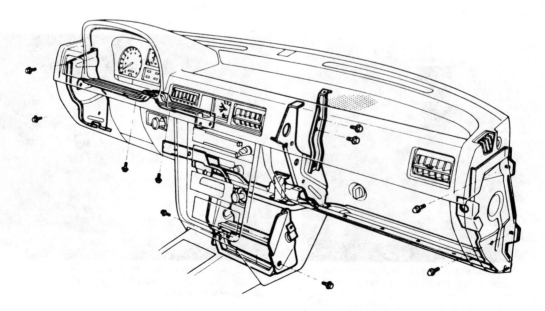

Fig. 12.17 Upper facia bolt location (arrowed) and plastic cover (Sec 22)

Fig. 12.18 Facia bracket locations (Sec 22)

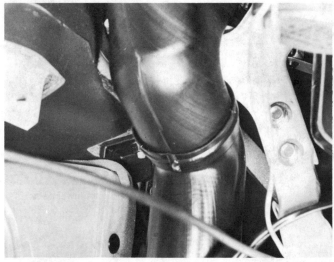

22.7 Facia centre vent hose

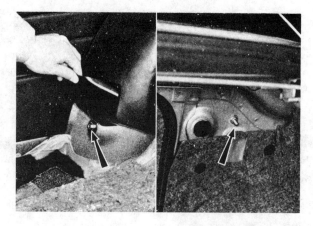

Fig. 12.21 Split rear seat filler pad bolt and nut location – arrowed (Sec 23)

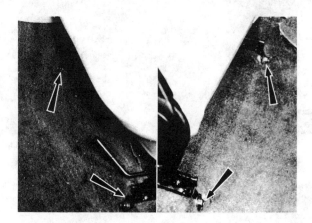

Fig. 12.19 Front seat mounting bolts – arrowed (Sec 23)

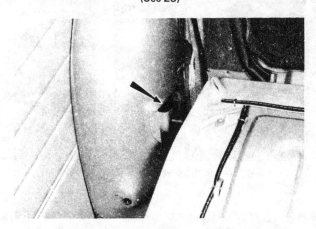

Fig. 12.22 Split rear seat hinge bush – arrowed (Sec 23)

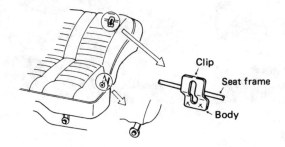

Fig. 12.20 Standard rear seat fastenings (Sec 23)

6   On all models refitting is a reversal of removal, but additionally on US and Canadian models check the fitting dimensions given in Fig. 12.16 with all the tyres inflated to the correct pressure.

22 Facia panel – removal and refitting

1   Remove the combination switch as described in Chapter 10.
2   Remove the instrument panel as described in Chapter 10.
3   Remove the glovebox as described in Section 24.
4   Remove the switch panel as described in Chapter 10.
5   Remove the facia centre panel as described in Chapter 10.
6   Remove the screws and prise the plastic cover from the centre console. Remove the retaining screws and withdraw the centre console over the handbrake lever after removing the knob.
7   Disconnect the side vent hoses and centre vent hoses (photo).
8   Unscrew the steering column-to-facia bolts.
9   Prise out the plastic covers and unscrew the upper facia bolts.
10 Unscrew the side mounting bolts, then withdraw the facia panel approximately 6 in (152 mm) and disconnect the remaining wiring, at the same time noting its location.
11 Withdraw the facia panel from the car.
12 Refitting is a reversal of removal.

23 Seats – removal and refitting

1   To remove the front seat, slide the seat forward and unscrew the rear runner mounting bolts, then slide the seat rearward and unscrew the front runner mounting bolts. Remove the seat from the car.
2   To remove the standard rear seat, first unscrew the cushion front mounting bolts and lift out the cushion. Unscrew the seat back lower mounting bolts and slide the back from the retaining clips in an upward direction.
3   To remove the split rear seat, first unscrew the cushion front mounting bolts and lift out the cushion. Unscrew the nuts and bolts and remove the seat back filler pads (nuts in boot compartment). Pull the seats forward and detach the floor mat, then lift each seat from the hinge bushes.
4   Refitting of front and rear seats is a reversal of removal.

24 Glovebox – removal and refitting

1   Open the glovebox and remove the bottom securing screws.

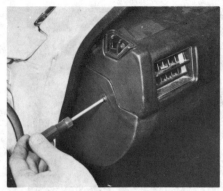

24.2 Glovebox side retaining screw location

24.3 Removing glovebox

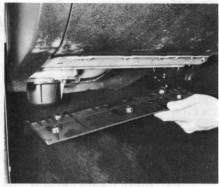

25.2 Removing heater motor lower panel

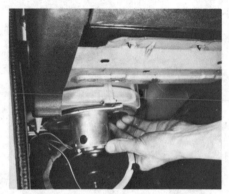

25.3A Removing heater motor cover ...

25.3B ... and heater motor

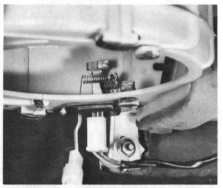

25.4A Heater motor wiring and control coils

25.4B Heater motor intake assembly

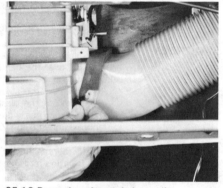

25.10 Removing air supply hose clip

25.11 Heater unit lower mounting nut location

2   Remove the side screw, then the four upper screws, noting that the middle screws retain the striker plate (photo).
3   Withdraw the glovebox from the facia (photo).
4   Refitting is a reversal of removal.

25 Heater – removal and refitting

1   Disconnect the battery negative lead.

Heater motor
2   The heater motor is located beneath the left-hand side of the facia panel. First remove the lower panel (photo). Remove the wiring from the retaining clip and note the location of the clip.
3   Remove the screws and lower the cover and motor from the air intake manifold (photos).
4   Disconnect the wiring and withdraw the heater motor (photos).
5   Refitting is a reversal of removal.

Heater unit and matrix assembly
6   Remove the facia as described in Section 22.
7   Remove the heater control mounting screws.
8   Drain the cooling system as described in Chapter 2.
9   Identify then disconnect the two hoses from the left-hand side of the heater unit.
10   Prise out the plastic clip and disconnect the air supply hose (photo).
11   Unscrew the mounting nuts and withdraw the heater unit from the car (photo).
12   Refitting is a reversal of removal. Refer to Chapter 2 for the cooling system refilling procedure.

26 Air conditioning system – general

1   On models equipped with air conditioning, the maintenance operations must be limited to the items given in the following

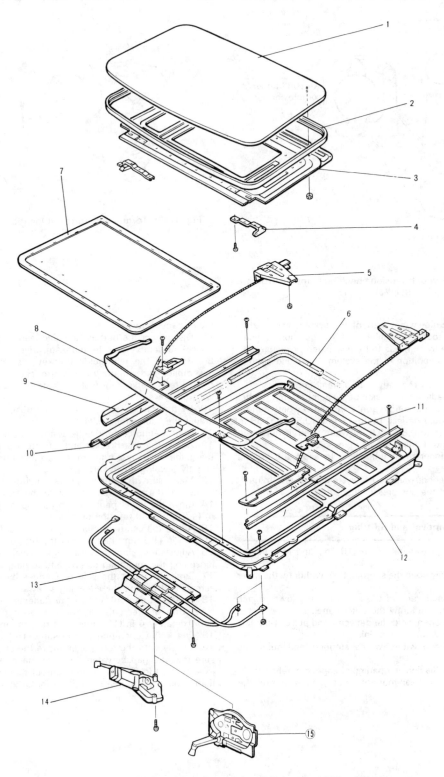

Fig. 12.23 Exploded view of the sliding sunroof (Sec 27)

1	Outer panel	5	Rear guide bracket	9	Rail cover	13	Tube assembly
2	Weatherstrip	6	Packing	10	Side rail	14	Motor
3	Lower panel	7	Inner trim	11	Stopper	15	Regulator
4	Front guide bracket	8	Deflector	12	Frame		

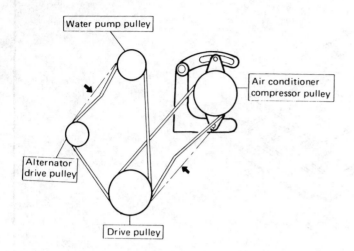

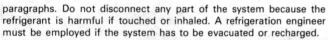

Fig. 12.24 Showing drivebelt tension checking points – arrowed
(Sec 26)

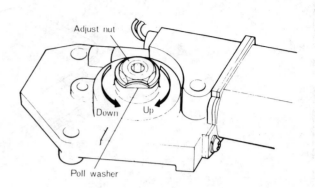

Fig. 12.25 Torque adjusting nut location on the sunroof motor
(Sec 27)

paragraphs. Do not disconnect any part of the system because the refrigerant is harmful if touched or inhaled. A refrigeration engineer must be employed if the system has to be evacuated or recharged.

2   Regularly check the condition of the system hoses and connections.

3   Clean the condenser fins regularly with a small brush.

4   Regularly check and adjust the tension of the compressor drivebelt – when pressed firmly with the thumb at a point midway between the two pulleys, the bolt should deflect 14 to 17 mm (0.55 to 0.65 in) when new or 20 to 23 mm (0.8 to 0.9 in) when used. If necessary adjust the tension by repositioning the compressor.

5   Keep the air conditioner drain tube clear to allow the internal condensation to disperse.

6   During the winter period, operate the system for a few minutes every two weeks to keep the compressor lubricated.

27 Sliding sunroof – removal and refitting

1   Open the sunroof approximately 4 in (10 cm) and remove the inner trim clips.

2   Pull the trim down, fully open the sunroof, then withdraw the inner trim.

3   With the sunroof closed, remove the nuts from the lower panel, slightly lift the panel, then withdraw the outer panel.

4   With the lower panel open, hold the deflector and pull out the link connector. Withdraw the deflector and link.

5   Remove the screws and withdraw the stoppers and guide rail covers.

6   Close the lower panel leaving an opening of approximately 1.85 in (47 mm), then unscrew the rear mounting nuts and withdraw the

lower panel upward.

7   Disconnect the battery negative lead, then remove the overhead console assembly and the motor or drive gear located in the recess.

8   Remove the rear guide bracket assemblies from the side rail assemblies and withdraw the control cables.

9   To refit the sunroof first lubricate the cables and sliding surfaces with grease.

10 Fit the cables into the tube assembly, install the side rails, and adjust the cables for position.

11 Refit the motor or drive gear, and the overhead console assembly.

12 Adjust the rear bracket and refit the lower panel. Make sure that the guide rollers are in the rails, then fully open the lower panel while slightly pushing downward.

13 Make sure that the stoppers are fitted to the correct sides as shown on the reverse side and with the arrow pointing forward.

14 Close the lower panel, leaving an opening of approximately 1.85 in (47 mm), and refit the outer panel.

15 Adjust the centre rear edge of the sunroof so that it is a maximum of 0.06 in (1.5 mm) higher than the roof panel.

16 Adjust the side forward edges level with the roof panel by loosening the mounting screws and turning the adjusting screws.

17 Similarly adjust the side rear edges by loosening the mounting screws and turning the adjusting screws.

18 Open the sunroof and fit the deflector, then carefully insert the inner trim between the frame and lower panel. Open the sunroof approximately 4 in (100 mm) and refit the inner trim.

19 Check the operation of the sunroof; if the rear edge interferes excessively with the roof panel, move the stopper forward, but make sure that the gap between the outer panel and roof panel does not exceed 0.20 in (5 mm). If the sunroof movement is too hard or too light, adjust the torque nut on the motor as necessary.

Chapter 13 Supplement:
Revisions and information on 1982 models

Contents

1 Introduction

This supplement contains specifications and changes that apply to vehicles produced in 1982.

Where no differences (or very minor differences) exist between 1982 models and 1981 models, no information is given here. In those instances, the original material included in Chapters 1 through 12 should be used.

2 Specifications

Note: *The specifications listed here include only those items which differ from those listed in Chapters 1 through 12. For information not specifically listed here, refer to the appropriate Chapter.*

General dimensions, capacities

Overall length	4415 mm (174 in)
Manual transmission oil capacity	
1600	1.0 litre (1.8 pint)
2000	1.1 litre (1.9 pint)

Engine

Valve spring free length	
Standard	40.6 mm (1.598 in)
Limit	39.4 mm (1.551 in)
Valve spring trueness of right angle (limit)	1.43 mm (0.056 in)

Fuel system

Carburetor main jet sizes (USA only)	
Primary	107
Secondary	145
Fast idle adjustment clearance	0.45 to 0.75 mm (0.018 to 0.030 in)
Float level adjustment	11.5 mm (0.453 in)

Braking system

Torque specifications	lbf-ft	Nm
Caliper slide pin (lower)	36	50
Caliper slide pin (upper)	62	85

Suspension and steering

Steering geometry	
King pin inclination	10° 36'
Camber	1° 14' ± 30'
Caster	3° 27' ± 45'

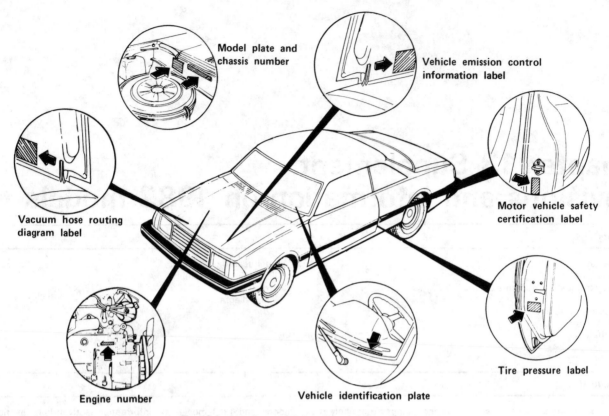

Fig. 13.1   Locations of the various information labels

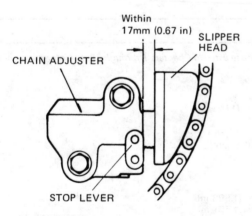

Fig. 13.2   The new timing chain adjuster features a
ratchet design to eliminate slack in the chain

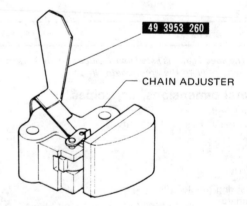

Fig. 13.3   The adjuster is shown here with the special
retaining tool properly positioned, ready for installation to
the engine, followed by chain adjustment

3   Vehicle identification numbers

Various indentification labels have been added. These labels contain valuable information concerning the maintenance and servicing of your vehicle. See Fig. 13.1 for a representative sampling of the various labels and their locations.

4   Engine

Timing chain adjuster

1   An alteration of the chain adjuster mechanism has taken place for the 1982 models. The new design features a ratchet-action operation.

Engine disassembly

2   When disassembling the engine, before removing the timing chain components, measure the protrusion of the chain adjuster as shown in Fig. 13.2. If the distance is greater than 17mm (0.67 in), a new timing chain should be fitted.

Timing chain adjustment

3   Whenever the engine has been disassembled or new timing chain components have been installed, a new procedure must be followed for adjusting the timing chain.

4   Move the stop lever on the chain adjuster towards the slipper head.

5   If the adjuster is installed on the engine, turn the engine crankshaft counterclockwise slightly.

6   Push in the slipper head and install the chain adjuster retaining tool (Mazda 49 3953 260). This special tool will hold the adjuster in the

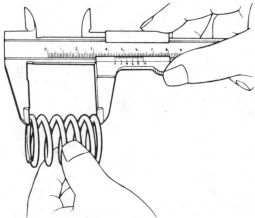

Fig. 13.4   Measuring valve spring free length

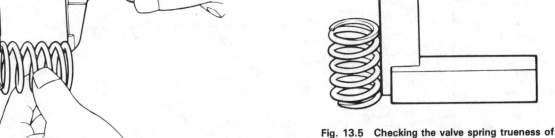

Fig. 13.5   Checking the valve spring trueness of
right angle

retracted position.

7   Continue assembling the engine as described in Chapter 1, Section 35, Steps 10 through 21. Note that Allen head screws are now used to secure the timing chain guide (the screws which should be left finger-tight during reassembly).

8   With the access plugs on the timing cover removed, slightly rotate the crankshaft in a clockwise direction.

9   Working through the access holes, carefully press the top of the chain guide strip with a screwdriver and tighten the Allen head guide strip attaching screws.

10   Remove the retaining tool previously installed.

11   The timing chain is now tensioned properly and final engine assembly, Chapter 1, can be completed. However, take note of the new camshaft design in Steps 14 through 16 below.

Valve springs

12   The inner and outer type of valve spring has been replaced by a new design which eliminates the inner spring.

13   When inspecting these new valve springs, check the free length as well as the right angle trueness (see accompanying Figs.).

Camshaft

14   A new camshaft design has been introduced which does away with the sprocket retaining nut at the front of the camshaft. Refer to Chapter 1, Section 38 and photograph 38.14 for the following.

15   In place of the camshaft sprocket lock tab and retaining nut, a spacer is located between the sprocket and distributor drive gear.

16   The lockwasher and locknut remain on the end of the camshaft to secure all components.

---

5   Manual gearbox

Dismantling/reassembly

1   Spring pins instead of bolts now secure the shift forks and shift

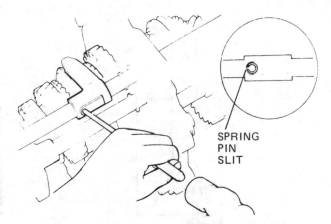

SPRING
PIN
SLIT

Fig. 13.6   Spring pins should be driven into place to
secure the shift forks and shift rod ends (note the
direction of the slit in relation to the shift rod)

rod ends to the shift rods.

2   When assembling these components only, new spring pins should be used. Additionally, the slit in the spring pin must be installed in the direction of the shift rod axis (see Fig. 13.6).

---

6   Electrical system

Wiring diagrams

Changes to the various electrical circuits on affected models can be seen in the accompanying wiring diagrams. Unless included in this Chapter, the wiring remains as for the 1981 models in Chapter 10.

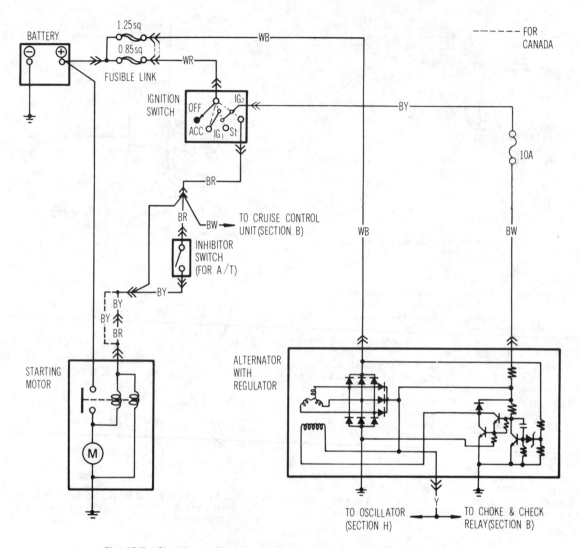

Fig. 13.7 Charging and starting systems wiring diagram (North America)

Key to Figs. 13.7 to 13.19 inclusive

Colour code

Where a wire is shown to be coded with two colours, the first is the basic colour, the second is the stripe colour

B — Black	L — Blue	R — Red
Br — Brown	Lb — Light blue	W — White
G — Green	Lg — Light green	Y — Yellow
Gy — Gray	O — Orange	

Abbreviations

St — Start	Hi — High	V — Volt	SW — Switch
IG — Ignition	RH — Right hand	A — Amp	Sq — Square millimeter
ACC — Accessory	LH — Left-hand	W — Watt	A/T — Automatic transmission
AS — Auto stop	FR — Front right	R — Resistance	M/T — Manual transmission
INT — Intermittent	FL — Front left	Tr — Transistor	NO — Normal open
Lo — Low	RR — Rear right	M — Motor	NC — Normal closed
Mi — Middle	RL — Rear left		

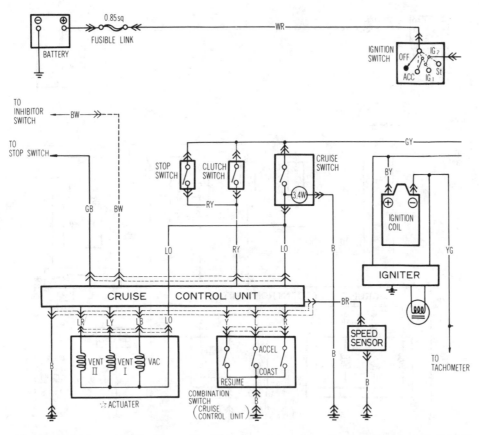

Fig. 13.8 Cruise control/ignition and emissions systems wiring diagram (USA models) (1 of 2)

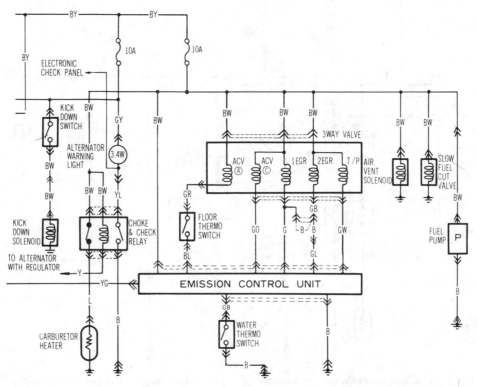

Fig. 13.9 Cruise control/ignition and emissions systems wiring diagram (USA models) (2 of 2)

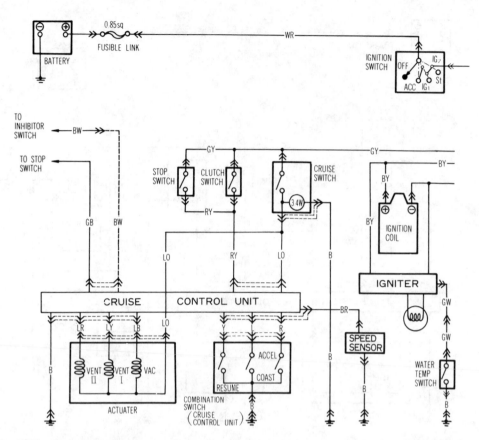

Fig. 13.10   Cruise control/ignition and emissions systems wiring diagram (Canadian models) (1 of 2)

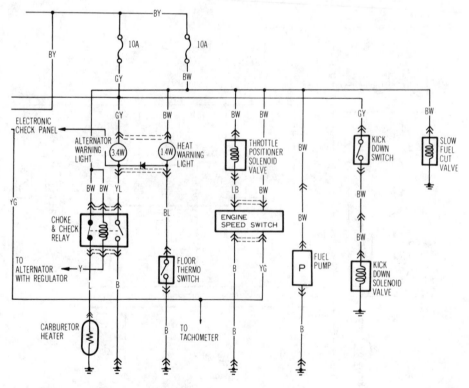

Fig. 13.11   Cruise control/ignition and emissions systems wiring diagram (Canadian models) (2 of 2)

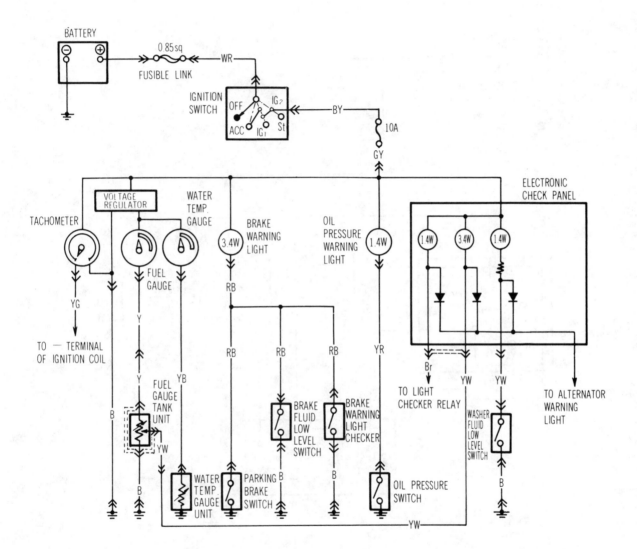

Fig. 13.12 Meter/warning systems and electronic check panel wiring diagram (North America)

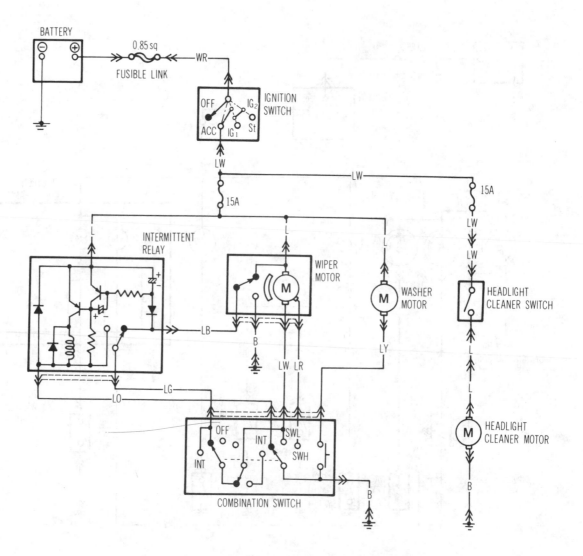

Fig. 13.13 Wiper/washer/headlight cleaner systems wiring diagram (North America)

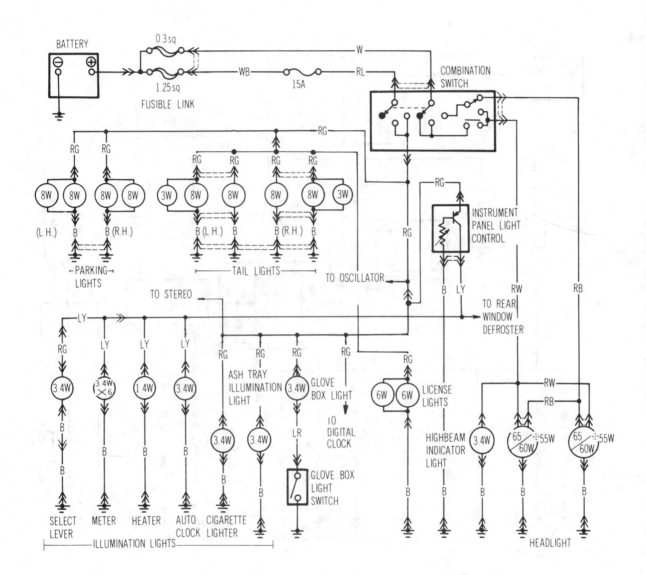

Fig. 13.14 Lighting systems wiring diagrams (North America)

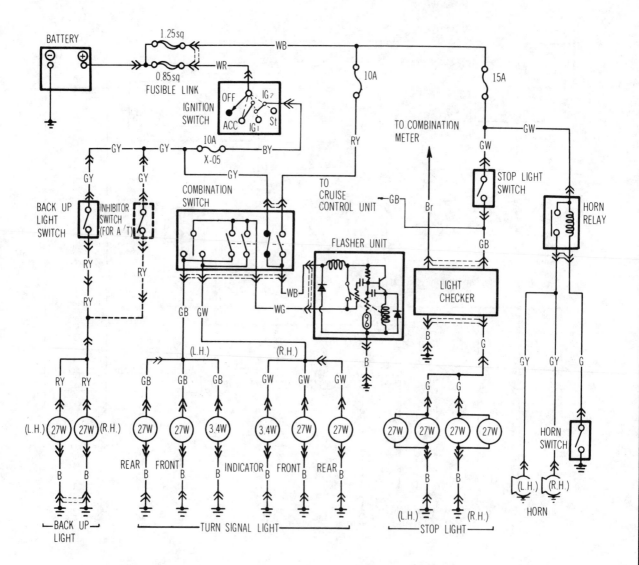

Fig. 13.15 Turn signal/back-up lights/stop lights wiring diagram (North America)

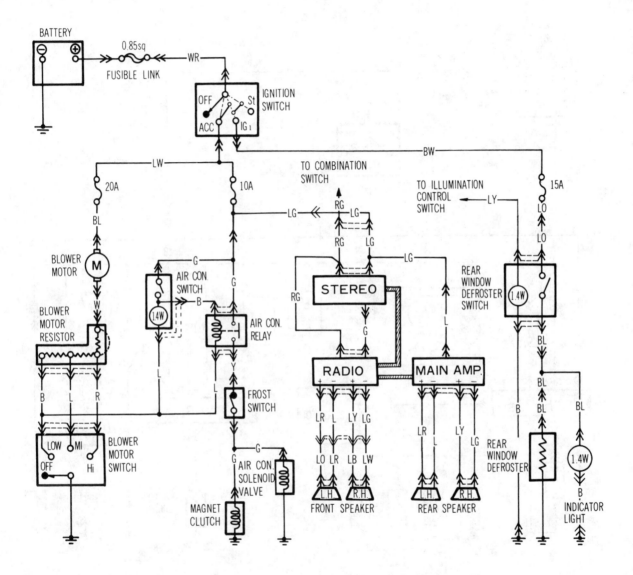

Fig. 13.16 Air conditioning/radio/stereo and rear window defroster wiring diagram (North America)

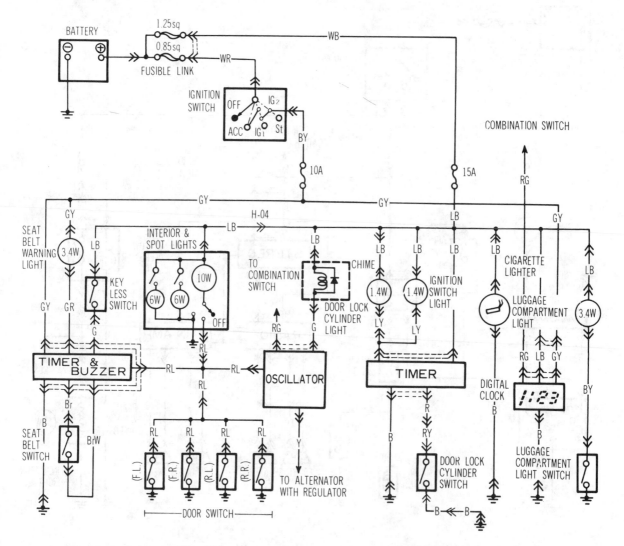

Fig. 13.17 Seat belt warning/spot light/clock/interior courtesy lamps wiring diagram (North America)

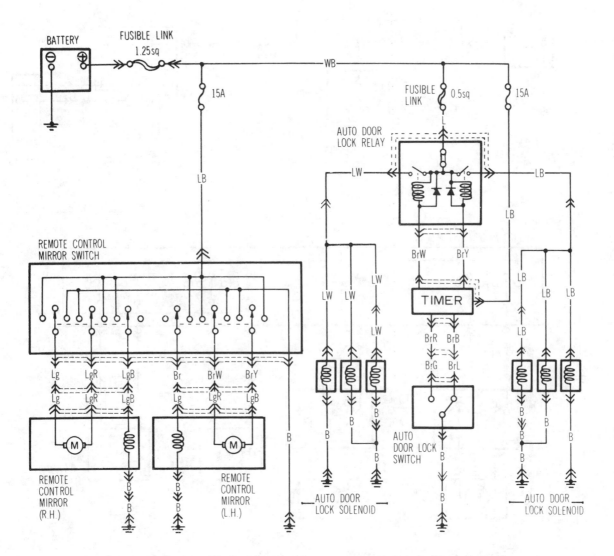

Fig. 13.18 Outside mirror and automatic door lock wiring diagram (North America)

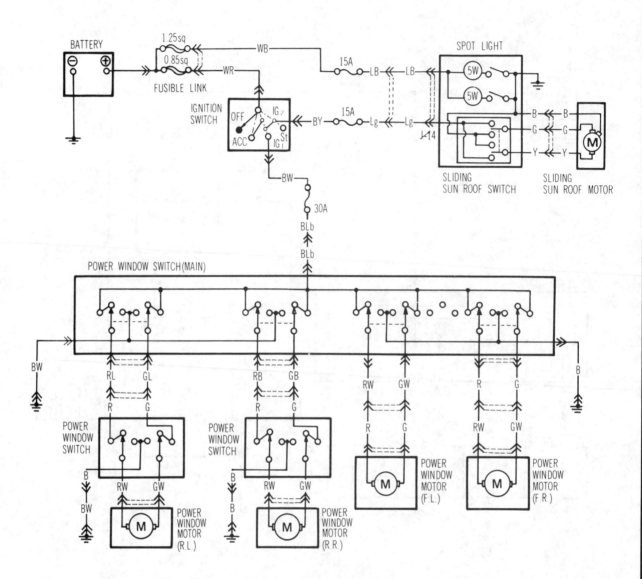

Fig. 13.19 Power window and sliding sunroof wiring diagram (North America)

Conversion factors

Length (distance)

Inches (in)	X	25.4	= Millimetres (mm)	X 0.0394	= Inches (in)
Feet (ft)	X	0.305	= Metres (m)	X 3.281	= Feet (ft)
Miles	X	1.609	= Kilometres (km)	X 0.621	= Miles

Volume (capacity)

Cubic inches (cu in; in³)	X	16.387	= Cubic centimetres (cc; cm³)	X 0.061	= Cubic inches (cu in; in³)
Imperial pints (Imp pt)	X	0.568	= Litres (l)	X 1.76	= Imperial pints (Imp pt)
Imperial quarts (Imp qt)	X	1.137	= Litres (l)	X 0.88	= Imperial quarts (Imp qt)
Imperial quarts (Imp qt)	X	1.201	= US quarts (US qt)	X 0.833	= Imperial quarts (Imp qt)
US quarts (US qt)	X	0.946	= Litres (l)	X 1.057	= US quarts (US qt)
Imperial gallons (Imp gal)	X	4.546	= Litres (l)	X 0.22	= Imperial gallons (Imp gal)
Imperial gallons (Imp gal)	X	1.201	= US gallons (US gal)	X 0.833	= Imperial gallons (Imp gal)
US gallons (US gal)	X	3.785	= Litres (l)	X 0.264	= US gallons (US gal)

Mass (weight)

Ounces (oz)	X	28.35	= Grams (g)	X 0.035	= Ounces (oz)
Pounds (lb)	X	0.454	= Kilograms (kg)	X 2.205	= Pounds (lb)

Force

Ounces-force (ozf; oz)	X	0.278	= Newtons (N)	X 3.6	= Ounces-force (ozf; oz)
Pounds-force (lbf; lb)	X	4.448	= Newtons (N)	X 0.225	= Pounds-force (lbf; lb)
Newtons (N)	X	0.1	= Kilograms-force (kgf; kg)	X 9.81	= Newtons (N)

Pressure

Pounds-force per square inch (psi; lbf/in²; lb/in²)	X	0.070	= Kilograms-force per square centimetre (kgf/cm²; kg/cm²)	X 14.223	= Pounds-force per square inch (psi; lbf/in²; lb/in²)
Pounds-force per square inch (psi; lbf/in²; lb/in²)	X	0.068	= Atmospheres (atm)	X 14.696	= Pounds-force per square inch (psi; lbf/in²; lb/in²)
Pounds-force per square inch (psi; lbf/in²; lb/in²)	X	0.069	= Bars	X 14.5	= Pounds-force per square inch (psi; lbf/in²; lb/in²)
Pounds-force per square inch (psi; lbf/in²; lb/in²)	X	6.895	= Kilopascals (kPa)	X 0.145	= Pounds-force per square inch (psi; lbf/in²; lb/in²)
Kilopascals (kPa)	X	0.01	= Kilograms-force per square centimetre (kgf/cm²; kg/cm²)	X 98.1	= Kilopascals (kPa)
Millibar (mbar)	X	100	= Pascals (Pa)	X 0.01	= Millibar (mbar)
Millibar (mbar)	X	0.0145	= Pounds-force per square inch (psi; lbf/in²; lb/in²)	X 68.947	= Millibar (mbar)
Millibar (mbar)	X	0.75	= Millimetres of mercury (mmHg)	X 1.333	= Millibar (mbar)
Millibar (mbar)	X	0.401	= Inches of water (inH₂O)	X 2.491	= Millibar (mbar)
Millimetres of mercury (mmHg)	X	0.535	= Inches of water (inH₂O)	X 1.868	= Millimetres of mercury (mmHg)
Inches of water (inH₂O)	X	0.036	= Pounds-force per square inch (psi; lbf/in²; lb/in²)	X 27.68	= Inches of water (inH₂O)

Torque (moment of force)

Pounds-force inches (lbf in; lb in)	X	1.152	= Kilograms-force centimetre (kgf cm; kg cm)	X 0.868	= Pounds-force inches (lbf in; lb in)
Pounds-force inches (lbf in; lb in)	X	0.113	= Newton metres (Nm)	X 8.85	= Pounds-force inches (lbf in; lb in)
Pounds-force inches (lbf in; lb in)	X	0.083	= Pounds-force feet (lbf ft; lb ft)	X 12	= Pounds-force inches (lbf in; lb in)
Pounds-force feet (lbf ft; lb ft)	X	0.138	= Kilograms-force metres (kgf m; kg m)	X 7.233	= Pounds-force feet (lbf ft; lb ft)
Pounds-force feet (lbf ft; lb ft)	X	1.356	= Newton metres (Nm)	X 0.738	= Pounds-force feet (lbf ft; lb ft)
Newton metres (Nm)	X	0.102	= Kilograms-force metres (kgf m; kg m)	X 9.804	= Newton metres (Nm)

Power

Horsepower (hp)	X	745.7	= Watts (W)	X 0.0013	= Horsepower (hp)

Velocity (speed)

Miles per hour (miles/hr; mph)	X	1.609	= Kilometres per hour (km/hr; kph)	X 0.621	= Miles per hour (miles/hr; mph)

Fuel consumption*

Miles per gallon, Imperial (mpg)	X	0.354	= Kilometres per litre (km/l)	X 2.825	= Miles per gallon, Imperial (mpg)
Miles per gallon, US (mpg)	X	0.425	= Kilometres per litre (km/l)	X 2.352	= Miles per gallon, US (mpg)

Temperature

Degrees Fahrenheit = (°C x 1.8) + 32

Degrees Celsius (Degrees Centigrade; °C) = (°F - 32) x 0.56

It is common practice to convert from miles per gallon (mpg) to litres/100 kilometres (l/100km), where mpg (Imperial) x l/100 km = 282 and mpg (US) x l/100 km = 235

Index

HAYNES AUTOMOTIVE MANUALS

NOTE: New manuals are added to this list on a periodic basis. If you do not see a listing for your vehicle, consult your local Haynes dealer for the latest product information.

ALFA-ROMEO
531   Alfa Romeo Sedan & Coupe '73 thru '80

AMC
    Jeep CJ – see JEEP (412)
694   Mid-size models, Concord, Hornet, Gremlin & Spirit '70 thru '83
934   (Renault) Alliance & Encore '83 thru '87

AUDI
615   4000 '80 thru '87
428   5000 '77 thru '83
1117   5000 '84 thru '88
207   Fox '73 thru '79

AUSTIN
049   Healey 100/6 & 3000 Roadster '56 thru '68
    Healey Sprite – see MG Midget (265)

BLMC
260   1100, 1300 & Austin America '62 thru '74
527   Mini '59 thru '69
*646   Mini '69 thru '88

BMW
276   320i all 4 cyl models '75 thru '83
632   528i & 530i '75 thru '80
240   1500 thru 2002 exceptTurbo '59 thru '77
348   2500, 2800, 3.0 & Bavaria '69 thru '76

BUICK
    Century (front wheel drive) – see GENERAL MOTORS A-Cars (829)
*1627   Buick, Oldsmobile & Pontiac Full-size (Front wheel drive) '85 thru '90 Buick Electra, LeSabre and Park Avenue; Oldsmobile Delta 88 Royale, Ninety Eight and Regency; Pontiac Bonneville
*1551   Buick Oldsmobile & Pontiac Full-size (Rear wheel drive) Buick Electra '70 thru '84, Estate '70 thru '90, LeSabre '70 thru '79 Oldsmobile Custom Cruiser '70 thru '90, Delta 88 '70 thru '85, Ninety-eight '70 thru '84 Pontiac Bonneville '70 thru '86, Catalina '70 thru '81, Grandville '70 thru '75, Parisienne '84 thu '86
627   Mid-size all rear-drive Regal & Century models with V6, V8 and Turbo '74 thru '87
    Regal – see GENERAL MOTORS (1671)
    Skyhawk – see GM J-Cars (766)
552   Skylark all X-car models '80 thru '85

CADILLAC
*751   Cadillac Rear Wheel Drive all gasoline models '70 thru '90
    Cimarron – see GM J-Cars (766)

CAPRI
296   2000 MK I Coupe '71 thru '75
283   2300 MK II Coupe '74 thru '78
205   2600 & 2800 V6 Coupe '71 thru '75
375   2800 Mk II V6 Coupe '75 thru '78
    Mercury Capri – see FORD Mustang (654)

CHEVROLET
*1477   Astro & GMC Safari Mini-vans '85 thru '90
554   Camaro V8 '70 thru '81
*866   Camaro '82 thru '90
    Cavalier – see GM J-Cars (766)
    Celebrity – see GM A-Cars (829)
625   Chevelle, Malibu & El Camino all V6 & V8 models '69 thru '87
449   Chevette & Pontiac T1000 '76 thru '87
550   Citation '80 thru '85
*1628   Corsica/Beretta '87 thru '90
274   Corvette all models '68 thru '82
*1336   Corvette '84 thru '89
704   Full-size Sedans Caprice, Impala, Biscayne, Bel Air & Wagons, all V6 & V8 models '69 thru '90
    Lumina – see GENERAL MOTORS (1671)
319   Luv Pick-up all 2WD & 4WD '72 thru '82
626   Monte Carlo all V6, V8 & Turbo '70 thru '88
241   Nova all models '69 thru '79
*1642   Nova & Geo Prizm front wheel drive '85 thru '90
*420   Pick-ups '67 thru '87 – Chevrolet & GMC, all V8 & in-line 6 cyl 2WD & 4WD '67 thru '87
*1664   Pick-ups '88 thru '90 – Chevlolet & GMC all full-size (C and K), '88 thru '90
*1727   Sprint & Geo Metro '85 thru '91
*831   S-10 & GMC S-15 Pick-ups '82 thru '90
*345   Vans – Chevrolet & GMC, V8 & in-line 6 cyl models '68 thru '89
208   Vega except Cosworth '70 thru '77

CHRYSLER
*1337   Chrysler & Plymouth Mid-size front wheel drive '82 thru '89
    K-Cars – see DODGE Aries (723)
    Laser – see DODGE Daytona (1140)

DATSUN
402   200SX '77 thru '79
647   200SX '80 thru '83
228   B-210 '73 thru '78
525   210 '78 thru '82

206   240Z, 260Z & 280Z Coupe & 2+2 '70 thru '78
563   280ZX Coupe & 2+2 '79 thru '83
    300ZX – see NISSAN (1137)
679   310 '78 thru '82
123   510 & PL521 Pick-up '68 thru '73
430   510 '78 thru '81
372   610 '72 thru '76
277   620 Series Pick-up '73 thru '79
    720 Series Pick-up – see NISSAN Pick-ups (771)
376   810/Maxima all gas models '77 thru '84
124   1200 '70 thru '73
368   F10 '76 thru '79
    Pulsar – see NISSAN (876)
    Sentra – see NISSAN (982)
    Stanza – see NISSAN (981)

DODGE
*723   Aries & Plymouth Reliant '81 thru '89
*1231   Caravan & Plymouth Voyager Mini-Vans '84 thru '89
699   Challenger & Plymouth Saporro '78 thru '83
236   Colt '71 thru '77
419   Colt (rear wheel drive) '77 thru '80
610   Colt & Plymouth Champ (front wheel drive) '78 thru '87
*556   D50 & Plymouth Arrow Pick-ups '79 thru '88
*1668   Dakota Pick-up all models '87 thru '90
234   Dart & Plymouth Valiant all 6 cyl models '67 thru '76
*1140   Daytona & Chrysler Laser '84 thru '89
*545   Omni & Plymouth Horizon '78 thru '90
*912   Pick-ups all full-size models '74 thru '90
*349   Vans – Dodge & Plymouth V8 & 6 cyl models '71 thru '89

FIAT
080   124 Sedan & Wagon all ohv & dohc models '66 thru '75
094   124 Sport Coupe & Spider '68 thru '78
310   131 & Brava '75 thru '81
479   Strada '79 thru '82
273   X1/9 '74 thru '80

FORD
*1476   Aerostar Mini-vans '86 thru '90
788   Bronco and Pick-ups '73 thru '79
*880   Bronco and Pick-ups '80 thru '90
014   Cortina MK II except Lotus '66 thru '70
295   Cortina MK III 1600 & 2000 ohc '70 thru '76
268   Courier Pick-up '72 thru '82
789   Escort & Mercury Lynx all models '81 thru '90
560   Fairmont & Mercury Zephyr all in-line & V8 models '78 thru '83
334   Fiesta '77 thru '80
754   Ford & Mercury Full-size, Ford LTD & Mercury Marquis ('75 thru '82); Ford Custom 500, Country Squire, Crown Victoria & Mercury Colony Park ('75 thru '87); Ford LTD Crown Victoria & Mercury Gran Marquis ('83 thru '87)
359   Granada & Mercury Monarch all in-line, 6 cyl & V8 models '75 thru '80
773   Ford & Mercury Mid-size, Ford Thunderbird & Mercury Cougar ('75 thru '82); Ford LTD & Mercury Marquis ('83 thru '86); Ford Torino, Gran Torino, Elite, Ranchero pick-ups, LTD II, Mercury Montego, Comet, XR-7 & Lincoln Versailles ('75 thru '86)
*654   Mustang & Mercury Capri all models including Turbo '79 thru '90
357   Mustang V8 '64-1/2 thru '73
231   Mustang II all 4 cyl, V6 & V8 models '74 thru '78
204   Pinto '70 thru '74
649   Pinto & Mercury Bobcat '75 thru '80
*1026   Ranger & Bronco II gasoline models '83 thru '89
*1421   Taurus & Mercury Sable '86 thru '90
*1418   Tempo & Mercury Topaz all gasoline models '84 thru '89
1338   Thunderbird & Mercury Cougar/XR7 '83 thru '88
*1725   Thunderbird & Mercury Cougar '89 thru '90
*344   Vans all V8 Econoline models '69 thru '90

GENERAL MOTORS
*829   A-Cars – Chevrolet Celebrity, Buick Century, Pontiac 6000 & Oldsmobile Cutlass Ciera '82 thru '89
*766   J-Cars – Chevrolet Cavalier, Pontiac J-2000, Oldsmobile Firenza, Buick Skyhawk & Cadillac Cimarron '82 thru '90
*1420   N-Cars – Buick Somerset '85 thru '87 Pontiac Grand Am and Oldsmobile Calais '85 thru '90; Buick Skylark '86 thru '90
*1671   GM: Buick Regal, Chevrolet Lumina, Oldsmobile Cutlass Supreme, Pontiac Grand Prix, all front wheel drive models '88 thru '90

GEO
    Metro – see CHEVROLET Sprint (1727)
    Tracker – see SUZUKI Samurai (1626)
    Prizm – see CHEVROLET Nova (1642)

GMC
    Safari – see CHEVROLET ASTRO (1477)
    Vans & Pick-ups – see CHEVROLET (420, 831, 345, 1664)

HONDA
138   360, 600 & Z Coupe '67 thru '75
351   Accord CVCC '76 thru '83
*1221   Accord '84 thru '89
160   Civic 1200 '73 thru '79
633   Civic 1300 & 1500 CVCC '80 thru '83
297   Civic 1500 CVCC '75 thru '79
*1227   Civic all models '84 thru '90
*601   Prelude CVCC '79 thru '89

HYUNDAI
*1552   Excel '86 thru '89

ISUZU
*1641   Trooper & Pick-up all gasoline models '81 thru '90

JAGUAR
098   MK I & II, 240 & 340 Sedans '55 thru '69
*242   XJ6 all 6 cyl models '68 thru '86
*478   XJ12 & XJS all 12 cyl models '72 thru '85
140   XK-E 3.8 & 4.2 all 6 cyl models '61 thru '72

JEEP
*1553   Cherokee, Comanche & Wagoneer Limited '84 thru '89
412   CJ '49 thru '86

LADA
*413   1200, 1300. 1500 & 1600 all models including Riva '74 thru '86

LAND ROVER
314   Series II, IIA, & III all 4 cyl gasoline models '58 thru '86
529   Diesel '58 thru '80

MAZDA
648   626 Sedan & Coupe (rear wheel drive) '79 thru '82
*1082   626 & MX-6 (front wheel drive) '83 thru '90
*267   B1600, B1800 & B2000 Pick-ups '72 thru '90
370   GLC Hatchback (rear wheel drive) '77 thru '83
757   GLC (front wheel drive) '81 thru '86
109   RX2 '71 thru '75
096   RX3 '72 thru '76
460   RX-7 '79 thru '85
*1419   RX-7 '86 thru '89

MERCEDES-BENZ
*1643   190 Series all 4-cyl. gasoline '84 thru '88
346   230, 250 & 280 Sedan, Coupe & Roadster all 6 cyl sohc models '68 thru '72
983   280 123 Series all gasoline models '77 thru '81
698   350 & 450 Sedan, Coupe & Roadster '71 thru '80
697   Diesel 123 Series 200D, 220D, 240D, 240TD; 300D, 300CD, 300TD, 4- & 5-cyl incl. Turbo '76 thru '85

MERCURY
See FORD Listing

MG
475   MGA '56 thru '62
111   MGB Roadster & GT Coupe '62 thru '80
265   MG Midget & Austin Healey Sprite Roadster '58 thru '80

MITSUBISHI
*1669   Cordia, Tredia, Galant, Precis & Mirage '83 thru '90
    Pick-up – see Dodge D-50 (556)

MORRIS
074   (Austin) Marina 1.8 '71 thru '80
024   Minor 1000 sedan & wagon '56 thru '71

NISSAN
1137   300ZX all Turbo & non-Turbo '84 thru '89
*1341   Maxima '85 thru '89
*771   Pick-ups/Pathfinder gas models '80 thru '88
*876   Pulsar '83 thru '86
*982   Sentra '82 thru '90
*981   Stanza '82 thru '90

OLDSMOBILE
    Custom Cruiser – see BUICK Full-size (1551)
658   Cutlass all standard gasoline V6 & V8 models '74 thru '88
    Cutlass Ciera – see GM A-Cars (829)
    Cutlass Supreme – see GM (1671)
    Firenza – see GM J-Cars (766)
    Ninety-eight – see BUICK Full-size (1551)
    Omega – see PONTIAC Phoenix & Omega (551)

PEUGEOT
161   504 all gasoline models '68 thru '79
663   504 all diesel models '74 thru '83

PLYMOUTH
425   Arrow '76 thru '80
    For all other PLYMOUTH titles, see DODGE listing.

PONTIAC
    T1000 – see CHEVROLET Chevette (449)
    J-2000 – see GM J-Cars (766)
    6000 – see GM A-Cars (829)

1232   Fiero '84 thru '88
555   Firebird all V8 models except Turbo '70 thru '81
*867   Firebird '82 thru '89
    Full-size Rear Wheel Drive – see Buick, Oldsmobile, Pontiac Full-size (1551)
    Grand Prix – see General Motors (1671)
551   Phoenix & Oldsmobile Omega all X-car models '80 thru '84

PORSCHE
*264   911 all Coupe & Targa models except Turbo '65 thru '89
239   914 all 4 cyl models '69 thru '76
397   924 including Turbo '76 thru '82
*1027   944 including Turbo '83 thru '89

RENAULT
141   5 Le Car '76 thru '83
079   8 & 10 with 58.4 cu in engines '62 thru '72
097   12 Saloon & Estate 1289 cc engines '70 thru '80
768   15 & 17 '73 thru '79
081   16 89.7 cu in & 95.5 cu in engines '65 thru '72
598   18i & Sportwagon '81 thru '86
    Alliance & Encore – see AMC (934)
984   Fuego '82 thru '85

ROVER
085   3500 & 3500S Sedan 215 cu in engines '68 thru '76
*365   3500 SDI V8 '76 thru '85

SAAB
198   95 & 96 V4 '66 thru '75
247   99 including Turbo '69 thru '80
*980   900 including Turbo '79 thru '88

SUBARU
237   1100, 1300, 1400 & 1600 '71 thru '79
*681   1600 & 1800 2WD & 4Wd '80 thru '89

SUZUKI
1626   Samurai/Sidekick and Geo Tracker '86 thru '89

TOYOTA
*1023   Camry '83 thru '90
150   Carina Sedan '71 thru '74
229   Celica ST, GT & liftback '71 thru '77
437   Celica '78 thru '81
*935   Celica except front-wheel drive and Supra '82 thru '85
680   Celica Supra '79 thru '82
1139   Celica Supra in-line 6-cylinder '82 thru '86
361   Corolla '75 thru '79
961   Corolla (rear wheel drive) '80 thru '87
*1025   Corolla (front wheel drive) '84 thru '91
*636   Corolla Tercel '80 thru '82
230   Corona & MK II all 4 cyl sohc models '70 thru '82
360   Corona '74 thru '82
*532   Cressida '78 thru '82
313   Land Cruiser '68 thru '82
200   MK II all 6 cyl models '72 thru '76
*1339   MR2 '85 thru '87
304   Pick-up '70 thru '78
*656   Pick-up '79 thru '90

TRIUMPH
112   GT6 & Vitesse '62 thru '74
113   Spitfire '62 thru '81
028   TR2, 3, 3A, & 4A Roadsters '52 thru '67
031   TR250 & 6 Roadsters '67 thru '76
322   TR7 '75 thru '81

VW
091   411 & 412 all 103 cu in models '68 thru '73
159   Beetle & Karmann Ghia all models '54 thru '79
238   Dasher all gasoline models '74 thru '81
*884   Rabbit, Jetta, Scirocco, & Pick-up all gasoline models '74 thru '89 & Convertible '80 thru '89
451   Rabbit, Jetta & Pick-up all diesel models '77 thru '84
082   Transporter 1600 '68 thru '79
226   Transporter 1700, 1800 & 2000 all models '72 thru '79
084   Type 3 1500 & 1600 '63 thru '73
1029   Vanagon all air-cooled models '80 thru '83

VOLVO
203   120, 130 Series & 1800 Sports '61 thru '73
129   140 Series '66 thru '74
244   164 '68 thru '75
*270   240 Series '74 thru '90
400   260 Series '75 thru '82
*1550   740 & 760 Series '82 thru '88

SPECIAL MANUALS
1479   Automotive Body Repair & Painting Manual
1654   Automotive Electrical Manual
1480   Automotive Heating & Air Conditioning Manual
1763   Ford Engine Overhaul Manual
482   Fuel Injection Manual
1666   Small Engine Repair Manual
299   SU Carburetors thru '88
393   Weber Carburetors thru '79
300   Zenith/Stromberg CD Carburetors thru '76

See your dealer for other available titles

Over 100 Haynes motorcycle manuals also available

4-1-91

* Listings shown with an asterisk (*) indicate model coverage as of this printing. These titles will be periodically updated to include later model years — consult your Haynes dealer for more information.

Haynes Publications Inc., P.O. Box 978, Newbury Park, CA 91320 ● (818) 889–5400 ● (805) 498–6703